UBH

AF529414

FINANCIAL SECTOR: CONTEMPORARY ISSUES

FINANCIAL SECTOR: CONTEMPORARY ISSUES

Editors

Dr. Jyotirmayee Kar

Dr. Pradeepta Kumar Samanta

Faculty Members, IBS Bhubaneswar

SERIALS PUBLICATIONS

NEW DELHI (INDIA)

© Editors

First Published – 2009

ISBN: 978-81-8387-281-2

The content and context of the articles are written by the authors. Although every care has been taken to avoid errors and omissions, this compendium is being published on the condition and understanding that the information given in this book is merely for reference and must not be taken having authority of or binding in any way on the author(s), editor(s), or publisher.

All rights reserved with the Publisher, including the right to translate or reproduce this book or parts thereof except for brief quotations in critical articles or reviews.

Published by

SERIALS PUBLICATIONS
4800/24, 1st Floor, Ansari Road
Darya Ganj, New Delhi-110002 (India)
Phone : 23245225. Fax : 91-11-23272135
E-mail: serials@satyam.net.in

CONTENTS

FOREWORD

Finance being the fuel for growth, financial sector is one of the most important keys to a country's growth process, more so in the case of a growing economy like India, which is rapidly getting integrated with the global trade and finance. The BoP crisis of 1991 was the trigger to reforms, among others, of the financial sector. Since then, the financial sector in India has made remarkable strides barring occasional hiccups, which is a natural corollary of a growth process. Success stories of the sector are galore, especially since the reform process started. The government and other related agencies have contributed immensely to the emerging architecture of the financial sector.

In the above context and the current turmoil in the global market, the National Conference organised by IBS Bhubaneswar sought to address the issues under three sections: Banking & Insurance, Microfinance and Financial Market.

BANKING

In India, the State dominated the banking sector, from the beginning. In the post-reforms era, the impact of banking sector reform has been slow. Competition from the new generation private sector banks and foreign banks became the main driver of the most effective changes in the depth and quality of banking services apart from the effect of globalisation, limited deregulation and technology application. There was a significant increase in the use of information and communication technologies resulting in up-gradation in the quality of banking services and their outreach. Large and mid-corporates benefitted enormously from deregulation and disintermediation. The urban middle class also benefitted from the retail boom. Along with this, banking sector expanded. The number of customers and footfalls increased exponentially. The number of bank branches increased and almost all the inhabitants in metro and urban areas now have bank accounts. Alternative delivery channels, mostly due to technology innovation and application multiplied and were gradually refined; these brought in convenience banking. The turnaround time of banking product delivery improved enormously.

There are, however, some areas of concern which need more attention. India ranks way below, on the index of financial inclusion. This implies that access to and availability and usage of formal financial sector by all members of the economy have remained marginal. There is no doubt that, banking penetration in metro, urban and semi-urban areas is high, microfinance has somewhat broadened its outreach, a good number of SHGs have been established and linked to banks and MFIs; but these initiatives have not been able to embrace most of the rural poor, who still remain unable to utilize the benefits of growth and development.

Banks have no price incentive for suo-motto initiative and expand into priority sector lending, including agriculture and allied activities, which are the mainstay of the majority of the rural people. Wherever they have good intention and want to take initiative, the banks face severe competition from the easily accessible informal sector whose services are readily available at the door step, sans a clutter of formalities and procedures (though at exorbitant rates). Whatever may be the reasons, the banks, perhaps, are losing a significant and perhaps, profitable market segment.

The banks in rural areas should rise to the occasion - there is wealth at the bottom of the pyramid. This is common knowledge now, but banks have to evolve appropriate business and delivery models, so that the cost of operation remains low and there is substantial net earning. All these and many more issues have been extensively dealt with in a few papers relating to Banking and Insurance sectors.

INSURANCE

The insurance sector in India was dominated by public sector monopolies–Life Insurance Corporation in the life insurance sector and General Insurance Corporation in the general insurance sector. The reforms of this sector began with setting up of the Insurance Regulatory and Development Authority (IRDA) by an Act of Parliament in 1999. With IRDA in place, the next step taken was exposing the sector to a competitive market structure, and free market pricing. The two visible outcomes of this effort are an increase in the number of insurance companies and varied user-friendly and competitive products available to the Indian public. Instead of only public sector monopolies, over a dozen insurance companies now vie for business with each other. Bank assurance has improved the credibility of and confidence in the products and has enlarged the outreach.

However, the insurance industry continues to be hobbled by basic problem. In terms of PLC framework, this sector is still at a nascent stage. There is a blue ocean out there with enormous potential, but also unforeseen risks in unchartered waters. On its way through the growth stage to maturity, hopefully, more user friendly, cost effective products and efficient delivery models will be developed and outreach expansion will take place.

MICROFINANCE

Microfinance should respond to financing gaps faced by small borrowers both in the rural as well as the fringes of the urban society; however, it has remained a marginal sector. It has not until now, been able to touch the poorest that have highly fluctuating incomes and the lowest, having almost no ability to save. Informal sector continues to dominate the rural financial sector of India.

There appears to be no substantial correlation between the spread of SHGs and poverty and HDI (Human Development Index) in India. The SHG-bank linkage seems to be riding piggy-back on the expanding presence of NGOs in various states rather than using elimination of deprivation and poverty as a measuring standard of the success of this initiative. In quite a few pockets, through SHGs, real empowerment, especially of poor, rural women has taken place. Various issues requiring attention regarding SHG-bank linkage model are adequacy of loan size, timeliness of credit and also the need for the bank manager or the promoter of a local movement adopting certain standards and processes for forming and nurturing an SHG before credit linking the group. In poverty reduction, microcredit has not made much noticeable impact despite microfinance movement having taken roots quite some years back.

There are several challenges facing the microfinance sector, and among those are the lack of transparency in lending and the price at which credit is available. SHG-Bank linkage programme is yet to delve into details like how to succeed in capacity building, building partner agencies and training inputs. Moreover, there is limited integration between the informal and formal sectors in so far as thrift and credit are concerned. Care needs to be taken to prevent microfinance degenerating into programme lending. The papers under this section have elaborately dealt with these issues.

CAPITAL AND DERIVATIVE MARKET

The State had a low involvement in the commodity and still less in the equity market where reforms have made huge strides because mostly of institutional development and changes in the regulatory framework. India's economy is expected to benefit enormously from the process of gradual capital market liberalization. Emerging market economies that have heralded changes in their financial market structure experienced higher growth and investment. The case of India is no exception. With rising domestic investment, during the post-liberalization period, per-capita GDP has improved. The sharp rise in the width and depth of India's stock market during the last few years reflect its improving macroeconomic fundamentals. India's financial market infrastructure has improved. But in contrast to several developed countries and Asian economies, India's capital market is still shallow, implying that further reforms are needed to make our capital market more visible and attain global standards.

During the last two decades, India's capital market, which consists primarily of debt and equity has played an increasingly significant role in mobilizing funds to meet public and private entities' financial needs. The advent of exchange-traded derivative instruments in 2000, such as options and futures, has enabled investors to hedge their positions better and reduce risks. But the derivative market is still in an embryonic stage. A number of reforms and initiatives are needed to promote India as a major commodity trading hub in tune with its status of being amongst the top five producers of most of the commodities and also a major consumer of precious metals and energy. Unlike Banking & Insurance and Microfinance, awareness about the capital market and about the benefits and the attendant risks, among common men is very low. Therefore, the usage has remained confined to a few. Deregulation in this area should perhaps be accompanied by initiative through appropriate agencies to create awareness regarding how and why to access the capital market. A few papers, under this section have analysed all these and have made excellent suggestions.

As the Indian economy ascends a higher growth path, and is subjected to greater opening to and financial integration with the rest of the world, the financial sector- Banking & Finance, Microfinance and Financial Market-in all its aspects will need further considerable development, along with corresponding measures in the area of regulatory modernization and strengthening. During the course of this process, the money market, equity market and capital market may face some occasional crises, both because of internal shocks and because of the impact of integrating these markets with the global markets. Continual readjustment and repositioning will be required to ensure that these small crises do not snowball into big crashes.

An exercise involving diagnostics and prescriptions for the Financial Sector by practitioners and academicians is more relevant now then ever before, in the context of the convulsions in the sector, especially during the past year or so. Quite a few of the papers have analyzed the impact of the turmoil and have hazarded suggestions in these areas, which are, prima facie, excellent. Some of these, I am confident, are achievable and will stand the test of time. We all know, it all started in a pronounced manner with the US sub-prime blues claiming its first major important victims at the highest places in centuries old excellently rated financial behemoths. Rest is current history. The euphoria of continuous growth until the last year gave way to abysmal helplessness–nobody seemed to be in control ; there has been, as they say, financial tsunami, equity market destruction, liquidity freeze and bruised public confidence. Nobody knows whether the bottom has been reached and when the bleeding will stop. Amidst this global chaos, the government and the regulators believe that India is the only country, which can decouple from the unpredictable impacts of the global contagion. Let us hope, the vigil, which the government, the regulators, the other related agencies and the public at large have maintained, have not been wasted. Yet care also must be taken to ensure that too much 'vigilance' does not obstruct the growth process, which India has so assiduously ushered in. Measured growth, tempered by adequate regulation probably is the recipe for the future.

Prof. Prafulla K. Dash
Dean, IBS Bhubaneswar

ACKNOWLEDGEMENTS

To conduct the National Conference and to bring out the precious ideas in book form, we are thankful to many eminent personalities and organizations. NABARD extended funds support to publish the book. CGM of NABARD, Shri C R Patnaik, CGM of State Bank of India Shri M N Rao, MD and CEO of SBI Life Shri U S Roy graced the occasion with their highly informative and thought provoking address. We are extremely thankful to them.

We are thankful to Shri Vivek Pattnaik, Ex Civil Servant and Chairman, Board of Management, Bhubaneswar Stock Exchange, for the valedictory lecture which broadened the ideas on Stock Market in the context of current financial situation.

We are thankful to Shri Bhaskar Niyogi of SBI, Shri Lalit Kumar Dash of LIC, Shri Subal Acharjee of the UCO Bank, Shri Parsuram Nayak of Swayamshree Micro Credit, Shri Neeraj Sati of Axis Bank, Dr N C Kar, Professor of MBA, Utkal University and Shri Debraj Biswal, Chief Executive of Bhubaneswar Stock Exchange for their valuable deliberations.

We acknowledge with gratitude the contribution of all the paper writers for their priceless ideas.

We are extremely thankful to the faculty, staff members and students of IBS Bhubaneswar who not only made the conference successful but helped a lot in preparing the book.

Jyotirmayee Kar
Pradeepta Kumar Samanta

SECTION–I

INSTITUTIONAL FINANCE

1

ACCESS TO BANK FINANCE AND REDUCTION OF POVERTY AND DEPENDENCY ON THE PRIMARY SECTOR

Jyotirmayee Kar

INTRODUCTION

Over dependence on the primary sectors like agriculture, forestry etc has prompted the government to launch various schemes to provide off-farm employment avenues. Yet such programmes have not succeeded in reducing primary sector dependency. Apart from other reasons, non-availability of timely finance has come up as a major obstacle. Without enough financial support it is difficult to take up any non-farm job. With tremendous opportunity for employment and income generation the non-farm sector remains untapped because of non availability of adequate finance. Recently taken steps towards financial inclusion, subsidized credit and group lending schemes have succeeded in encompassing quite a large number under the purview of the formal financial sector. Yet quite a substantial portion still relies on easily and timely available informal finance, despite sky high cost.

With this development the present exercise attempts to address the following issues: 1. what obstructs the rural poor in getting bank finance? 2. Will access to bank finance encourage participation in off-farm jobs and reduce pressure on agricultural and forest land?

The aim of this article is to first assess what are the benefits of formal finance to the rural poor and why rural people fail to access it. This is presented in the next section. Section III builds up a theoretical underpinning identifying individual access to formal finance and participation in off-farm jobs. Section IV contains empirical test of the theoretical development on the basis of primary data collected from two villages of Mayurbhanj district, a tribal dominated less developed area in Orissa. The last section is conclusion and policy implication.

FORMAL FINANCE AND THE POOR

A well developed financial sector, no doubt helps the poor by contributing to overall economic development of the country in which they live. A strong financial sector can mobilize opportunities. Appropriate saving schemes can enable them to undertake risky and high income earning avenues of investment. Access to credit support is an added advantage in this direction. Micro credit programmes have proven success in undertaking large scale high risk activities by pooling and pricing risk. Suitable insurance schemes can reduce their vulnerability to adverse income shocks.

The study by Levin, Loayza and Beck (2000) uses dynamic panel data technique to analyze the causal relationship between banking sector development and economic growth. Using data for 63 countries averaged over the period 1960-95, and after controlling for potential endogeneity bias, the authors find that 'the data suggest a strong positive link between financial intermediary development and economic growth.' They have quantified the contribution of formal financial sector to economic growth and have concluded that doubling of bank credit to the private sector (as a ratio of GDP) adds almost 2 percentage points to the long term growth rate. Rutherford (2000) has observed that poor convert their irregular flow of saving into a lump sum average amount so as to increase the level of investment and acquire productive assets. Jalilian and Kirkpatrick (2005) have examined contribution of financial development and economic growth. Their empirical study indicates that, up to a threshold level of economic development, financial sector growth contributes to poverty reduction through growth enhancing effect. Financial services also help in reducing other dimensions of poverty, like extension of education and healthcare facilities, improving gender equity and empowering women. Another significant contribution of financial services is in the area of environmental protection. Studies have indicated a positive correlation between environment and poverty. Extension of financial services makes the poor more dependent on other means of earning a livelihood rather than on environment.

In fact poor need a range of financial services. Contribution of micro credit is significant in this aspect but the extremely poor remain in the outreach because of their greater risk aversion and limited access to investment opportunities. For these groups saving and insurance schemes are more essential as these can reduce vulnerability while facilitating the households to take up riskier ventures.

The actual scenario is, however, not much conducive. The financial sector in the developing countries often fails to work for the poor. As revealed by the World Bank Report (2002), domestic credit provided by the banking sector in the low income countries was only 43 per cent of GDP in1999 as against 148 per cent in high income countries.

Solanki (2008), on the basis of techno-economic studies on the unorganized sector of rural artisans, carpenters, blacksmiths, weavers etc has underlined inability to get bank loans has hampered their work and earn a livelihood. Sarkar (2008) has observed that in India, despite prompt repayment 78.7 percent of the SHGs who were previously financed by the mainstream banks did not receive additional credit in 2005-06. Only 21.29 percent of the SHGs were provided with a repeat loan during the same year. As regards access to bank finance, women have remained largely marginalized (Chavan, 2008).

The Raguram Rajan Committee on Financial sector reforms has pointed out the gray areas of the Indian Banking system. One of the major flaws is low usage of technology, which increases transaction cost of borrowing. EPW Research Foundation (EPW, Oct 18, 2008) has advocated for fundamental changes in the banking and financial sector. It has stressed on relationship banking as the most viable foundation. Under this the relatively close banker borrower contact obviates information asymmetry. Moreover, these banking practice do not need over dependency on Basel norms. The Research foundation has also observed that for emerging markets, excessive emphasis on these norms have also been found to be not only expensive but also harmful in pursuing better credit delivery for informal sector. The weaknesses in the organizational structure of commercial banks in the post reforms period have also manifested themselves in the neglect of agriculture, small and micro enterprises and other informal sector.

Nonetheless, extension of sound banking facility does not mean that banking services will be availed by the poor, so as to facilitate themselves to take up non-farm activities. It has been observed that the poor exhibit a strong alignment towards the informal sector, rather than the low cost formal one, where procedural delay and huge paper work act as deterrent factors. This makes the banking sector defunct in the most needed rural areas. Few studies have looked into the consumer specific reasons for not obtaining formal finance. Present one is an attempt fill the gap and examines underlying causes of non-access of the poor to formal finance.

The next section examines a theoretical model of the individual opting for formal finance, which is empirically tested in the next section on the basis of a field study.

OPPORTUNITY COST OF FARM EMPLOYMENT

Working individuals have two sources of income: farm (from agriculture, forest etc) and off-farm (from small business, art and craft, animal rearing, micro enterprises etc.)

Let total income of the person be

$Y_t = y^{fl} + y^{ofl}$

Y^{fl} = farm labour

Y^{ofl} = off farm labour

Total time available with the person $L_i = T - t_i^l - t_i^{fl} - t_i^{ofl}$

The subscript indicates time devoted to leisure, farm income and off-farm income. Labour devoted towards off-farm activities will depend on availability of finance, which is contingent upon interest cost and transaction cost of borrowing.

Income from off-farm activities will have a direct effect as an opportunity cost to be engaged in farm activities. For individuals not going for off-farm labour opportunity cost will be zero. If the income from off-farm labour is high and cost of credit is low, opportunity cost of farm employment will increase and he will opt for non- farm employment. Further more, if the income from farm labour is high, they will move to agriculture.

Then net income of the individual could be given as

$Y_i = py_i^{ofl} - [w_i (y_i^{fl}, I_i^{ofl}) I_i + â (ec). y_i^{ofl}$

I_i = the labour of individual i

p = the price of the off farm products

w = the opportunity cost of the individual and it is determined by his income

β = the probability of getting a bank finance

ec = the effective cost (interest and transaction cost) of borrowing, which is proportionately related to access to formal finance.

To maximize income the first order condition will be

$$\partial Yi/\partial Ii - \partial\{py_i^{ofl} - [w_i(.)\, l_i + \beta(ec).\, y_i^{ofl}]\}/\partial Ii = 0$$

$$\frac{\partial\, pyi(li)}{\partial li} = \frac{\partial}{\partial li}[wi(.)l_i + \beta(ec).yi^{ofl}(l_i)]$$

$$\frac{\partial py'_i(li)}{MR} = \frac{wi(.) + \beta(ec).y'(li)}{MC + BC}$$

MC is the individual opportunity cost and BC is borrowing cost, which can be termed as EMC (Effective Marginal Cost). The former is determined by individual opportunity cost and the latter by access to formal finance. A high EMC will discourage farm employment. Income from farm employment is low as there is marked disguised unemployment in this sector. If $w_i = 0$, off-farm employment will entirely depend upon cost of borrowing. This indicates that high price of non-farm products and low cost of borrowing will encourage non-farm employment. As market prospect of these products is high price will not be a constraint. But high borrowing cost, especially transaction cost, will prohibit individuals to go for this alternative.

Observing a good demand for the off farm products we assume MC to be low. The option to go for off farm employment depends on BC. One component, interest cost of BC is given and subsidized. So it is transaction cost which plays a major role. Transaction cost in the present study incorporates travel cost, loss of wage due to visit to the bank, documentation cost and other expenses incurred during visit to the bank. It is not possible to measure transaction cost directly because of inaccurate record of the same. Moreover, exact quantification of farm and off-farm income, loss of income due to visit the bank office, documentation cost etc is difficult. An indirect measurement was conducted by the study as it is influenced by a number of factors like income and asset possession, educational attainment, proximity of the bank, membership in SHGs etc.

EMPIRICAL STUDY

The study is based on primary information collected through household survey conducted in two villages in Mayurbhanj, a tribal dominated district of Orissa. Primary information about the socio-economic backdrop of the households, their occupation and participation in farm and off-farm jobs were obtained through structured questionnaire administered to 130 households, selected at random. The households surveyed were largely dependent on agriculture and forest products to earn a livelihood. There is ample scope for off-farm activities like preparation of doormats, carpets and other fancy items from Sabai grass, which is cultivated plentily in this area. These products have very good market in the urban areas. People of the area, mainly women were engaged in this work, but this craft has gradually vanished because of poor financial support and little access of the craftsmen to market for these. Some of the households own a small grocery or tea shop. Household depended on animal husbandry, with one or two milking cows, some goats and hen as a secondary source of income. All these groups were unequivocal about constraints posed by inadequate finance. By and large they depended on informal sector at the time of need. Even a reverse interest rate was observed to prevail in the area. The extra income from a days work or by selling a goat or chicken was given to the shopkeepers who claimed some amount to keep the money in safe custody. It is observed that of the 130 households in the sample, 34 (26 per cent) have obtained some formal finance while the rest 74 percent have not.

Factors Influencing Transaction Cost

Now, which factors influence individual participation in off-farm activities? The villagers are largely dependent on agriculture and forest products to earn a living. It was observed that when land holding at the disposal of the households is large, they depended on agriculture. Still per capita return from the field being very less they prefer some off farm activity. Possession of landed property facilitates them to obtain formal finance at a lower transaction cost. This increases the possibility of earning from off-farm activities and escalates opportunity cost of farm labour. Educational attainment and skill improves access to bank finance as the financiers are convinced about the repayment potential of the borrower. Education also makes the borrower feel at ease with the banking procedures and formalities. Wide social network improves information dissemination which facilitates in improving mobility of labour, increases scope for off-farm employment. Thin credit market along with dearth of information due to weak social network and low educational attainment restricts access to formal finance and thereby limits the scope of off-farm self employment.

Land Holding and Access to Bank Finance

Majority (55 percent) of the sample households are landless. They work as wage earners, collect forest products or earn a livelihood by animal herding. Of the 34 households with access to formal finance 35 percent possess landed property above 5 acres. Land in these areas is mainly hilly and absence of adequate irrigation facility affects productivity. Even though rice is the chief cultivation, people prefer cultivation of Sabai grass, which is woven into rope and sold to businessmen. For this the remuneration is not high. So the villagers prefer some off farm engagement. Land being accepted as good collateral they can get finance easily by providing document. The borrowers have also observed that with a valid collateral number of visits to the bank is also less. A statistically significant chi-square establishes a strong relationship between possession of landed property and access to bank finance at a low transaction cost, which in turn reduces opportunity cost of off-farm jobs. (Table 1).

Table 1
Land Holding and Access to Bank Finance

Size of Land Holding	*No*	*Yes*	*Total*
No Land	72	0	72
	(75.00)	(0)	(55.38)
0 to1	15	6	21
	(15.63)	(17.25)	(16.15)
1 to 2	5	7	12
	(5.21)	(20.59)	(9.23)
2 to 5	2	9	11
	(2.01)	(26.47)	(8.46)
Above 5	2	12	14
	(2.01)	(35.29)	(10.77)
Total	96 (100)	34 (100)	130 (100)

Source: Computed from survey data.
Note: Values in parentheses are percentages to total. Chi-square value 61.11, significant at one percent level.

Educational Attainment and Access to Bank Finance

Access to bank finance is largely dependent on educational attainment and inherited or acquired skill. Low educational attainment restricts access to market information and mobility necessary for any off farm job. It also makes the borrower averse to the paper work necessary for bank finance. Transaction cost of borrowing increases, if there is no other member in the family help them out. And this reduces scope of off farm employment. However, higher educational attainment by any member of the family was observed to have positive effect on the other members. Therefore, the study has considered highest years of schooling by any member in the household. As education level below class 10 hardly influences bank borrowing, all members educated up to this level are grouped in one category. Persons above class 10 and educated in the general line are categorized as general graduates. Those with some skill based or technical training are grouped in one category.

Table 2
Educational Attainment and Access to Bank Finance

Educational Attainment	*No*	*Yes*	*Total*
Illiterate	2	0	2
	(2.08)	(0)	(1.54)
Up to class 10	46	5	51
	(47.92)	(14.71)	(39.23)
General Graduates	28	11	39
	(29.16)	(32.35)	(30.00)
Skill based training	20	18	38
	(20.83)	(52.94)	(29.23)
Total	96	34	130
	(100)	(100)	(100)

Source: Computed from survey data. Note: Values in parentheses are percentages to total. Chi-square value 64.11, significant at one percent level.

Of the 130 sample households 2 households did not have any educated member. These households did not obtain any bank finance. It was observed that a skill based training increases scope of availing bank finance as nearly 53 percent of the households who obtained bank finance possess some skill. However, these loans are given to the trained person. Of the rest loan applicants 11 (32.35 per cent) households had graduates. The data reveals that the banks prefer higher educational attainment and this reduces transaction cost of borrowing. The persons who have obtained loan have stated some business, mainly auto/cycle repairing shop, tailoring shops, grocery shop, food stalls or have purchased auto-rickshaws. Those educate up to class 10 have added to their stock of cow and goat.

SHG Membership and Access to Bank Finance

The study attempted to examine relationship between SHG membership and access to formal finance. The villagers formed SHGs under the supervision of some NGOs and contribute to the stipulated monthly saving. However, wide variation was observed in the performance of the village specific SHGs, depending on the economic status of the members and their involvement in the productive activities. Women of most of the households were observed to be members of these groups, but their borrowing capacity is largely restricted. Members from the households with a larger amount of landed property, income from service and relatively more educated ones received a better deal. They are able to get funds for productive purposes which improve their repayment capability. They could be termed as 'A' category. Yet, they face the problem of short duration of loan for which they have to repay the loan even when it is badly needed. These members are primarily engaged in activities like preparation of food items, floriculture, plates from Sal leaves. Access to formal finance has taken care of their livelihood problems.

There is another category 'B' category, of members who borrow but use the fund for repayment of previous loans. This reduces their high cost informal indebtedness but does not improve their economic position. This reduces their ability to repay and hence, the continuous flow of finance, which restricts their ability to take up any non-farm activity. Even though these members are not able to start some off farm activity, formal loan improves their income position indirectly by reducing dependency on high cost informal borrowing.

In the 'C' category are people who are neither able to access bank finance nor to form a group. Due to lack of any collateral support or educational attainment they are not able to prove their creditworthiness. High transaction cost of formal finance increases opportunity cost of non-farm employment and therefore, these people entirely depend on wage work, collection of forest product or cattle herding to earn a livelihood. They are mainly tribal and ignorant about the nuances of forming a group, obtaining finance and using the same for income earning activities.

This shows that formation of SHGs facilitate access to bank finance at a low transaction cost. The members are made aware of banking facilities. They do not have to pay visit to the banks which saves both travel cost as well as wage loss. However, full benefit of SGH membership is not realized because the periodicity of the loan is too low. The needy ones do not have access to it. Nearly 6 percent of the women in the sample go without work. They have voiced for some credit support, so that they can at least add to their stock of goats or buy a cow.

Proximity of the Bank and Access to Bank Finance

Proximity of the bank reduces transaction cost as it reduces travel cost. Majority of the sample households (32 per cent) live beyond 5 kilometers from the bank. Only 18 percent live in an area within 1 km, and the largest number of the households who availed bank finance belongs to this category. However, no concrete relationship could be established between proximity of the bank and access to bank finance. Most of the borrowers travelled by bicycle and hence longer distance did not entail higher travel cost. In this aspect SHG members are at an advantage as the secretaries of the group negotiate with the bank for credit and the borrower need not move to the bank office for official formalities. During the survey, respondents beyond 5 kms from the bank expressed their hesitance to move to the bank as time cost escalates. They have to spend a long time, at times, more than 2 hours, which affects their daily wage. It also forces them to forgo a day's work.

Table 3
Proximity of the Bank and Access to Bank Finance

Distance of the Household from the Bank	*No*	*Yes*	*Total*
< 1 km	14	10	24
	(14.58)	(29.41)	(18.46)
1 to 2 kms	26	8	34
	(27.08)	(23.53)	(26.15)
2 to 5 kms	24	8	32
	(25.00)	(23.53)	(24.62)
> 5 kms	32	8	40
	(33.33)	(23.53)	(30.77)
Total	96	34	130
	(100)	(100)	(100)

Source: Computed from survey data. *Note:* Values in parentheses are percentages to total. Chi-square value 22.11.

Access to Bank Finance by Women and Tribal

Of the total 130 sample households 298 are in the working age group. Form those 156 were male and 142 are female. Of the female, a majority, 36 per cent are engaged in collection of forest products, like firewood, Sal leaves, Mohua etc, 16 percent in animal herding, 14 per cent are working as wage labourers, 7 per cent are in some petty business and 6 percent have no work. Women have a better access to finance through SHGs. However, women in the aforementioned works, though desirous to get some credit facility, did not have access to it. They are not even able to form SHG because of inadequate saving. This shows that the needy ones don't have access to finance.

Identical is the case of the tribal people. Mayurbhanj district is dominated by tribal population. In the sample households 78 are ST, 24 are SC and 28 are general, of which nearly 2%, 5% and 19% had access to formal finance. Despite sincere effort for financial inclusion, the socially marginalized groups continue to remain in the outreach of formal finance.

Multivariate Analysis

A multivariate analysis was conducted to assess the strength of association between each independent variable with the dependent variable. A logistic regression was computed with the specification: Access to Bank Finance = *f* (Land holding, Human capital, SHG membership, Distance from the bank).

The logit model was estimated in SPSS, with the dependent variable as binary and rest others excepting proximity to bank are categorical. Distance from the bank is measured in kilometers.

Table 4
Specification of Variables in the Logit Model

Variables	*Specification*
Access to Bank Finance	1, if at least one member in the household has obtained bank finance, else 0
Land Holding	1, if the household is without any land, else 0
Human Capital	1, if general education, else 0
SHG membership	1, if no member of the household is a member of SHG, else 0
Distance from the bank	Measured in kilometers

Table 5
Logistic Regression on Household Involvement in Forest Degradation by Selected Household's Characteristics

Variables	*Model I*	*Model II*
Land Holding		
With Land	7.56*	8.42*
Without Land [R]	1.00	1.00
Human Capital		
Skilled	8.75*	9.46*
Without Skill [R]	1.00	1.00
SHG Membership		
Yes		26.35*
No [R]		1.00
Distance	1.00	1.00
-2 log likelihood	98.28	86.98
Model Chi-Square	74.56	68.54
N	130	130

* p =< 0.01
[R] = Reference Category

These results are identical with the findings of the bi-variate analysis.

Results of the computation are presented in the Table 5. these results are in conformity with our earlier findings. Households which are landless, with low and unskilled education, and not members of SHG are found to have low access to formal finance. Access to bank finance by the households reveals a positive relationship with possession of land. Households with some land are 8 times more likely to get formal finance. Those with a person having skill based education are 9 times more likely to get bank finance. SHG membership increases the scope of bank borrowing by 26 percent. But this type of borrowing does not cater to the needs of the borrowers due to less time for which it is sanctioned.

CONCLUSION

Over supply of labour in rural areas causes disguised unemployment in the farm sector and suppresses wage rate. There remains ample scope for off-farm self employment. But these could not be harnessed due to low access to bank credit. Even though interest cost on bank credit is subsidized, high transaction cost restricts access to it and forces labourers to depend on farm jobs. This provides a basis for poor man's over dependence on the farm sector and high transaction cost of bank finance which prohibits them to participate in these jobs and reduces opportunity cost of farm work participation.

The study reveals that high transaction cost of bank borrowing escalates opportunity cost of non-farm employment. The household who are in need of some financial support do not get it and those who manage to get it feel the inadequacy. This shows that the subsidized credit facilities will not succeed unless some of the basic problem like education, awareness etc are addressed. The surveyed area faces dearth of skilled workers like mechanics, plumbers, drivers etc. Government can take steps in this direction to open training centres, which will not only upgrade skill of the local people but also facilitate in getting finance and start self employment ventures. Mayurbhanj has a large forest area, with a lot of non-timber forest products, like *kendu* leaves used for making bidi, mahua flower, a nutritious food material also used for preparation of local liquor, sal leaves for making plates and *sabai* grass for making various useful products. Moreover, the district is situated adjascent to the national park Similipal, offering a huge scope of earning from eco-tourism. The local people are not fully aware of these. Government can take active step in promoting these activities. Imparting training in these areas along with sanction of loan while attaching a part of the sales revenue for repayment could provide a sustainable source of livelihood. Trained people could be organized in groups which will strengthen their performance.

In this aspect the formal financial institutions have a strong role to play. Recently advocated models of Business Correspondent, Business facilitators by encompassing individuals with local knowledge, such as, retired teachers, retired government officials and active NGOs are yet come into practice in the surveyed area. However, these agencies could thrive on mutual confidence and trust with the rural folk who could be persuaded to deposit their meager saving and also to repay the loans in time without expecting for any waiver scheme. Application of information technology in the form of rural kiosks has a remote possibility of being accepted by the local people with a low educational attainment. Trained person from the village could be assigned to run these so that the villagers could trust them.

REFERENCES

Chavan, P. (2008), Gender Inequality in Banking Services, *Economic and Political Weekly*, Nov. 22.

Economic Research Foundation (2008), Paradigm Shift in Financial Policies: Need of the Hour, *Economic and Political Weekly*, Oct., 18.

Jalilian, H., and C. Kirkpatrick (2005), Does Financial Development Contribute to Poverty Reduction?, *The Journal of Development Studies*, Vol. 41, No. 4.

Levine, R., Loayza, N., and T. Beck (2000), Financial Intermediation and Growyh: Causality and Causes, *Journal of Monetary Economics*, 46, 31-77.

Rutherford, S. (2000), The Poor and Their Money, Oxford University Press, New Delhi

Sarkar, D. (2008), Indian Microfinance: Lessons from Bangladesh, *Economic and Political Weekly*, Jan. 5,

Solanki, S. S. (2008), Sustainability of Rural Artisans, *Economic and Political Weekly*, May 10, Vol. XLIII, No. 19.

World Bank (2002), World Development Indicators, Washington D C.

2

TECHNOLOGY AND INNOVATION IN THE BANKING SECTOR: THE CASE OF INTERNET BANKING IN INDIA

Manoranjan Dash & Anil Mishra

INTRODUCTION

The Indian banking system has undergone a technological makeover over time. The banking system in India has created a niche for itself in the current competitive global arena where adoption of new and innovative technological development carries the key to expansion of business and its future development. The revolutionary advent of internet banking has empowered banks with new ways to cater to the needs of customers. Banks have attained more lee-way on the technology front than ever before. From just being a business enabler, IT is now a business driver for the banking sector. At the heart of the banking technology lies the Core Banking Solutions implemented by most banks. At present out of the total IT spending undertaken by banks, around 75 % goes towards maintenance of existing systems and ensuring that the business of the bank goes through smoothly. Hence a major exercise in upgrading core banking architecture is something many banks may not be able to afford at present. To gain an edge over their competitors and address customer demands effectively, banks need to do a balancing act by replacing old systems with new platforms. The Indian banking system has come a long way from being a player restricted to domestic boundaries to a leading giant in the world of financial services across the globe. Credit for this goes to a mix of factors like ,the introduction of various economic reforms which gave a boost to the banking sector, adoption of new technology by banks in order to stream line their line of businesses and increases profits by improving cost efficiency and offering doorstep banking convenience to their customers. Today almost all scheduled commercial banks are connected to all the branches on a real time basis extending the any where banking facility to the customers, which means that it is not necessary for a customer now to visit the branch personally in order to conduct a transaction. Now a customer has various options available with him i.e. internet banking ,mobile banking,ATMs,phone banking etc.The future of Indian banking system lies in increased investment in technology platforms and a greater focus on end-to-end solutions provided by IT majors like core banking products, vertical specific CRM and risk management software. As the new technology spreads across various sectors, businesses as well as academicians are tempted to assess the opportunities created by the new technology in a comparative manner with the existing operations. It is foreseen by many that competition will get tougher in the financial industry owing to the rapid technological change and globalization of financial markets. As increasing competition between the financial institutions has forced many of the players to offer similar prices on deposits and loans, the efforts for gaining competitive advantage were shifted towards non-price factors. In this context, new forms of distribution channels are invaluable outlets for financial institutions since they provide the opportunity for cutting costs without diminishing the existing service levels. As time passes, financial institutions world-wide become more interested in diversifying their traditional service delivery channels, basically the branch network, which is known to be associated with high staff and overhead costs.

The advent of new channels has contributed not only to the adoption of multi-channel strategies by the existing institutions but also the emergence of new forms of financial businesses such as "virtual banks". In today's digital sphere the number of people browsing the internet is increasing daily. Banking in India has gone electronic over the last few years, in line with the global trends. Today, banks are not only automating their core banking operations, but also increasingly using Internet Technology for better customer service operations and resulting in rising rates of productivity growth. Banks and financial institutions in India are in the process of web-enabling their services in order to offer Internet banking to its customer's .With the advantages of enhanced productivity, also some of the risks is associated with the Internet infrastructure. Internet platform offer new markets for web-based services such as internet banking. Internet banking has experienced fiery growth in many countries and has transformed traditional banking practice. By offering internet banking services, banks are adopting paper less work, lowering operational costs, improving consumer banking services, retaining the customers' and expanding their customer base. Internet banking customers gain more benefits than the traditional banking customers as they can access 24-hours services in everywhere. The Internet is the driving engine of the new digital economy and it has given birth to Internet Banking. Internet banking is predicted to transform the traditional banking. The internet offers banks the opportunity to better meet customer needs through enhanced interaction, data mining and customization. By use of the internet, it is possible for banks to offer a number of banking services, such as checking status of account, fund transfer, bill payment and banking services 24 hours a day. Internet based services are believed to be superior to those delivered through the regular channels due to convenience, interactivity, relatively low costs etc. In recent years more and more number of traditional brick and mortar banks has been moving to the internet, in order to sustain their competiveness in the global market place. Promoting quick response, just in time deliveries of services in electronic market place improve information sharing between the bank and its customers. Instead of banks controlling the relationship with the customer, today customers have more control of their banking needs via interaction with website. Banking online is both convenient and time saving .Customer satisfaction has always been a necessary condition of this organization. Internet banking is defined as the conducting of banking transaction through the internet .Banking services can be acquired through the public network of the internet. A customer can have accessed to his/her bank account through the Internet. Internet banking means any user with a personal computer and a web browser can get connected to his banks website to perform any of the banking transaction functions. All the services that the bank provides are displayed on the banks website. Innovation in technology and world-wide revolution in information and communication technology are perceived to be the catalyst of productivity growth. The relationship between IT and Banking is fundamentally symbiotic. It is expected to reduce costs, increase volumes and facilitate customized products. Technology adoption is a dire necessity for the public sector banks to complete with new generation private sector and foreign banks. It is a `compulsion' rather than a `choice'. Retention of existing customer is the primary concern of majority of the banks today. The Reserve Bank of India constituted a working group on Internet Banking. The group divided the internet banking products in India into 3 types based on the levels of access granted. They are: *Information Only System* - General purpose information like interest rates, branch location, bank products and their features, loan and deposit calculations are provided in the banks website. There exist facilities for downloading various types of application forms. The communication is normally done through e-mail. There is no interaction between the customer and bank's application system. No identification of the customer is done. In this system, there is no possibility of any unauthorized person getting into production systems of the bank through internet. *Electronic Information Transfer System*-The system provides customer-specific information in the form of account balances, transaction details, and statement of accounts. The information is still largely of the read only format. Identification and authentication of the customer is through password. The information is fetched from the bank's application system either in batch mode or off-line. The application systems cannot directly access through the internet. *Fully Electronic Transactional System* - This system allows bi-directional capabilities. Transactions can be submitted by the customer for online update. This system requires high degree of security and control. In this environment, web server and application systems are linked over secure infrastructure. It comprises technology covering computerization, networking and security, inter-bank payment gateway and legal infrastructure.

INTERNET BANKING IN INDIA

The banking industry in India is facing unprecedented competition from non-traditional banking institutions, which now offer banking and financial services over the Internet. The deregulation of the banking industry coupled with the emergence of new technologies, are enabling new competitors to enter the financial services market quickly and efficiently. Indian banks are going for the retail banking in a big way. However, much is still to be achieved. According to a study it shows, throughout the country, the Internet Banking is in the growing stage of development. In general, these Internet sites offer only the most basic services. 55% are so called 'entry level' sites, offering little more than company information and basic marketing materials. Only 8% offer 'advanced transactions' such as online funds transfer, transactions & cash management services. Foreign & Private banks are much advanced in terms of the number of sites & their level of development. Internet banking has gained wide acceptance internationally and seems to be fast catching up in India with more and more banks entering the fray. Due to technology innovations, Internet banking for the retail segment is a recent phenomenon that has generated a lot of interest in the Indian banking industry. Private and foreign banks have been the early adopters while the PSU banks are also beginning to latch on to the bandwagon.As per IDC estimates, the total number of registered users for Internet banking in India is over two million. India has a little less than a million active Internet banking users. And though this is just 0.096 per cent of the total population, it represents 15 per cent of the India's Internet user population. Thus indicating that the concept of Internet banking is surely catching on. Internet Banking Market will develop which will be driven by factors like:

(1) Demand side pressure due to increasing access to low cost electronic services.
(2) Emergence of open standards for banking functionality.
(3) Growing customer awareness and need of transparency.
(4) Global players in the market.
(5) Eliminate geographic boundaries.

As in all forms of technology innovations, Public sector banks have remained laggards in the race for adopting Internet banking practices. There are very few nationalized banks like State Bank of India, Bank of Baroda, Allahabad Bank, Syndicate Bank and Bank of India that offer Internet banking services. SBI's Internet banking initiative, launched in July 2001, is in fact doing quite well and has over 18,000 registered customers across 150 branches. The enthusiastic response has encouraged the SBI management to extend the service to an additional 500 branches. But despite positive news like this, PSU banks still have a lot of catching up to do on the Internet banking services front.

LITERATURE REVIEW

Attitudes and motives are among the fundamental factors influencing consumers' buying behaviour and have, therefore, attracted considerable attention from researchers probing the behaviour of bank customers and their relationship with these institutions. In the context of technologically based distribution channels, attitudes and motives have generally been used as segmentation variables to define distinct customer groups whose attitudinal profiles showed similarities within the group. Using 11 attitudinal dimensions concerning technology and information, Machauer and Morgner (2001) defined four clusters of bank consumers. These were "transaction oriented", "generally interested", "service oriented", and "technology opposed" groups. Barczak et al. (1997) studied the consumer motives for use of technologically based banking services and distribution channels and found that customers could be clustered on their money management philosophies. Their results describing four motivational clusters including "security conscious", "maximizers", "instant gratification", and "hassle avoiders" indicated that the four motivational segments had different attitudes and behaviours towards different banking technologies.Karjaluoto et al. (2002) found that attitude towards online banking and actual behaviour were both influenced by prior experience of computers and technology as well as attitudes towards computers. Moutinho and Smith (2000) who studied the behaviour of established bank customers in the UK and concluded that ease of banking and convenience were the two important expectations. Mattila et al. (2003) added that household income and education had a significant effect on the adoption of IB among mature consumers in Finland, whereas perceived difficulty in using computers combined with the lack of personal service in e-banking were the main barriers. For corporate customers, however, the main barrier was seen as security concerns (Rotchanakitumnuai and Speece, 2003). Sathye (1999) investigated the adoption of internet banking by Australian consumers and identified security concerns and lack of awareness about internet banking as the main obstacles to non-adoption. Black et al. (2001) reinforced the importance of the perceived innovation attributes in the adoption process but also drew attention to additional dimensions such as "societal issues" and "the sense of fatalism" which required further research. Mukherjee and Nath (2003) concentrated on the concept of trust in online relationship marketing in India and tested a model of trust in which "shared value", "communication", and "opportunistic behaviour" were taken as antecedents of trust. They concluded that both shared value and communication played a significant positive role on trust and that trust had a significant positive influence on commitment. Joseph and Stone (2003) argued that the ability to deliver services via technology appears to be correlated with high satisfaction with services deemed most important to customers.

RESEARCH OBJECTIVES

- To identify the main types of financial transactions the Customers carry out with their respective public and private sector banks.
- To determine the factors for adoption of internet banking.
- To model the customers' adoption of internet banking using Structural equation model.

METHODOLOGY

This study aims to determine the factors the customers keep in their mind while using internet banking .A specifically designed questionnaire was used as a tool for collecting the data. Seven point scale was used to measure all the statements (1 = Strongly agree to 7 = Strongly disagree). Respondents were asked to express the level of their agreement/disagreement with attributes identified. The total sample size was 100. The statements covered various attributes of internet banking and the responses given by the respondents were based on their perceptions about some attributes of the internet banking. Data were analyzed using factor analysis for identifying consumer's perception about internet banking using SPSS 16.0 software and SEM modeling using AMOS 16.0 software.

30% of the respondents expressed that they have accessed their banks websites for financial transactions. 70% of the respondents expressed that they have not used internet banking for their financial transactions. Out of the 70% respondents, 26% of the respondents opined that they will be using internet banking in the future. The respondents' preferences are computed in terms of frequency analysis. According to the study it was found that the main types of financial transaction carried out by the customers in internet banking are Balance Enquiry in Accounts, Display of Transaction for a Specific Period, Marketing Services i.e. new product/services/customer feed Back etc, download or print Statement. The highest number of customers prefers to balance enquiry in accounts followed by download or print statement. The least preferred financial transaction is marketing services and display of transaction for specific period. The respondents were requested to rank the statements on a 7-point scale basis (1=Strongly agree, 4=Neutral, 7=Strongly disagree).The 16 statements are as follows:

Statement	*Name of Variable*
Bank's website design and navigation makes comfortable to conduct a transaction.	A1
Bank's website executes transaction quickly and efficiently.	A2
Bank's website can be accessed -24 hours/day when needed.	A3
The Bank provides assurance of internet banking integrity	B1
Privacy statement on bank's website guarantees privacy of personal data	B2
The Bank's website displays the logo of certifying authority.	B3
Changing the way to establish relationship with banks.	C1
Having friends and colleagues that conduct internet banking.	C2
No Longer satisfied with the quality of the current bank branch service.	C3
Being required to try out and use a new technology based product.	D1
Being required to integrate internet banking with lifestyle and the working environment.	D2
The website provides up-to-date information	E1
The website provides innovative products or services	E2
Internet Banking avoids interaction with bank employees.	F1
Interaction with Bank employees gives more confidence than internet banking.	F2
Employees in bank do thing for me which internet banking cannot.	F3

The adequacy of the data is evaluated on the basis of the results of Kaiser-Meyer-Olkin Measure of Sampling Adequacy (KMO) and Bartlett's Test of Sphericity.The KMO measure of sampling adequacy is .578 indicating that the present data are suitable for factor analysis. Bartlett's Test of Sphericity is significant ($p<.001$), indicating sufficient correlation exists, between variables for the factor analysis. The Bartlett's Test statistics is approximately distributed and is accepted.

KMO and Bartlett's Test

Kaiser-Meyer-Olkin Measure of Sampling Adequacy.		.578
Bartlett's Test of Sphericity	Approx. Chi-Square	301.896
	df	120
	Sig.	.000

The first 6 components i.e. factors in the above table have an Eigen values over 1 and they account for about 80 per cent of the observed variation in the consumers' perception about internet banking. According Kaiser Criterion ,only the first 6 factors should be used because other Eigen values are more than one.

Rotated Component Matrix (a)

	Component					
	1	2	3	4	5	6
B1		.910				
B2		.927				
B3		.685				
A1	.941					
A2	.954					
A3	.957					
C1			.613			
C2			.766			
C3	-.513		-.659			
F1					.811	
F2				.594		.413
F3						.807
D1	-.355	-.702		.305		
D2		-.792		.422		
E1		.863			.359	
E2		.812			.367	

Extraction Method: Principal Component Analysis. Rotation Method: Varimax with Kaiser Normalization.
a Rotation converged in 9 iterations.

From the above table, the attributes like A1, A2, A3 have loading factor .941, .954, .957 on Factor 1.This concludes that Factor 1 is a combination of these 3 variables. Therefore, the factor can be interpreted as internet banking has perceived ease

Total Variance Explained

	Initial Eigenvalues			*Extraction Sums of Squared Loadings*			*Rotation Sums of Squared Loadings*		
Component	*Total*	*% of Variance*	*Cumulative %*	*Total*	*% of Variance*	*Cumulative %*	*Total*	*% of Variance*	*Cumulative %*
1	3.901	24.379	24.379	3.901	24.379	24.379	3.499	21.867	21.867
2	2.561	16.006	40.386	2.561	16.006	40.386	2.682	16.764	38.632
3	2.330	14.561	54.947	2.330	14.561	54.947	2.355	14.716	53.348
4	1.667	10.422	65.369	1.667	10.422	65.369	1.717	10.729	64.077
5	1.415	8.843	74.212	1.415	8.843	74.212	1.499	9.367	73.444
6	1.002	6.260	80.472	1.002	6.260	80.472	1.124	7.028	80.472
7	.924	5.776	86.248						
8	.744	4.653	90.901						
9	.464	2.898	93.799						
10	.255	1.592	95.390						
11	.245	1.531	96.922						
12	.211	1.319	98.241						
13	.142	.887	99.127						
14	.077	.484	99.611						
15	.047	.294	99.905						
16	.015	.095	100.000						

Extraction Method: Principal Component Analysis.

of use and usefulness. Factor 1 alone contributed 24% variations in consumers' perception about internet banking. The attributes like B1, B2, and B3 have a high loading i.e. .910, .927, .685 indicating that Factor 2 is a combination of these variables. These variables are combined into a factor called perceived risk and privacy. Factor 2 i.e. perceived secure and privacy alone contributed 16% variations in consumers' perception about internet banking. The attributes like C1, C2, C3 have a high loading i.e. .613, .766 indicating that Factor 3 is a combination of these variables. These variables are combined into a factor called perceived for culture. Factor 3 i.e. perceived culture alone contributed 14% variations in consumers' perception about internet banking. The attributes like D1, D2 have a high loading i.e. .305, .422 indicating that Factor 4 is a combination of these variables. These variables are combined into a factor called perceived for personal preference. Factor 4 i.e. perceived personal preference alone contributed 10% variations in consumers' perception about internet banking. The attributes like E1, E2 have a high loading i.e. .359, .367 indicating that Factor 5 is a combination of these variables. These variables are combined into a factor called perceived for innovation. Factor 5 i.e. perceived for innovation alone contributed 8% variations in consumers' perception about internet banking. The attributes like F1, F2 have a high loading i.e. .413, .807 indicating that Factor 6 is a combination of these variables. These variables are combined into a factor called perceived for interaction. Factor 6 i.e. perceived for interaction alone contributed 6% variations in consumers' perception about internet banking.

OVERVIEW OF STRUCTURAL EQUATION MODELLING:

Structural equation modeling (SEM) grows out of and serves purposes similar to multiple regression, but in a more powerful way which takes into account the modeling of interactions, nonlinearities, correlated independents, measurement error, correlated error terms, multiple latent independents each measured by multiple indicators, and one or more latent dependents also each with multiple indicators. SEM may be used as a more powerful alternative to multiple regression, path analysis, factor analysis, time series analysis, and analysis of covariance. Advantages of SEM compared to multiple regression include more flexible assumptions, use of confirmatory factor analysis to reduce measurement error by having multiple indicators per latent variable, the attraction of SEM's graphical modeling interface, the desirability of testing models overall rather than coefficients individually, the ability to test models with multiple dependents, the ability to model mediating variables rather than be restricted to an additive model, the ability to model error terms, the ability to test coefficients across multiple between-subjects groups, and ability to handle difficult data

SEM supports two types of variables

(1) Measured/Observed/Indicator

(2) Latent

First category has numeric data, responses to a rating scale in a questionnaire which can be ranked. Data cannot be categorical .The second category i.e. latent variables cannot be observed. Latent variables are modeled using observed variables. In SEM terminology one uses endogenous for latent variables and exogenous for measured/independent variables. Model in SEM are shown in the form a path diagram. Observed variables are drawn as rectangles, latent variables are drawn as circles. Errors that are estimated which are not directly measured are shown as circles. When one variable is believed to cause another variable the relation is shown as directed arrow from cause and effect. This assumption is made by the modeler. One can also model correlation between variables which is shown as double headed arrow. For each arrow there may be an estimated weight similar to co-efficient in regression. There is also called path co-efficents.Latent variables can be used as dependent or independent variables. Normally latent variables are usually modeled using two or more observed variables. Objective of factor analysis is to reduce a set of variables to a smaller number. In factor analysis the loading of any observed variables on any factor can assume any value i.e. no constraints are imposed. In SEM modeler specifies which path co-efficient are free and which are to be fixed. One can also specify whether variables are independent or other co-vary.

Benefits of using SEM:

(1) Latent variables or unobserved variables which measures a concept that cannot be reliably measured can be modeled using measured or observed variables and one can validate to what extent the concept is captured using measured variables.

(2) One latent variable can drive another latent variable.

(3) Correlation among independent variables can be taken into account.

(4) Errors or reliability of each measured variables and also latent variables can be analyzed.

(5) Direct and indirect effects in path diagram can be explicitly analyzed.

The path diagram is shown below:

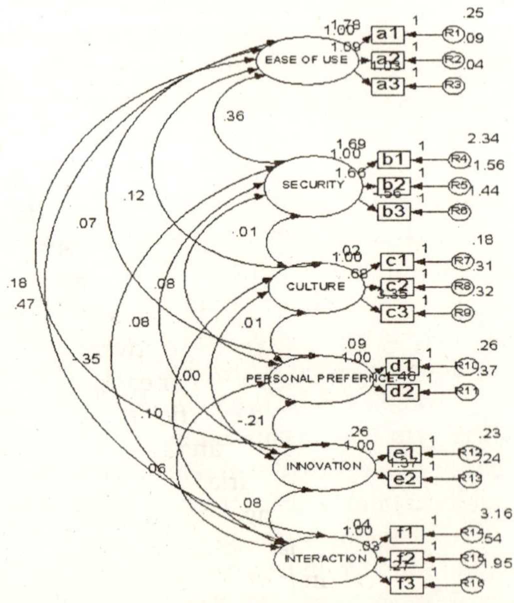

CONCLUSION

Awareness of internet banking services is essential in the early adoption stages. To access more potential adopters, information about internet banking should be provided by bank tellers and bank assistants at branches. The information should include references to "time saving", "convenience" at anywhere any time, "low costs", and "information availability". A perception of quality service will increase the bank's image for good services, accuracy and effectiveness. Failure of execution not only causes dissatisfaction and uncertainty to the customer but also makes the whole internet banking process more complex and less comprehensible. Banks should develop internet diffusion strategies by adopting pull strategies. Increased diffusion will increase the number of internet banking adopters since they are likely to come from the internet population. Furthermore, support from the government and the industry regulator will positively affect internet banking services by increasing the confidence of the adopters. The bank has to create a mass awareness campaign about the various merits of internet banking among customers, so that internet banking will be used as an alternative channel for delivering financial services. They need to satisfy customer needs , face up to increased competition from within the sector and from new entrants coming into the financial services market and they must continually invent new products and services in light of the technological change and innovation. Banks feel that customers lack the necessary confidence in internet banking so they have to use customer centric techno-innovative approach in building customer loyalty towards the adoption of internet banking.

REFERENCES

Dannesnberg, M. and Kellner, D. (1998), "The Bank of Tomorrow with Today's Technology", *International Journal of Bank Marketing*, Vol. 16 No. 2, pp. 90-7.

Doll, W.J. and Torkzadeh, G. (1988), "The Measurement of End User Computing Satisfaction", *MIS Quarterly*, Vol. 12, pp. 259-74.

Black, N.J., Lockett, A., Winklhofer, H., Ennew, C. (2001), "The Adoption of Internet Financial Services: A Qualitative Study",

International Journal of Retail & Distribution Management, Vol. 29 No. 8, pp. 390-8.

Devlin, J.F. (1995), "Technology and Innovation in Retail Banking Distribution", *International Journal of Bank Marketing*, Vol. 13, No. 4, pp. 19-25.

Gerrard, P., Cunningham, J. B. (2003), "The Diffusion of Internet Banking Among Singapore Consumers", *International Journal of Bank Marketing*, Vol. 21, No. 1, pp. 16-28.

Howcroft, B., Hamilton, R., Hewer, P. (2002), "Consumer Attitude and the Usage and Adoption of Home-based Banking in the United Kingdom", *The International Journal of Bank Marketing*, Vol. 20, No. 3, pp. 111-21.

Jun, M., Cai, S. (2001), "The Key Determinants of Internet Banking Service Quality: A Content Analysis", *International Journal of Bank Marketing*, Vol. 19, No. 7, pp. 276-91.

Kolachi, N. (2006), "Internet Banking System in Pakistan: Some Crucial Weaknesses and Suggestions for Improvement", *Journal of Institute of Bankers Pakistan*, Vol. 73, No. 2, pp. 23–32.

Liao, Z., Cheung, M.T. (2002), "Internet-based E-banking and Consumer Attitudes: An Empirical Study", *Information & Management*, Vol. 39, No. 4, pp. 283-95.

Laforet, S., and Xiaoyan Li. (2005), "Consumers' Attitudes Towards Online and Mobile Banking in China", *International Journal of Bank Marketing*, Vol. 23, No. 5, pp. 362-380.

White, H., Nteli, F. (2004), "Internet Banking in the UK: Why are There Not More Customers?", *Journal of Financial Services Marketing*, Vol. 9, pp. 49-57.

Yakhlef, A. (2001), "Does the Internet Compete with or Complement Bricks-and-Mortar Bank Branches?", *International Journal of Retail & Distribution Management*, Vol. 29, No. 6, pp. 272-81.

Kervin, J.B ,"Methods for Business Research (2nd Edition)",New York, Happer Collins.

Lewis,Ph,thornhill, A "Research Methods for Business Students", Prentice Hall.

Devlin J.F., "Technology and Innovation in Retail Banking Distribution", *International Journal of bank Marketing*, Vol. 17, No. 3, p. 19-25

www.onlinebankingreport.com

Bollen K.A Structural equation modellling with latent variables,John Wiley, 1989.

http://www2.chass.ncsu.edu/garson/pa765/structur.htm

Hoyle R. (1995), Structural Equation Modeling ,Concepts, Issues and Application ,Thouisant Publications.

Moutinho, L. and Smith, A. (2000), "Modelling Bank Customers' Satisfaction Through Mediation of Attitudes Towards Human and Automated Banking", *International Journal of Bank Marketing,* Vol. 18, No. 3, pp. 124-34.

Mukherjee, A. and Nath, P. (2003), "A Model of Trust in Online Relationship Banking", *International Journal of Bank Marketing,* Vol. 21, No. 1, pp. 5-15.

Nath, R., Schrick, P. and Parzinger, M. (2001), "Bankers' Perspectives on Internet Banking", *E-Service Journal,* Vol. 1, No. 1, pp. 21-36.

Polatoglu, V.N. and Ekin, S. (2001), "An Empirical Investigation of the Turkish Consumers'Acceptance of Internet Banking Services", *International Journal of Bank Marketing,* Vol. 19, No. 4, pp. 156-65.

3

FINANCIAL PERFORMANCE OF BANKS IN INDIA

Biswo Ranjan Mishra & Manidatta Ray

INTRODUCTION: INDIAN BANKING SECTOR

Without a sound and effective banking system in India it cannot have a healthy economy. The banking system of India should not only be hassle free but it should be able to meet new challenges posed by the technology and other external and internal factors.

For the past three decades India's banking system has several outstanding achievements to its credit. The most striking is its extensive reach. It is no longer confined to only metropolitans or cosmopolitans in India. In fact, Indian banking system has reached even to the remote corners of the country. This is one of the main reasons of India's growth process.

Currently banking in India is fairly mature in terms of supply, product range and reach. In terms of quality of assets and capital adequacy, Indian banks are considered to have a strong and transparent position. As the growth in Indian economy is expected to be strong for quite some time, especially in its service sector, the demand for banking services sector, is also expected to be stronger.

INDIAN BANKING SECTOR- BANKING ON REFORMS

The Indian financial system in the pre-reform period (i.e., prior to Gulf crisis of 1991), essentially catered to the needs of planned development in a mixed-economy framework where the public sector had a dominant role in economic activity. The strategy of planned economic development required huge development expenditure, which was met through Government's dominance of ownership of banks, automatic monetization of fiscal deficit and subjecting the banking sector to large pre-emptions-both in terms of the statutory holding of Government securities (statutory liquidity ratio, or SLR) and cash reserve ratio (CRR).

Besides, there was a complex structure of administered interest rates guided by the social concerns, resulting in cross-subsidization. These not only distorted the interest rate mechanism but also adversely affected the viability and profitability of banks by the end of 1980s. There is perhaps an element of commonality of such a 'repressed' regime in the financial sector of many emerging market economies. It follows that the process of reform of financial sector in most emerging economies also has significant commonalities while being specific to the circumstances of each country. A narration of the broad contours of reform in India would be helpful in appreciating both the commonalities and the differences in our paths of reforms.

The Indian banking system has witnessed significant changes during the last decade. There have been new banks, new instruments, mergers and takeovers and, along with all these new challenges.

While deregulation of banks opened up new vistas to augmented revenues, it has also posed greater competition and risks. The financial sector reforms introduced early in 1990s as a part of the structural reforms have affected almost all the banking operations. The broader objectives of the financial sector reforms were to enhance efficiency and productivity.

Financial sector reforms were carried out in two phases:

- To create productive and profitable institutions; and
- To strengthen the financial system and put it on a par with global standards.

Financial sectors reforms in India started with deregulation of interest ratio. Banks now have complete flexibility to decide their rate of interest and manage their assets and liabilities accordingly. The SLR has been gradually reduced from a peak of 38.5% to 25%. CRR was reduced from its peak level of 15% maintained during 1989-92 to 4.5% in June 2003; presently it is at 6%.

In the second phase, persistent efforts have been made towards the adoption of international benchmarks by RBI. As a part of the financial sector reforms, the regulatory norms with respect to capital adequacy, income recognition, asset classification and provisioning have moved towards convergence with the accounting standards. In turn, these measures have enhanced the transparency of the balance sheet of bank and infused accountability in their functioning.

Securitization and Reconstruction of Financial Assets and Enforcement of Security Interest (SARFAESI) Act, 2002 has helped to reduce the level of NPAs targeted, towards improvement risk management practices. The minimum capital to risk asset ratio (CRAR) was set and the banks which are not able to comply with new norms were allowed to raise capital from the market.

In line with the amendment to incorporate market risk in Basel I, separate charge for market risks was also introduced in 2004.

The banks are required to disclose capital adequacy, asset quality and maturity distribution of selected items on assets and liability, profitability, country risk exposure as per the accounting standards.

RBI issued guidelines on asset-liability management and risk management systems in banks in 1999, guidance on credit risk management and market risks management in October 2002, and the guidance risk on operational risk management in 2005.

RBI set guidelines for the establishment of new banks in the private sector and foreign banks with a view to enhance productivity and efficiency through competition. Foreign Direct Investment (FDI) in private sectors is now allowed to 74%.

The smooth functioning of the payment and settlement system is a pre-requisite for financial stability. The Board of Regulation of Payment and Settlement Systems (BPSS) were set up in March 2005 for giving policy direction in the area of payment and settlement system. A risk free payment and settlement system in government securities and foreign exchange was established by the Clearing Corporation of India Limited (CCIL), which is set up by the banks.

In the post-reform period, assets/liabilities of bank have grown consistently at a high rate. The financial performance of banks also improved as reflected in their increased profitability. Another important development is the sharp reduction in the NPA to net advances.

It is evident that we are at the beginning of this new phase in the Indian banking, but with a competitive pressure, both domestic and external, public sector banks have to push hard.

RESEARCH METHODOLOGY

Problem Statement

The development of industries depends on several factors such as human, technology, and quality marketing and financial, among which the financial aspect assumes a significant role in determining the growth of industries. In this context, the researcher is interested in undertaking an analysis of the financial performance of the banking sector companies to examine and understand how management of finance plays a crucial role in the growth. Hence, the present study entitled as "Financial Performance of Banks in India: Some Evidence to Select Banks" has been undertaken.

OBJECTIVES OF THE STUDY

- To study the growth and development of Indian banking sector.

- To study the behavior of profitability of select banks; and
- To analyze the factors determining the profitability.

TESTING OF HYPOTHESIS

- When Return on Investment (ROI) increases, Earnings Before Interest and Taxes (EBIT) remain the same.
- When Interest income increases, ROI remains the same.
- When ROI increases, Net NPA to Net advances remains the same.
- When interest coverage ratio increases, debt equity ratio remains the same.

DATA AND THE SOURCE

The study is entirely based on secondary data. All the banks of BANKEX Index are sample units. Data regarding performance of banks was collected for a period of six years. i.e. 2001-06. Necessary data was obtained from CMIE - PROWESS.

FRAMEWORK OF ANALYSIS

For the purpose of analysis, various ratios are studied extensively. Statistical measures like correlation analysis, multiple regression (linear) analysis and testing of hypothesis are used for comparison.

SIGNIFICANCE OF THE STUDY

The study will throw light on the overall financial performance of banking sector as a whole in the past five years.

HIGHLIGHTS OF THE RATIO ANALYSIS

The primary objective of any business is to earn. The investors want adequate return on their investment Tables 1, 2, 3, 4, 5, 6, 7, 8 and 9) throw light on the various dimensions of business.

ANALYSIS OF DATA

- Table 1-shows that the interest coverage ratio is continuously increasing, which indicates the company's ability to meet the interest obligations.

Table 1
Ratio Analysis

Interest	*2001*	*2002*	*2003*	*2004*	*2005*	*2006*
Mean	119.375	123.625	127.125	137.5	133.8125	132.4375
Median	112.5	118	127	137	132	131
Standard Deviation	25.07555	31.49365	19.70744	34.18187	22.51583	018.25
Sample Variance	628.7833	991.85	388.3833	1168.4	506.9625	333.0625
Kurtosis	11.26099	009.630193	002.600671	005.421835	001.230355	003.31296
Skew ness	3.238613	002.474353	000.620503	-1.355460	-0.529310	-0.62204
Minimum	103	70	92	36	79	84
Maximum	207	229	178	199	73	17
Largest (1)	207	229	178	199	73	170
Smallest (1)	103	70	92	36	79	84

- Table 2-displays net profit ratio which shows a continuous decline, nearly 7% in the past five years.

Table 2
Net Profit Ratio

NP Ratio %	*2001*	*2002*	*2003*	*2004*	*2005*	*2006*
Mean	70.80688	69.68563	69.02688	64.61813	62.04125	63.8925
Median	70.27	71.495	70.565	66.89	63.35	68.775
Standard Deviation	5.281681	6.779461	5.809152	13.70915	9.312341	9.621619
Sample Variance	27.89616	45.96109	33.74625	187.9408	86.71969	92.57555
Kurtosis	2.447236	6.592492	1.190823	9.219947	7.121573	7.211428
Skew ness	1.152431	-2.26922	-0.96472	-2.52976	-2.20516	-2.47414
Range	22.47	28.17	23.82	66.04	41	38.46
Minimum	62.6	48.25	54.81	18.85	32.28	32.9
Maximum	85.07	76.42	78.63	84.89	73.28	71.36
Largest (1)	85.07	46.42	78.63	84.89	73.28	71.36
Smallest (1)	62.6	48.25	54.81	18.85	32.28	32.9

- Table 3-is the ratio of debt to equity. Debt equity ratio was highest in year 2003 and later reduced to reach a level of 1:1 apex.

Table 3
Ratio of Debt to Equity

DE Ratio %	*2001*	*2002*	*2003*	*2004*	*2005*	*2006*
Mean	138.5625	164.375	172.9375	118.9375	101	106.0625
Median	91.5	94	93.5	84.5	80	91
Standard Deviation	135.3814	212.7784	214.2477	108.7943	73.08169	64.96773
Sample Variance	18328.13	45274.65	45902.06	11836.2	5340.933	4185.796
Kurtosis	5.27882	10.2227	5.129249	9.402674	5.833998	-1.02578
Skew ness	2.348741	3.079709	2.405769	2.93009	2.228481	0.525596

Table 3(a)
Ratio of Debt to Equity

DE Ratio %	*2001*	*2002*	*2003*	*2004*	*2005*	*2006*
Range	524	849	751	445	189	63.8925
Minimum	15	45	45	41	28	68.775
Maximum	539	894	796	486	217	9.621619
Largest (1)	539	894	796	486	217	92.57555
Smallest (1)	15	45	45	41	28	7.211428

- Table 4-displays the return on net worth which shows an exceptionally poor performance in the year 2004.

Table 4
Return on Net worth (RONW)

RONW %	*2001*	*2002*	*2003*	*2004*	*2005*	*2006*
Mean	14.76938	14.51875	17.95688	4.220625	17.89063	15.80438
Median	12.57	21.53	24.51	25.43	17.315	16.31
Standard Deviation	7.7605	27.48248	23.83017	86.36268	12.08318	9.914521
Sample Variance	60.22535	755.2866	567.8772	7458.512	146.0034	98.29773
Kurtosis	0.200013	12.85136	6.317239	15.74735	2.43356	3.896808
Skew ness	0.200013	-3.44404	-2.24625	-3.95515	-0.65545	-1.08713
Range	29.91	118.51	100.6	358.16	51.68	45.91
Minimum	1.28	-84.07	-56.66	-318.58	-13.61	-11.94
Maximum	31.19	34.44	43.94	39.58	38.07	33.97
Largest (1)	31.19	34.44	43.94	39.58	38.07	33.97
Smallest (1)	1.28	-84.07	-56.66	-318.58	-13.61	-11.94

- Table 5-Capital adequacy ratio remains more or less constant over a period of time.

Table 5
Capital Adequacy Ratio

Capital Adequacy Ratio %	*2001*	*2002*	*2003*	*2004*	*2005*	*2006*
Mean	10.82188	12.3675	12.40938	12.44813	12.89813	12.31938
Median	10.975	11.03	12.02	12.59	12.49	12.205
Standard Deviation	3.392276	5.070484	4.378714	1.819924	2.576559	1085642
Sample Variance	11.50754	25.70981	19.17314	3.312123	6.638656	1.17862
Kurtosis	7.456338	12.6389	7.570327	2.776364	8.697602	-1.52536
Skew ness	-2.06137	3.344905	1.506838	-1.22811	2.5285	0.165405
Range	16.49	23.73	22.95	7.76	12.21	3.25
Minimum	0	6.74	3.02	7.49	9.21	10.75
Maximum	1649	30.47	25.97	15.25	21.42	14
Largest (1)	16.49	30.47	25.97	15.25	21.42	14
Smallest (1)	0	6.74	3.02	7.49	9.21	10.75

- Table 6-Interest income in proportion to working funds is reducing overall though marginally.

Table 6
Interest Income in Proportion to Working Funds

Interest Income to Working Funds W%	*2001*	*2002*	*2003*	*2004*	*2005*	*2006*
Mean	9.32375	9.515625	9.195625	8,304375	7.55625	7.403125
Median	9.815	9.455	9.15	8.215	7.535	7.3
Standard Deviation	2.579475	0.808166	0.808166	0.795244	0.75401	0.466086
Sample Variance	6.653692	0.653133	0.653133	0.632413	0.568532	0.217236
Kurtosis	13.37411	-0.74762	-0.74762	2.235845	3.787752	-0.74216
Skew ness	-3.51546	-0.02514	-0.02514	1.055679	1.584356	0.408411
Range	11.54	2.6	2.6	3.23	3.03	1.49
Minimum	0	7.89	7.89	7.19	6.71	6.69
Maximum	11.54	10.49	10.42	10.42	9.74	8.18
Largest (1)	11.54	10.49	10.42	10.42	9.74	8.18
Smallest (1)	0	7.89	7.19	7.19	6.71	6.69

- Table 7-Operating profit is very low and sustained at 2% not showing any signs of growth.
- Table 8-Non-performing assets are continuously reducing in percentage to net advances.
- Table 9-Return on Investment (ROI) is also reducing, which is not a good sign.

Table 7
Operating. Profit

Operating Profit Ratio %	*2001*	*2002*	*2003*	*2004*	*2005*	*2006*
Mean	1.569375	2.48	2.668125	2.916875	2.3875	2.20875
Median	1.47	2.17	2.605	2.965	2.5	2.185
Standard Deviation	0.652119	1.327584	0.953361	0.859494	0.617754	0.348824
Sample Variance	0.42526	1.76248	0.908896	0.73873	0.38162	0.121678
Kurtosis	1.54802	6.763178	3.891249	4.54265	3.990322	-0.00493
Skew ness	-0.30294	2.03314	0.721173	-1.64983	-1.3017	-0.41337
Range	2.83	6.33	4.63	3.72	2.87	1.26
Minimum	0	0.32	0.61	0.38	0.65	1.49
Maximum	2.83	6.65	5.24	4.1	3.52	2.75
Largest (1)	2.83	6.65	5.24	4.1	3.52	2.75
Smallest (1)	0	0.32	0.61	0.38	0.65	1.49

Table 8
Non-Performing Assets

NPA to Net Advances %	*2001*	*2002*	*2003*	*2004*	*2005*	*2006*
Mean	5.116875	4.93875	3.9	2.188125	1.505625	0.8525
Median	5.435	5.4	4.18	2.61	1.42	0.855
Standard Deviation	3.146752	2.761125	2.226187	1.447472	0.900577	0509608
Sample Variance	9.90205	7.623812	4.955907	2.095176	0.81104	0.2597
Kurtosis	-0.31725	0.845846	-0.45443	-0.99339	-1.16679	-0.28708

Table 8(a)
Non-Performing Assets

NPA to Net Advances %	*2001*	*2002*	*2003*	*2004*	*2005*	*2006*
Skew ness	0.243572	0.203729	-0.1355	-0.09841	-0.11569	0.319159
Range	11.23	11.09	7.81	4.5	2.6	1.87
Minimum	0	0	0.11	0	0.2	0
Maximum	11.23	11.09	7.92	4.5	2.8	1.87
Largest (1)	11.23	11.09	7.92	4.5	2.8	1.87
Smallest (1)	0	0	0.11	0	0.2	0

Table 9
Return on Investment (ROI)

ROI %	*2001*	*2002*	*2003*	*2004*	*2005*	*2006*
Mean	7.6302	7.118744	7.31265	8,304375	5.105294	5.094881
Median	7.02125	7.14095		7.20585	8.215	5.1366
5.13445						
Standard Deviation	1.954304	1.735144	0.777802	0.795244	0.526581	0.434716
Sample Variance	3.819302	3.010726	0.604976	0.632413	0.277288	0.188978
Kurtosis	9.42432	5.29169	-0.12886	2.235845	-0.67277	-1.08627
Skew ness	2.780251	-1.83366	0.142676	1.055679	0.266146	-0.38724
Range	8.8005	7.6181	3.0065	3.23	1.6864	1.3697

Contd.

ROI %	*2001*	*2002*	*2003*	*2004*	*2005*	*2006*
Minimum	5.4237	1.865	5.8015	7.19	4.3679	4.3466
Maximum	14.2242	9.4831	8.0808	10.42	6.0573	5.7163
Largest (1)	14.2242	9.4831	8.0808	10.42	6.0573	5.7163
Smallest (1)	5.4237	1.865	5.8015	7.19	4.3679	4.3466

HIGHLIGHTS OF THE CORRELATION ANALYSIS

Correlation analysis helps in understanding how two variables are related to each other and how a cause and effect relation can be established among them (Table 10).

- Interest coverage ratio has a strong negative correlation with net profit ratio, debt equity ratio, interest income to working funds ratio, ROI and net NPA to net assets ratio.

MULTIPLE REGRESSION ANALYSIS

The following multiple regression equation is used in the model to describe the relationship between dependent and independent variables:

$$Y = \alpha + \beta_1 X_1 + \beta_2 X_2 + \beta_3 X_3 + \beta_4 X_4 + \beta_5 X_5 + \beta_6 X_6$$

Where

Y	=	Earnings before interest and Tax (EBIT) (dependent variable)
α	=	Intercept
β_1	=	Coefficient of Interest Coverage Ratio
β_2	=	Coefficient of Dept Equity Ratio
β_3	=	Coefficient of Capital Adequacy Ratio
β_4	=	Coefficient of Net NPA to Net Advances Ratio
β_5	=	Coefficient of Interest Income to Working Funds Ratio
β_6	=	Coefficient of ROI
X_1	=	Interest Coverage Ratio
X_2	=	Debt Equity Ratio
X_3	=	Capital Adequacy Ratio
X_4	=	Net NPA to Net Advances Ratio
X_5	=	Interest Income to Working Funds Ratio
X_6	=	ROI

Table 10
Correlation Analysis

	Interest Converge Ratio	*Net Profit Ratio*	*Debt Equity Ratio*	*Capital Adequacy Ratio*	*Interest Income to Working Funds*	*Operating Profit to Working Funds*	*Net NPA to Net Advance Ratio*	*ROI*
Interest CoverageRatio	1	–	–	–	–	–	–	–
Net ProfitRatio	- 0.8921*	1	–	–	–	–	–	–
Debt EquityRatio	- 0.64467*	- 0.64467*	1	–	–	–	–	–
Capital AdequacyRatio	0.735902*	-0.68321*	-0.21535	1	–	–	–	–
Interest Income to Working Funds	- 0.77931*	0.950428*	0.902935*	-0.50258	1	–	–	–
Operating Profit to Working Funds	0.681754*	-0.36383	0.100254	0.798289*	-0.18406	1	–	–
Net NPAto Net Advance Ratio	- 0.87111*	- 0.953617*	0.821529*	-0.60461*	0.976463*	-0.31872	1	–
ROI	- 0.81614*	0.971849*	0.867313*	-0.6309	0.974271*	-0.25223	0.962074*	1

Note: * Correlation is significant at the 0.01 level (2-tailed)

While it has a positive relation with the operating profit to working funds.

- Net profit ratio has a strong negative relation with capital adequacy while strong positive relations with debt equity. Interest income to working funds, net NPA to Net advances and ROI.
- Debt equity ratio has positive relations with interest income to working funds, net NPA to net advances and ROI.
- Capital adequacy ratio is linked with net NPA to net advances.
- Interest income to working funds is having a strong degree of positive relation with net NPA to net advance and ROI.

It is observed from the multiple regression equation for the period (2001-06) that the correlation coefficient was 0.476 (Table 11). The six selected independent variables in the study collectively contributed 22.6% to earnings before interest and taxes. The analysis of variance (multiple regressions) in Table 12 shows "F" value of 0.439; it indicated that the multiple regression equation is not significant.

Table 11
Model Summary (2001-06)

Model	*R*	*R Square*	*Adjusted R Square*	*Std. Error of the Estimate*
6	0.476	0.226	-0.289	6536.38

Table 12
Analysis of Variance (ANOVA)

Model	*Sum of Squares*	*df*	*Mean Square*	*F*	*Sig.*
Regression	112434297.658	6	18739049.610	0.439	0.836 (1)
Residual	384401127.428	9	42711236.381	–	–
Total	496835425.086	15	–	–	–

TESTING OF HYPOTHESIS

Hypothesis is an assumption to be tested. The statistical testing of hypothesis is the most important technique in statistical inference. Hypothesis tests are widely used in business and industry for making decision. The following are the hypotheses framed and tested by using test of significance (t-test) at 1% level of significance (Tables 13, 14, 14(a), (b) and (c)).

Table 13
Coefficients

	Un-Standardized Coefficients	
ROI %	*B*	*Std.Error*
(Constant)	44261.027	57914.644
Interest Coverage Ratio	-171.765	224.295
Debt Equity Ratio	-7.806	18.814
Capital Adequacy Ratio	1467.863	2287.996
Net NPA to Net Advance Ratio	256.717	1820.615
Interest Income to Working Funds	-4182.836	4698.983
RO	63.747	4721.444

1. H_0 = When ROI increase, EBIT remains same.
   H_α = When ROI increases, EBIT also increases.

Table 14
Hypothesis – 1 : Paired Differences

t-Test	*Mean*	*Std. Deviation*	*Std.Error Mean*	*95% Confidences Interval of the Difference*		*t*	*df*	*Sig. (2 tailed)*
				Lower	*Upper*			
ROI0EBIT	-4416.861	5755.330	5755.832	-7483.66	-1350.06	-3069	15	0.0077

Calculated t value - 3.06 is more than table value 2.58 at 1% level of significance, so the null hypothesis cannot be accepted, i.e. when ROI increase EBIT remains the same which means that with increase in ROI, EBIT also increases.

2. H_0 = When interest increase, ROI remains the same.
   H_α = When interest income, ROI also increase.

Table 14 (a)
Hypothesis – 2 : Paired Differences

t-Test	*Mean*	*Std. Deviation*	*Std.Error Mean*	*95% Confidences Interval of the Difference*		*t*	*df*	*Sig. (2 tailed)*
				Lower	*Upper*			
Interest Income-ROI-	2.171	0.921	0.230	1.680	2.662	9.425	15	1.082

Calculated t value 9.42 is more than the table value 2.58 at 1% level of significance, so the null hypothesis cannot be accepted, i.e. when interest income increases, ROI remains the same which means that when interest income increases, ROI also increases.

3. H_0 = When ROI increases, Net NPA to Net advances remains same.
   H_α = When ROI increases, Net NPA to Net advances also increases.

Table 14 (b)
Hypothesis – 3 : Paired Differences

t-Test	*Mean*	*Std. Deviation*	*Std.Error Mean*	*95% Confidences Interval of the Difference*		*t*	*df*	*Sig. (2 tailed)*
				Lower	*Upper*			
Net NPA to Net Advance ROI	-3.29	1.90	0.475	-4.30	-2.281	-6.93	15	4.79

Calculated t value -6.93 is more than the table value 2.58 at 1% level of significance, so the null hypothesis cannot be accepted, i.e. when ROI increases net NPA to Net advances remains the same and we can say that when ROI increases, net NPA to net advances also increases.

4. H_0 = When interest coverage ratio increases, Debt equity ratio remains same.
   H_α = Higher the interest coverage ratio, Higher the debt equity ratio.

Table 14(c)
Hypothesis – 4: Paired Differences

t-Test	*Mean*	*Std. Deviation*	*Std.Error Mean*	*95% Confidences Interval of the Difference*		*t*	*df*	*Sig. (2 tailed)*
				Lower	*Upper*			
Interest Coverage Debt Equity	-4.66	118.280	29.57	-67.69	58.36	-0.157	15	0.876

Calculated t value -0.15 is less than the table value of 2.58 at 1% level of significance, so the null hypothesis cannot be rejected, i.e. when interest coverage ratio increases, debt equity ratio remains the same.

CONCLUSION

From the study of the financial performance analysis of selected banks, it can be concluded that the financial positions of banks is reasonable. Debt equity ratio is maintained at an adequate level throughout and NPAs also witnessed a decline during the study period. The ROI remains at a very low position, which is a worrying factor.

We can conclude that banks in India be it Public, Private Indian or Foreign, have to use the following three mantras for success and to meet the future challenges.

- Tapping into the rural market;
- Risk management under Basel perspective; and
- Consolidation.

REFERENCES[*]

Address by Mr. V. Leeladhar (2007), Deputy Governor of the Reserve Bank of India, at the Annual Washington Conference of the Institute of International Bankers, Washington DC, March 5.

Hamsalakshmi R and Manicham M. (2005), Financial, Performance Analysis of Selected Banks", *Finance India,* Vol. XIX, No. 3, September.

Khan M. Y. and Jain P. K. (2001), Financial Management, Text and Problems, Tata McGraw Hill Publishing Company Ltd., New Delhi.

Mayers and Berly (2005), Principles of Corporate Finance, Tata McGraw Hill Publishing Company Ltd., New Delhi.

Pandey I. M. (2001), Financial Management, Eighth Revised Edition, Vikas Publishing House Pvt. Ltd., New Delhi.

Ross (2005), Corporate Finance, Tata McGraw Hill Publishing Company Ltd., New Delhi.

Appendix

List of Banks Selected

S. No.	*Company Name*
1.	Allahabad Bank
2.	Andhra Bank
3.	Bank of Baroda
4.	Bank of India
5.	Canara Bank
6.	Centurion Bank of Punjab Ltd.
7.	Federal Bank Ltd.
8.	HDFC Bank Ltd.
9.	ICICI Bank Ltd.
10.	Indian Overseas Bank
11.	Kotak Mahindra Bank Ltd.
12.	Oriental Bank of Commerce
13.	Punjab National Bank
14.	State Bank of India
15.	UTI Bank Ld.
16.	Union Bank of India

4

RBI SCANNER AND SAHARA INDIA GROUP

(AN INTUITIVE VIEW ON RURAL POVERTY IN INDIA)

Sukanta Chandra Swain

INTRODUCTION

News flashes like Indian stock markets crashed and rupee touching all times lows have been very familiar for last couple of weeks or so. Before trying to uncover the ways to divest ourselves of those, it is apparent to explore what is happening in the market that is pulling the sensex downhill and forcing rupee to touch unprecedented lows as this scrutiny may endow with better elucidation for the current predicament in the Indian economy.

One of the most important causes behind the present market catastrophe in India is the extraction of Foreign Institutional Investments (FIIs) causing substantial outflow of Dollar and demand crunch in equity market. Many foreign institutions and hedge funds have become bankrupt in their domicile countries forcing them to vend Indian assets at offhand prices pulling our market down and depreciating our currency. Now the point is "Why do we rely on them so enormously that any setback of them creates identical or even further knotty state of affairs for us?" The answer is so simple.

In the pursuit of growth and development we covet to be in leading edge but our domestic savings and investment volumes are not adequate for the reason. So there is no way out to accomplish our intent of elevated growth rate except for soaring dependence on foreign investment. Foreign investment in the form of Foreign Direct Investment has been proved advantageous for Indian economy in many fronts but foreign institutional investment has been daunting lot many negatives in our economy as compared to positives. And our economy in recent years has been a very superior destination of foreign institutional investors because of incredibly strong macroeconomic rudiments catering favorable ambiance for them. As we have invited those, it is our duty to endure any sort of adversities there from.

On the exterior any one can effortlessly say that we are short of domestic savings and investments but if we strive to envisage intuitively, we may unearth the reality which may diverge radically from the accessible piece of information. It is not that the size of savings we do have now accurately represents our optimum latent. In rural areas still people are there who have savings potential but because of non-availability of financial institutions and/or lack of financial transaction habits they don't go for ceremonial savings. As an alternative they prefer hoarding or conspicuous consumption which is economically and socially unwanted for them, which can also be treated as an economic waste. Some instances are there where miniature depositors in rural areas keep their slight leftover earnings with their professed masters/zamindars who in return charge something from them. That is how emblematic reverse interest rate becomes operative. If we could have given our savings potential the shape of savings and channelize them in proper way probably our dependence on foreign investment would have been nil or miniscule and hence the present crisis would have been easily avoided. In this context the financial institutions (FI's) have a massive responsibility to execute. But most of our FIs fancy to concentrate in urban and sub-urban areas as business in those areas are safer and cost effective as compared to business in rural areas. On the other hand, the

FIs concentrating in rural areas, examples are the Sahara India Group led two institutions–Sahara India Investment Corporation Limited (SIICL) and Sahara India Financial Corporation Limited (SIFCL), are alleged to have functioned not in line with the Reserve Bank of India's guidelines. So those will die out from Indian financial market because of the RBI scanner. With the egress of FIs like SIICL and SIFCL, not only the problems of equity market and exchange rate will be unsolved but more intensively the hitch of poverty will exacerbate as they were working for the deprived and by the depriving too. While our focus now is on financial inclusion and micro finance in order to alleviate poverty, the sudden termination of institutions working for the same purpose, i. e., mobilization and channelization of surplus earnings of rural masses, will definitely furnish a gust to our splendid objective.

The idea of this paper is not to appraise the role of RBI being ruthless on those FIs rather on the economic upshot there from. In fact, this paper will explicitly focus on the effect of the immature demise of SIICL and SIFCL due to regulatory concerns of RBI on poverty alleviation and current market problem. It is a fact that those who are not in line, can never be tolerated but can't we think of something without going for their absolute desertion. Can't we imagine of bringing them in line as opposed to banning them? If the response is even very small yes, then we have to put all our efforts to stumble on the ways behind that yes so that we can contribute something in fulfilling a composite objective - poverty easing, exchange rate stabilization and equity market stabilization.

The sketch of this paper is as follows. While section-2 of this paper highlights Sahara India Group (specifically SIICL and SIFCL) as a catalyst in lessening reliance on FII and eradicating poverty, section-3 heaves light on facts concerning RBI scanner on SIICL and SIFCL. However, the Effects of RBI scanner on Sahara India Group and on economy are sited in section-4. Last but the imperative facet of this paper, i.e., conclusion and suggestions are incorporated in section 5 of the paper.

SAHARA INDIA GROUP AS A CATALYST:

Indian conglomerate Sahara India group with the market value of assets at more than $50 billion has been a major unit in the corporate world and has diversified business in the areas like finance, real estate, media and entertainment, tourism and services. However, its business in financial sector is the center of attention of this paper. Its two FIs–SIICL and SIFCL, which have been under sturdy surveillance of RBI, can precisely be interpreted as a catalyst in shrinking India's reliance on FII and fighting out poverty.

Sahara India Investment Corporation Limited (SIICL)

SIICL, a non-deposit taking non-banking finance company (NBFC), is one among a handful investment companies in India which had been operational in rural and semi-urban areas in collecting investment resources. In the vicinity of financial investment, it is not that uncomplicated for a private unit to mark its identity where many gigantic public players are already there. Because for winning the confidence of people, some deep-rooted agency or body is required in order to be professed as the guaranteer of people's investible funds. In case of public units, government is considered as the guarantee in the mind of customers. Therefore, without having a deep-seated body as the guarantee, SIICL started its investment business with preliminary losses as it was unable to be appreciated by people. But slowly and steadily it entered into the market and started gaining people's confidence and reported a net profit in 2006-07. In the process of mobilizing investible funds, it was also catering a good amount of employment opportunities to educated youth of rural areas in the form of agents, who were otherwise unoccupied. Thus it was channelizing both capital and manpower in prolific lines. Although the contribution of SIICL to economy's investable fund and employability was very insignificant, on the basis of the way it was marching, something immense could have been anticipated in near future. But before establishing its credibility and at a very precipitate stage, the exit door has been shown to it, the detail story of which is elucidated in next section.

Sahara India Financial Corporation Limited (SIFCL)

SIFCL, a residuary non-banking finance company (RNBC) that accepts public deposits, is the earliest RNBC of India to be granted a certificate of registration by the RBI. In raising public deposits, the RNBCs have an exceptional track record and so also in customer service. Many types of investors prefer them to banks albeit they do not get tax concessions or a significantly higher interest rate. The following table clearly exhibits how the RNBCs are having edge over other FIs in raising public deposits.

Table 1
(Data on Performance of RNBCs in India)

Rs. crore

Item	*NBFCs*	*Of which RNBCs*
Number of Reported Companies	466	3
Total Assets	57453	21891 (38.1)
Public Deposits	22842	20175 (88.3)
Net Owned Funds	6663	1183 (17.8)

Source: Trend and Progress of Banking in India, RBI-November 14, 2006.

Note:
1. Figures in brackets indicate percentages to respective total of NBFCs.
2. NBFCs include miscellaneous non-banking companies, unregistered and un-notified nidhis.

As evident from the table, while a very small number of RNBCs (although 3 in number, in reality, only two - Sahara & Peerless) has merely 17.8% of Net Owned Funds of NBFCs, they have bagged 88.3% of the total public deposits of NBFCs. It clearly shows two things. First, they are easily reaching to the people who are deprived of accessing modern banking facilities. Second, people are having tremendous confidence on them.

For the investors' security, the company maintains the invested scrips in safe custody with a nationalized bank and withdrawal takes place only for emancipation of liabilities to the depositors. It does not prefer speculative investment in order to afford definite return to the investors. It has invested only less than 1% of its total assets in listed equity shares. Again its attention on red carpet investment has been proved useful as it has only 0.04% non-perfoming asset ratio. Most imperative facet of its burly rudiments, which congregates the poise of public, is its capital adequacy ratio. While the statutory requirement of capital adequacy ratio is only 12%, SIFCL has been able to uphold it at 28.78% as on 31.03.2008. Its strong and strict fundamentals as mentioned above are mainly responsible for its wide popularity. It has already been well-accepted by the public and has also offered very good number of employment in the economy. With the help of 6.85 lakh workers in business promotion and 1508 service centers, it has been able to create 3.94 crore deposit accounts.

The target investors of the SIFCL are the common man–middle class, lower middle class and lower class of the society. The company has succeeded largely in inculcating the savings behavior of the common man even with a bare minimum daily deposit of Re 1. It has also been contributing to the national economy for the overall development of the country through money invested in government securities, banks and institutions.

SIFCL as a catalyst in solving the problems of poverty and present market munch can be well decorated on the basis of facts mentioned above. In the perspective of deposit accretion, SIFCL is a very proverbial name among the common masses as it gets to the depositors' doorstep through its large number of trained agents and collects the deposits from them at their convenience, that too, after proper motivation. In fact, because of this innovative scheme of collecting deposits, it has succeeded winning the hearts of the public. The amount the SIFCL is collecting as deposits from common masses has zero opportunity value as the next best use of that would be either wasteful consumption or expenses on unsocial activities like gambling. By doing this, the company is securing the future of the poor as the amount kept with it may be spent by the depositors during their rainy days and restraining them from doing unsocial acts. Addiction to anything insists to do many things. As people are now captivated with the saving habits initiated by SIFCL, they are trying to keep up that habit by earning more. It is a reality that minute depositors in rural areas are competing themselves to deposit more and that is mostly because SIFCL. In this way they are adding a lot in their productivity and lessening their unnecessary spare time. That way SIFCL is a genuine catalyst in mitigating poverty of common man.

By the way of providing employment to rural educated youth in the shape of agents, the company is contributing to the society in three ways–reducing the unemployment problem, lessening the pinch of poverty and most importantly denouncing the unsocial and anti-social activities. Educated unemployed are proved hazardous as they use their intelligence in disparaging activities out of poverty and annoyance. Most of the unsocial and anti-social activities including terrorism are happening because of this community. For the sake of meager earning, they are easily getting ready to do anything and the terrorist organizations are taking the advantage of that by making use of them for their reason. By recruiting some of them in business promotion activities of the company, SIFCL is helping them and the society too.

If the companies like SIFCL come forward and try to tap the unexplored section then huge amount of deposits, which are otherwise idle or waste, can be extracted and diverted towards investment–both direct and institutional. If it happens, time will come when we will be no more relying on foreign investment and facing the problems inherited there from. So the job of SIFCL is not only praiseworthy but also to be imitated for the sake of macro economic benefit.

SIICL AND SIFCL UNDER RBI SCANNER

As the monetary authority of the country RBI has the responsibility of ensuring the smooth functioning of the monetary sector. Smooth functioning also includes making out whether the depositors' money are protected or not with the FIs. In order to do this, RBI has been watchful on the operation of all FIs. Specifically it keeps an eye to know whether the private players in financial markets are doing their jobs within the framework prescribed. If it finds any anomaly in their way of working, it becomes harsh on them and forces them to quit the market. Two of the FIs of Sahara India Group is now the victim of RBI scanner.

Scanner on SIICL

On the basis of scanned result, on August 11, 2008 RBI cancelled the registration of Sahara India Investment Corporation for carrying on the business of a non-banking financial institution as it felt that the company was more like a paper company. Since there is cost involved in regulating NBFCs, RBI feels that it is just to spend on those which are adhering the RBI guidelines and not to allow others. Therefore, all NBFCs were merely asked to file their annual statements so that the credibility of the companies can easily be traced. In fact, to distinguish the paper companies from the companies in reality, RBI initiated that step. Because of this, many of the NBFCs voluntarily exited and SIICL also did the same. It is because; the assets of SIICL were not immediately available. RBIs step in cancelling the registration of SIICL is justified as it has been done to keep public money safe.

Scanner on SIFCL

On the other hand, Residuary Non-Banking Companies (RNBCs), a special type of NBFCs, are treated as a perplexing breed in the Indian financial system with almost certainly sparse RBI custody. While the monetary authority had approved them the liberty to take public deposit in the form of daily deposits, recurring deposits and fixed deposits devoid of any limit, the financial markets have been reasonably scratchy with their survival as the markets are oblivious of their financial status. As per the RNBC regulations, these companies are allowed to access borrowing from banks, financial institutions and corporate but they have only tapped public deposits and are performing stupendous in gathering public deposits. The maneuver of these companies had caused supervisory concerns to the RBI in the past. As RBI feels that they are not moving in line with the directions meant for them, it has become harsh for them by outlawing them to collect public deposits and withdrawing their discretionary investment power. The RNBCs are not free in the context of investment pattern like other NBFCs. They are required to invest only in the directed line of investments. Earlier, the discretionary investments of RNBCs were 20% but because of unscrupulous expansion in deposit accretion, the RBI, apprehending unfavourable circumstances for the depositors in the future, has denied them to have any discretionary investments. In fact, the idea of withdrawing RNBC's discretionary investments power was to channelize their investment in approved securities to lessen treacherous & grievous consequences.

There are three RNBCs in India out of which one is a miniature setup and the rest two are giants in their size. So while anybody speaks of RNBCs, they only mean these two giants; Sahara India Financial Corporation Ltd., Lucknow and Peerless General Finance & Investment Company Ltd., Kolkata. They are now required to invest 100 per cent of their deposits in approved securities which comprise government bonds, fixed deposits with banks and mutual funds. In continuation with the extraction of discretionary investments power and the banning of raising public deposits, the RBI has also asked the two RNBCs to put forward alternative business plans. Peerless has already streamlined its alternative courses of action but for the sake of wrapping up the business of RNBC and finalizing a suitable new business model, it had asked the RBI to allocate some more time. And Sahara has made representations to the RBI for relaxation of its norms. But the RBI is determined to mess up the two RNBCs to assure depositors of their principal, if not interest.

However, RBI has asked SIFCL to have zero liability by June, 30, 2015 and has permitted the company to go for investing deposits that mature in three years.

EFFECTS OF RBI SCANNER:

SIICL has already exited the market and SIFCL is just counting its days. Their untimely demise, when they were in full swing, will definitely have some effect on the Sahara India Group and on the economy too.

Effects on Sahara India Group

Like any private business house, being motivated by profit appropriation, Sahara India Group will never tolerate the assets deployed in these two FIs to be redundant. It will undeniably come across the alternative mode to channelize the resources withdrawn or to be withdrawn in near future in a healthier way. From its up to date courses of action it is clearly discernible that the Group will revolutionize its objective from finance to real estate, where in it has been a prominent player in India as it has a massive land reservoir in the country. Under its possession 217 townships ranging from 100 acres to 300 acres each are in the course of development. It has its own three entertainment television channels, one national news channel, 36 regional news channels and various newspapers and magazines in Hindi, English and Urdu as well. Thus it has scores of alternatives to fit the spare resources from these two FIs. Keeping the prospective of different sectors and the competency of Sahara India Group in mind, any one will certainly foretell that the Group (i.e., Sahara India Group) will reallocate the resources in favour of real estate. That way, the profitability of Sahara India Group will never be undermined.

In order to compensate the loss of business in the form of losing two of its FIs, the Chairman of Sahara India Group Subrata Roy has recently visited UAE to explore business and investment opportunities in that country. During the visit he had also met there prominent business people and industrialists and eyed at potential projects in various sector. Thus, the problem the Sahara India Group faced due to the RBI Scanner is just temporary and it would never impose any negative effect on the Group as many alternatives are open for it. It is just a matter of time. The group just needs some time to wind up the business in financial sector and to concentrate in best possible alternatives. It is now passing through a transition period and it will stretch for little more time as wrapping up a long-drawn-out business is not that simple. Materially it may not lose anything but definitely some real cost it has to put up with until it exits the financial sector.

Effects on Indian Economy

Shrink in Employment Opportunities

As mentioned in previous subsection, if the Sahara India Group will not keep the resources withdrawn from those FIs idle and will go for reallocation of those, from exterior, one may question: how can it shrivel employment opportunities? But in reality, it can. May be the amount of funds reallocated will be the same as the amount withdrawn but the employment opportunities in new heads of investment may not be as much as it was in financial sector. If the Group reallocates the withdrawn resources, as guessed, in real estate where it has already a recognized set up, definitely it will try to apt the economies of scope and hence very nominal employment opportunities may be created. Thus, there will be a sizeable shrink in the employment opportunities of the economy.

Again, this move of the Group from financial sector to real estate sector will cause a shift of employment opportunities from rural and semi-urban to urban areas. Basically in financial business of the Group, educated youth of rural areas, who are very conversant with the rural living style, get employment. As the Group changes the sector, for the sake of corporate social responsibility, it may try to help the old employees out. But its trial may not take the real shape for two reasons. First, employees of financial sector may not be fitted into the real estate sector, i.e., the problem of accommodation from the Group's side. Second, Even though the Group takes the responsibility to train them afresh in new line of requirements then also the objective may not materialize as the rural educated youth may not adapt themselves to the city life and may not cater as per the requirements of city jobs, i.e., the problem of accommodation from the employees' side. As in India, the incidence of poverty is highly concentrated in rural areas, if we want to reduce the gravity of poverty from the economy; we have to focus on employment generation in rural areas, where as this shifting of sector by the Group goes against it.

In the backdrop of the problems mentioned above, it is obvious that the transformation of the Group's objective towards real estate leaving the financial sector, which is just a move by coercion (from RBI's side on regulatory ground), will certainly have threats on livelihood of lakhs of people. That way it will aggravate the rural poverty too.

Distortion in Deposit Accretion

We feel proud for the fact that our country has been performing considerably well since last couple of years in our economic front. It is genuine as our rate of growth is getting augmented year by year and the country's foreign exchange reserve is accumulating rapidly. At the same time, we should not forget to attribute our economic success to the foreign capital which is the main factor behind it. Our dependence on foreign capital fingers two alternatives. Probably our domestic savings & investments are not enough to accumulate sufficient capital so as to meet the huge demand of massive population. Or probably we do have potentials to save & invest but our financial system is not well-diversified to mobilize those. But in our context both these alternatives are non-mutually exclusive. That means we lack in savings or saving potentials and also whatever small potential we do have is not properly tapped. Our limited saving potentials, as is inherited from our massive poverty & huge population, needs lot of things to do for its improvement. But mobilizing the existing potential is not a great task and can be easily done by a sound financial system. If we are unable to do so that means there is something lacking in our financial system. We speak a lot on retail banking and up gradation of banking services in India. But the point to see is whether all these are conducive for mobilization of saving potentials of the country. If we consider FIs excluding RNBCs, probably our answer will be no. That can be substantiated from the following facts.

As per the RBI's Handbook of Statistics on the Indian Economy (2006-07), there were 30,639 rural branches of Scheduled Commercial Banks (SCBs) in 2007, which were 4,750 less than the number in 1993. In an average, 26 bank branches in rural areas blackout each month. In other words, on every working day there is closure of one bank branch in rural areas. But branches in metros shot up from 5,753 to 11,826 in the same period, where as in other urban areas, the number climbed from 8,562 to 12,792 in this period. It clearly depicts that, modern banks for the sake of maximizing profits, are providing updated services with competitive offers to their sophisticated customers of urban areas neglecting the rural masses. They are least bothered about the savings of rural areas. Their expansion seldom solves the problem of mobilization of resources.

Deposit accretion will definitely be lowered after the exit of SIFCL from the financial market. Slow deposit accretion will in turn be a cause of poverty because when FIs are not available and/or not interested to collect deposits from the surplus income holders how can they be encouraged to give loans to the needy people over there in rural areas. Therefore, the poor but potential investors will be deprived of getting funds and hence the supply side of the market in those areas will be sticky. Further, the spending of surplus income, which were supposed to be saved, on consumption heads owing to lack of savings facilities will be resulted in augmentation in consumption demand. While in one hand, the supply in rural market will deteriorate because the potential investors can not go for production due to lack of funds resulted from less deposit accretion, the demand in rural market will surge for extra spending by the surplus income holders. This mismatch between the market demand and supply will stimulate the cost of living and undermine the standard of living of rural people. Thus the poor will be poorer. Further, it will have negative impact on the efficiency of rural depositors too. For the sake of depositing considerable amount, some of the rural people might have fascinated to earn more by improving their efficiency and reducing their wasteful leisure time. In that way they must have been acquainted with the financial transactions through the agents or advisors who know them very well. When they miss the services they were getting previously and don't find the FIs to deposit their surplus income, their zeal to earn more will definitely be spoiled. By this, they will lose their competence and will also involve themselves in many unsocial and anti-social activities as they will get much spare time to use for those purposes. However, the concept of micro finance may to some extent neutralize this effect and can help the poor but to what extent it can manage alone, that the time will say.

CONCLUSION

If anything is established as bad, that is to be banned. If it is doing bad but the hope of improvement is there, that is to be regulated. But if it is doing well but not in proper line then that is to be promoted for development by bringing that into the predetermined track or by determining a track specifically for that so as to cope up with its line of functioning. FIs of Sahara India Group, particularly SIFCL and SIICL are coming under last type. They are doing well so far as their services & confidence of the customers are concerned. But only problem with them is that they are not in line with the norms of the authority. If bankers and other financial institutions, in spite of functioning in proper line, are not able to do something which is important that these two FIs are doing with their interest and are also succeeding, the authority of the country should give them the status that is given to other FIs or it should create a special status for them with the power of raising deposits and discretionary investments.

As RNBCs like SIFCL are a good source of mobilizing the resources which are otherwise idle, they are to be encouraged. Encouragement to them does not mean to make them free. Rather they are to be given the facilities that are appropriated by other FIs and at the same time they are to be regulated by the regulatory authority. To solve the composite problem of resource mobilization, poverty alleviation and safety of the deposits of the public, the RBI should go for two authorities – development authority and regulatory authority. For the development of RNBCs and other FIs, the development authority should cater all possible facilities without any discrimination and to forbid any sort of deviation and exploitation in their functioning, the regulatory authority should apply all possible checks without hampering their development. However, regulation should follow development. But the recent move of the RBI in the context of SIICL and SIFCL does not foresee development, nor dare to confirm regulations but strong enough to spoil. This is the right time for the RBI to think over the issue in order to show the concerns for development.

SIICL has already been stopped and if RBI is determined to stop SIFCL for its careless approach towards the RBI guidelines, nobody will find any scope to utter a word against the authority, provided it does this after arranging some alternatives by which the rural segment will not impede. While we speak a lot on financial inclusion and its importance in Indian context, where maximum inhabitants are rural and are excluded financially for one or other reasons, by denouncing the FIs like SIICL and SIFCL, we are fairly favouring financial exclusion. Although micro finance is one means of financial inclusion, there is doubt in its sustainability as in this way we are trying to help the rural poor without taking the help of their untapped resources, which may lead to sub-prime crisis. So this is the right time for the authority to focus on rural areas through bilateral transactions. Because of exhaustion of corporate clients, the Indian banking sector is as such facing problem in finding borrowers. Still the banks are not keen to bank upon rural sector because of lack of credit worthiness. In the name of modernization most of the banks are expanding urban branches and catering ultra modern facilities but at the cost of rural branches. Thus if the banks prefer to be away from the rural sector for risk reason and the NBFCs and RNBCs are forced to be away from it for regulatory reasons, then how can we fight out poverty, the basic problem of Indian economy.

Poverty eradication is the ultimate challenge before the policy formulators of India. While the incidence of poverty is primarily concentrated in rural areas, poverty in urban sector is due to the emergence of slum population in towns and cities which is due to the migration of rural population to urban areas for sake of living and livelihood. To combat poverty, the focus of our government should be on rural areas. Accordingly many programmes have been initiated for the purpose but looking into the gravity of pauperization, the effort puts forth seems inadequate. As the rural sector have the maximum resource reservoir of the country, without making use of those, how long and how effectively the government can keep on helping the poor. This way of doing something for the poor is also backed by many allied problems like inflation, laziness and may be unsocial activities. Therefore, it is essential to utilize the resources of rural sector to upgrade its standard of living. Sahara India Group with its two FIs was doing the same. They were tapping the potential of rural sector in financial front. If they are banned because of their misaligned functioning, they are to be well substituted by some other institutions what has not happened so far in India. If at all the RBI encouraged and gave green signal to any institute to carry on the job of Sahara India Group in financial sector but under the RBI guidelines, who can guarantee that the new player will abide by every checks and balances? As an alternative, if the authority put efforts to bring the banned and would be banned FIs back to the track prescribed by it then we can give justice to the rural underprivileged and guiltless employees.

REFERENCES

www.rbi.org

www.sahara.in

www.saharamutual.com

www.newstrackindia.com

www.dnaindia.com

www.thehindubusinessline.com

www.abbyy.com

www.timesofindia.indiatimes.com

www.financialexpress.com

www.indianexpress.com
www.business-standard.com
www.indopia.in
www.moneycontrol.com
www.hindustantimes.in
www.today.com
www.abclive.in
www.hindu.com
www.merinews.com
www.outlookmoney.com
www.deccanherald.com

5

MOBILE BANKING: CHALLENGES AND OPPORTUNITIES FOR BANKING SECTOR

Manoranjan Dash, Jyotiranjan Das & Ashok Ku Dash

INTRODUCTION

Technological innovation has rapidly changed every aspect of our lives and the way of banking business during the last decade. One of the most innovative changes is the use of mobile devices in the banking transaction. The integration of the internet technology and mobile network creates new opportunities and applications. Mobile Banking refers to provision of bank-related financial services with the help of mobile telecommunication devices. The scope of offered services may include facilities to conduct bank and stock market transactions, to administer accounts and to access customized information. Mobile Banking enhances the number of existing channels of distribution that a bank employs to offer its services. The efficiency of a distribution channel can be measured by its fulfillment of three major objectives, which are closely related to each other. Mobile banking i.e. M-Banking, SMS Banking etc. is a term used for performing balance checks, account transactions, payments etc. via a mobile device such as a mobile phone. Mobile banking today is most often performed via SMS or the Mobile Internet but can also use special programs downloaded to the mobile device. Mobile Banking is considered to be one of the most value-added and important mobile service available. Mobile Banking is a service that allows you to do banking transactions through your mobile phone without making a call, using the SMS or WAP facility. You can check your balance, stop a cheque payment, or even pay your utility bills. Mobile Banking service gives you account information and real-time transaction capabilities from the mobile phones anywhere, anytime. Mobile phones as a medium for extending banking services have off-late been attaining greater significance. The rapid growth in users and wider coverage of mobile phone networks have made this medium an important platform for extending banking services to customers. With the rapid growth in the number of mobile phone subscribers in India (about 261 million as at the end of March 2008 and growing at about 8 million a month). banks have been exploring the practicability of using mobile phones as an alternative channel of delivery of banking services. Some banks have started offering information based services like balance enquiry, stop payment instruction of cheques, transactions enquiry, and location of the nearest ATM/branch etc. Acceptance of transfer of funds instruction for credit to beneficiaries of same/or another bank in favor of pre-registered beneficiaries have also commenced in a few banks. In order to ensure a level playing field and considering that the technology is relatively new, Reserve Bank has brought out a set of operating guidelines for adoption by banks. With the introduction of any new channel or technology such as the use of mobile devices for banking activity, financial institutions must ensure that the perceptions and the realities surrounding security are successfully managed, both to ensure adoption and protect customers and the institution from emerging threats. In today's click economy banks use the mobile phone to provide financial services to those without access to traditional banks. Mobile banking is still in the nascent stage but the scope it offers for low-cost transactions will make banks and customers warm up to it. At present, mobile banking focuses on low-value transactions and complements current mediums like the Internet. Mobile payments can be used in government payments, pension, micro-finance, loan disbursements, etc. While paying by the mobile for rail and air tickets, movie tickets, pizza, etc, will be need-based, a bigger chunk of the business will come from areas like micro-finance, paying suppliers, and remittances. The most critical use of mobile banking is in RBIs vision of creating financial inclusion in the under banked or unbanked sectors. RBI estimates that around 40% of Indians lack access to formal financial services, and are largely unbanked. The government is conducting mobile banking pilots and full-scale operations across twelve states, and the entire ecosystem is being managed with the help of the Reserve Bank of India, other banks, leading telecom operators, and technology implementation partners.ICICI Bank was one of the first banks to introduce mobile banking in India with its iMobile platform. Through iMobile, ICICI Bank customers can transfer funds to ICICI and non-ICICI Bank accounts, as well as pay utility bills and insurance premiums. The offering works on both GPRS and SMS options.

MOBILE BANKING BUSINESS MODELS

A broad range of Mobile or branchless banking models is sprouting. These models differ primarily on the question that who will establish the relationship i.e. account opening, deposit taking, etc. with the customer, the Bank or the Non- Bank/ Telecommunication Company . Models of branchless banking can be classified into three broad categories - Bank Focused, Bank-Led and Non Bank-Led.

Bank-Focused Model

The bank-focused model emerges when a traditional bank uses non-traditional low-cost delivery channels to provide banking services to its existing customers. Examples range from use of automatic teller machines (ATMs) to internet banking or mobile phone banking to provide certain limited banking services to banks' customers.

Bank-Led Model

The bank-led model offers a distinct alternative to conventional branch-based banking in that customer conducts financial transactions at a whole range of retail agents or through mobile phone instead of at bank branches or through bank employees. This model promises the potential to substantially increase the financial services outreach by using a different delivery channel i.e. retailers/mobile phones having experience and target market distinct from traditional banks, and may be significantly cheaper than the bank based alternatives. The bank-led model may be implemented by either using correspondent arrangements or by creating a joint venture between Bank and Telecommunication Company/non-bank. In this model customer account relationship rests with the bank.

Non Bank-led Model

The non-bank-led model is where a bank does not come into the picture and the non-bank i.e. telecommunication company performs all the functions.

MOBILE BANKING SERVICES

Banks offering mobile banking provides mostly the following services:

Account Information

- Mini-statements and checking of account history
- Balance Information i.e. view balances of your savings and current accounts.
- Monitoring of term deposits
- Access to loan statements
- Access to card statements

Payments & Transfers

- Domestic and international fund transfers
- Mobile recharging
- Bill payment processing

Investments

- Portfolio management services
- Real-time stock quotes

- Personalized alerts and notifications on security prices support
- Status of requests for credit, including mortgage approval, and insurance coverage
- Cheque book and bank statement requests

Content Services

- Loyalty-related offers
- Location-based services

TECHNOLOGIES FOR MOBILE BANKING

Mobile Banking is being deployed using mobile applications developed on one of the following technologies. The common mobile technology platforms are browser, J2ME, BREW etc ,enabling technologies are WPKI/WIM, SIM, Device OS, Interactive Technologies-Voice, WAP, SMS, USSD, i-mode and transport–GSM, CDMA, TDMA, GPRS, Bluetooth, Infrared, RFID.

SMS–Short Messaging Service

This is a text message standard to enable mobile applications based banking. Short messages are stored and forwarded by SMS centers. SMS messages have a channel of access to phone different from the voice channel. SMS can be used to provide information about the status of one's account with the bank i.e. informational or can be used to transmit payment instructions from the phone i.e. transactional. The way this works is that the customer requests for information by sending an SMS containing a service command to a pre-specified number. The bank responds with a reply SMS containing the specific information. For example, customers of the HDFC Bank in India can get their account balance details by sending the keyword 'HDFCBAL' and receive their balance information again by SMS. An SMS based service is hosted on a SMS gateway that further connects to the Mobile service providers SMS Centre.

Unstructured Supplementary Services Delivery (USSD)

Unstructured Supplementary Service Data (USSD) is a technology unique to GSM. It is a capability built into the GSM standard for support of transmitting information over the signaling channels of the GSM network. USSD provides session-based communication, enabling a variety of applications. USSD is session oriented transaction-oriented technology while SMS is a store-and-forward technology. Turnaround response times for interactive applications are shorter for USSD than SMS.

WAP – Wireless Access Protocol/GPRS(General Packet Radio Service)

General Packet Radio Service (GPRS) is a mobile data service available to GSM users. GPRS provides packet-switched data for GSM networks. GPRS enables services such as Wireless Application Protocol (WAP) access, Multimedia Messaging Service (MMS), and for Internet communication services such as email and World Wide Web access in mobile phones. Banks maintain WAP sites which customer's access using a WAP compatible browser on their mobile phones. WAP sites offer the familiar form based interface and can also implement security quite effectively. The banks customers can now have an anytime, anywhere access to a secure reliable service that allows them to access all enquiry and transaction based services and also more complex transaction like trade in securities through their phone .A WAP based service requires hosting a WAP gateway. Mobile Application users access the bank's site through the WAP gateway to carry out transactions, much like internet users access a web portal for accessing the banks services. The actually forms that go into a mobile application are stored on a WAP server, and served on demand. The WAP Gateway forms an access point to the internet from the mobile network.

Near Field Communication (NFC)

NFC is the fusion of contactless smartcard (RFID) and a mobile phone. The mobile phone can be used as a contactless card.

NFC enabled phones can act as RFID tags or readers.

MOBILE PAYMENT SCHEMES

Different mobile payment schemes are present

- eCash in a mobile environment
- GeldKarte
- BarclayCard solution
- M-Pay Bill
- Paybox
- ItiAchat
- EMPS (Electronic Mobile Payment System)

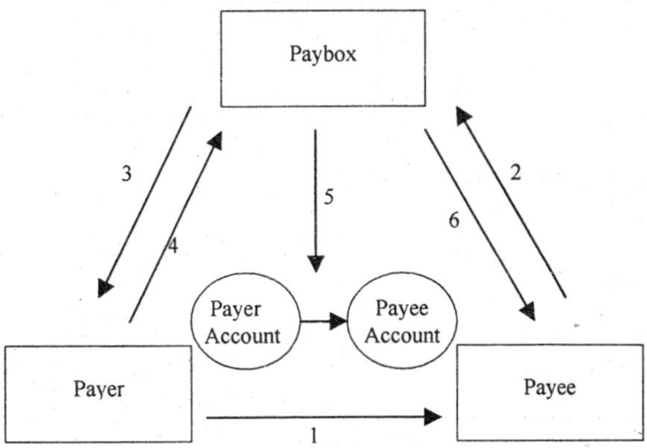

Paybox payment transaction (communication via mobile phone)

(1) Payer sends his mobile phone number

(2) Payee sends his mobile phone number, Payer's mobile phone number and payment amount x to Paybox

(3) Paybox seeks the confirmation of payment of amount x to Payee from Payer

(4) Payer confirms the payment by providing his PIN

(5) Paybox transfers amount x from payer's account to payee's account

(6) Paybox sends a Confirmation message to the Payee.

RESEARCH OBJECTIVES

(1) To what degree customers are using mobile banking.

(2) To identify the main types of financial transactions the customers carry out with their mobile.

(3) To find the factors associated with customers' perception towards the advantage of mobile banking.

RESEARCH METHODOLOGY

A specifically designed questionnaire was used as a tool for collecting the data. The survey questionnaire consisted of two parts. The first section recorded the subject's demographic information. The demographic variables included gender, age, level of education, profession and income. The second section asked each of the subject's perceptions of each variable using the seven point Likert scales from 1("strongly agree") to 7("strongly disagree"). For data collection, we designed and also implemented a Web survey. We asked mobile banking users to participate in the survey. Participants were asked to express the level of their agreement/disagreement with attributes/factors identified. Attributes covered respondents' present requirements, their awareness towards mobile banking, their expectations towards the benefits/advantages, and risks associated to the mobile banking. Data were analyzed via frequency analysis and factor analysis with the help of the SPSS software.

SOCIO-ECONOMIC PROFILE OF THE RESPONDENTS

(1) *Age Structure Of The Respondent:*

Respondents' age varies from 30 to 65 years. About 75 percent respondents are in the age group of 35 to 50 years.

(2) *Income Level Of The Respondent*:

Majority of the respondents range from upper middle class to higher class and monthly income greater than Rs15, 000 p.m.

(3) *Marital Status:*

10 percent of the respondents are unmarried.

(4) *Level Of Education*:

All the respondents are educated.45 percent of the respondents had completed their post graduation.5 percent of the respondents are under graduated.50 percent of the respondents are graduated.

(5) *Gender :*

The respondent sample consisted of 78 percent male and 22 percent female.

Mobile Banking Users Across Professions

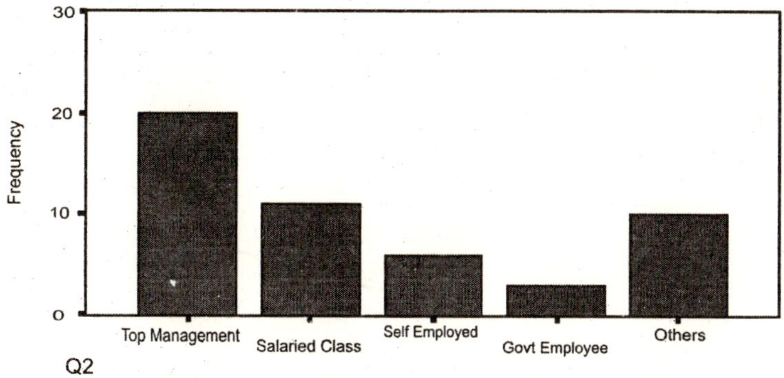

The above table presents the different types of mobile banking services by the customers in their respective mobiles. The respondents' preferences are computed in terms of frequency analysis. The highest number of customers prefers to mini statements and check balance enquiry in accounts followed by bill payment processing or cheque book request. The least preferred financial transaction are content services i.e. loyalty related offers.

Types of Mobile Banking Services Carried Out By Customers

		Frequency	*Percent*	*Valid Percent*	*Cumulative Percent*
Valid	Mini Statements And Check Balance	20	40.0	40.0	40.0
	Bill Payment Processing	10	20.0	20.0	60.0
	Portfolio Mgmt Services	10	20.0	20.0	80.0
	Cheque Book Request	7	14.0	14.0	94.0
	Content Services	3	6.0	6.0	100.0
	Total	50	100.0	100.0	

Factor analysis is a very used widely technique for reducing data complexity by reducing the number of variable being studied. Factor analysis is a good way of identifying latent or underlying factors from an array of seemingly important variables. Factor analysis is a set of techniques which by analyzing correlation between variables, reduces their number into fewer factors which explain much of the original data more economically. Even though a subjective interpretation can result from a factor analysis output, the procedure often provides an insight into relevant psychographic variables, and results in economical use of data collection efforts.

KMO and Bartlett's Test

Kaiser-Meyer-Olkin Measure of Sampling Adequacy		.596
Bartlett's Test of Sphericity	Approx. Chi-Square	276.284
	df	28
	Sig.	.000

The adequacy of the data is evaluated on the basis of the results of Kaiser-Meyer-Olkin Measure of Sampling Adequacy (KMO) and Bartlett's Test of Sphericity.The KMO measure of sampling adequacy is .596 indicating that the present data are suitable for factor analysis. Bartlett's Test of Sphericity is significant ($p<.001$), indicating sufficient correlation exists, between variables for the factor analysis. The Bartlett's Test statistics is approximately distributed and is accepted.

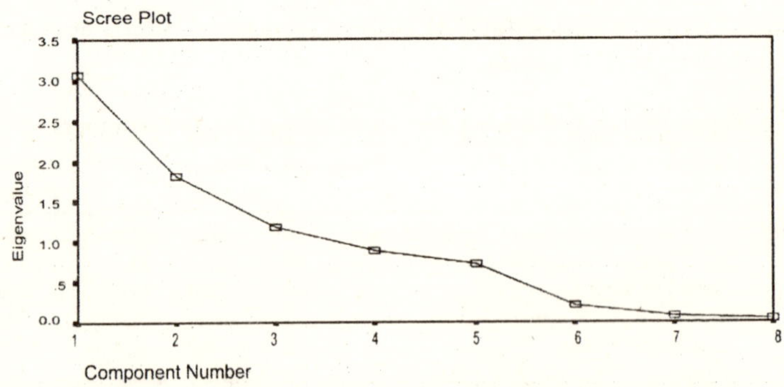

In the above analysis, Scree plot shows that three factors are going to be extracted.Catell's Scree test(1966) involves plotting each of the Eigen values of the factors and inspecting the plot to find a point at which the shape of the curve changes direction and becomes horizontal.Catell recommends retaining all factors above the elbow or break in the plot as these factors contribute the most to the explanation of the variance in the data set.

Rotated Component Matrix(a)

	Component		
	1	2	3
Time and Place Independent Purchase		.928	
Enhanced payment instrument availability and complement to cash		.892	
Queue Avoidance		.543	
Trust in Merchant	.957		
Trust in Telecom Operators	.965		
Trust in Financial Institutions/Banks	.980		
Concerns on Privacy and Reliability			.807
Transaction errors			.737

Extraction Method: Principal Component Analysis.
Rotation Method: Varimax with Kaiser Normalization.
a Rotation converged in 4 iterations.

Interpretation of results

From the table Rotated Component Matrix we find that attributes like time and place independent purchase, Enhanced payment instrument availability and complement to cash, Queue avoidance have loading .928,.892,.543 on Factor 1. This suggests that Factorl is a combination of these variables. Therefore this factor can be interpreted as mobile banking has ease of use and relative advantage. For factor 2, we see that trust in merchant, trust in telecom operators, trust in financial institutions/banks have a high loading .957,.965,.980 respectively, indicationg that Factor 2 is a combination of these variables. These variables can be grouped into a factor called trust towards mobile banking .For factor 3, we see that Concerns on privacy and reliability, transaction errors have a high loading .807, .737 respectively, indicationg that Factor 2 is a combination of these variables. These variables can be grouped into a factor called perceived security and risk towards mobile banking.

MANAGERIAL IMPLICATIONS

The new banking distribution channels to consumers i.e. mobile banking is still at early stages in India. The current target market for mobile banking is relatively small due to its low level of awareness. There were many critical issues, which stood out as being obstacles to consumer adoption of mobile banking among these were consumers' attitudes. Security factor was found the most important attribute that could motivate consumers' attitudes towards mobile banking in india. Other barriers to adoption of mobile banking were perceived risks, computer and new technological skills. As for mobile banking, lack of understanding of the concept and its benefits were the main barriers to its adoption. Users were also widely spread among the salaried employees, senior managers and small business owners. As such, more women of a particular customer profile may be targeted. Advertising messages could emphasize security and trust for mobile banking. Finally, as far as mobile banking is concerned, lack of understanding of its benefits was found significant. Therefore, perhaps while bankers should focus on security issue for mobile banking, their advertising should focus on the aspect for mobile banking. Bankers should also consider raising consumer awareness and acceptance of new technology-based banking services more, through advertising and promotion rather than word-of-mouth communication, as this might prove not to be effective since reference group's influence did not have any impact on mobile banking.

CONCLUSION

Mobile banking adoption will depend on more than just market timing. Financial institutions must implement their programs based on i.e. an understanding of what factors distinguish the mobile channel from existing ones and consumer segmentation criteria that put next to consumer preferences with attributes and benefits of mobile banking. Perceived risk, trust and ease of use had important effects on the adoption behavior of mobile banking. Consumers' trust in and the perceived usefulness of the mobile banking service had direct effects on their adoption behavior. That is, the consumer's trust of the bank, telecom provider, and wireless Internet had significant influence on their using mobile banking. Therefore, banking managers should concentrate on building trust as a prerequisite to mobile banking adoption and developing m-commerce relationships. In a management context, several of our findings are relevant to financial services providers to better understand diffusion of mobile banking services and characteristics of the prospective adopters.

REFERENCES

Anckar, Bill and D'Incau, Davide (2002), "Value Creation in Mobile Commerce: Findings from a Consumer Survey," *Journal of Information Technology Theory & Application,* Vol. 4 (1), 43-64.

Black, Nancy Jo, Lockett, Andy, Winklhofer, Heidi and Ennew, Christine (2001), "The Adoption of Internet Financial Services: a Qualitative Study," *International Journal of Retail and Distribution Management,* Vol. 29 (8), 390-398.

Churchill, Gilbert A. and Iacobucci, Dawn (2002), Marketing Research: Methodological Foundations. 8th edition. Orlando: Harcourt College Publishers.

Davis, Fred D. (1989), "Perceived Usefulness, Perceived Ease of Use, and User Acceptance of Information Technology," *MIS Quarterly,* Vol. 9, 319-339.

Howcroft, Barry, Hamilton, Robert and Hewer, Paul (2002), "Consumer attitude and the usage and adoption of home-banking in the United Kingdom," *International Journal of Bank Marketing,* Vol. 20 (3), 111-121.

Jonason, Andreas and Eliasson, Gunnar (2001), "Mobile Internet Revenues: an Empirical Study of the I-mode Portal," *Internet Research: Electronic Networking Applications and Policy,* Vol. 11 (4), 341-348.

Jun, Minjoon and Cai, Shaohan (2001), "The Key Determinants of Internet Banking Service Quality: a Content Analysis," *International Journal of Bank Marketing,* Vol. 19 (7), 276-291.

Mattila, Minna and Pento, Tapio (2002), "Development of Electronic Distribution Channels in Finland–M-banking Usage and Consumer Profiles," *Die Banking und Information Technologie,* Vol. 2, 41-49.

Mols, Niels Peter (2001), "Organization for the Effective Introduction of New Distribution Channels in Retail Banking," *European Journal of Marketing,* Vol. 35 (5), 661-686.

West, Louse (2001), "SWIM Makes a Splash in Mobile Banking," Bank Technology News, December 2001.

Pedersen, P. E. and Ling, R. (2003), "Modifying Adoption Research for Mobile Internet Service Adoption: Cross-disciplinary Interactions," Proceedings of the 36th Hawaii International Conference on System Sciences (HICSS'03).

Anckar, B & D'Incau, D. (2002), Value Creation in Mobile Commerce: Findings From a Consumer Survey, *Journal of Information Technology Theory & Application,* Vol. 4 (1), pp. 43-64.

T. Dahlberg, *et al.*, (2007), Past, Present and Future of Mobile Payments Research: A Literature Review, Electronic Commerce Research and Applications.

GSM Association Aims for Global Mobile Payments Using NFC Card Technology Today,Volume 19, Issue 2, February 2007, Pages 1, 3

Visa and SK Telecom to Launch Mobile Payments Card Technology Today, Volume 19, Issue 2, February 2007, p. 6.

6

CRM IN NEW AGE BANKING

S. C. Bihari

INTRODUCTION

'RELATIONSHIP MANAGEMENT' is the name of the game in the banking industry today and customers never had it so good before. In a savings-driven economy like ours, banks have finally come of age and the emphasis is now on making the customer feel that he is the king.

With newer platforms emerging everyday to facilitate banking services, ranging from the, internet, mobile commerce to higher-end technology applications such as WAP etc, the traditional role of the bank which used to be that of 'money lending' has assumed broader dimensions.

The process of developing a cooperative and collaborative relationship between the buyers and sellers is called customer relationship management shortly called CRM.

CRM aims at focusing all the organizational activities towards creating and maintaining a customer. CRM is a new technique in marketing where the marketer tries to develop long term collaborative relationship with customers to develop them as life time customers. CRM aims to make the customer climb up the ladder of loyalty.

CUSTOMER FOCUS IN BANKING SERVICES

As the intense competition becomes a way of doing business, it is the customer who calls the shot in deciding the nature of products and services offered in the market. The customers are becoming demanding, dominant and selective. In fact the perceptions and the expectations of the customers have undergone a sea change, with the availability of banking services to the customers at their door steps through the help of technology.

Marketing of customer services aims at two important goals: prosperity to the bank and satisfied customers. Banks offer tangible services like loan schemes, interest rates and kinds of account and the intangible services like behavior and efficiency of staff, speed of transactions and the ambience. The banks may need to include customer oriented approach or customer focus in their five areas of businesses such as Cash accessibility, asset security, money transfer, deferred payment and financial advices.

There are four strategies available to customer relations' managers:

- To win back or save customers
- To attract new and potential customers
- To create loyalty among existing customers and
- To up sell or offer cross services.

The future of banking business very much depends upon the ability of the banks to develop close relationship with the customers. In order to develop close relationship with the customers the banking industry has to focus on the technology oriented innovations that offer convenience to the customers. Today customers are offered ATM services, access to internet banking and phone banking facilities and credit cards. These have elevated banking beyond the barriers of time and space.

THE NEW AGE BANKS-NEW ORIENTATION

Unlike in the past, the banks today are market driven and market responsive. The top concern in the mind of every bank's

CEO is increasing or at least maintaining the market share in every line of business against the backdrop of heightened competition. With the entry of new players and multiple channels, customers have become more discerning and less "loyal" to banks. This makes it imperative that banks provide best possible products and services to ensure customer satisfaction. To address the challenge of retention of customers, there have been active efforts in the banking circles to switch over to customer-centric business model. The success of such a model depends upon the approach adopted by banks with respect to customer data management and customer relationship management.

Over the years, Indian banks have expanded to cover a large geographic and functional area to meet the developmental needs. They have been managing a world of information about customers - their profiles, location, etc. They have a close relationship with their customers and a good knowledge of their needs, requirements and cash positions. Though this offers them a unique advantage they face a fundamental problem. During the period of planned economic development, the bank products were bought in India and not sold. Marketing is a customer-oriented operation. What is needed is the effort on their part to improve their service image and exploit their large customer information base effectively to communicate product availability.

Achieving customer focus requires leveraging existing customer information to gain a deeper insight into the relationship a customer has with the institution, and improving customer service-related processes so that the services are quick, error free and convenient for the customers. Furthermore, banks need to have very strong in-house research and market intelligence units in order to face the future challenges of competition, especially customer retention. Marketing is a question of demand (customers) and supply (financial products and services, customer services through various delivery channels). Both demand and supply have to be understood in the context of geographic locations and competitor analysis to undertake focused marketing efforts.

Focusing on region-specific campaigns rather than national media campaigns would be a better strategy for a diverse country like India.

Customer-centricity also implies increasing investment in technology. Throughout much of the last decade, banks world-over have re-engineered their organizations to improve efficiency and move customers to lower cost, automated channels, such as ATMs and online banking. But this need not be the case.

As is proved by the experience, banks are now realizing that one of their best assets for building profitable customer relationships especially in a developing country like India is the branch-branches are in fact a key channel for customer retention and profit growth in rural and semi-urban set up. However, to maximize the value of this resource, our banks need to transform their branches from transaction processing centers into customer-centric service centers. This transformation would help them achieve bottom line business benefits by retaining the most profitable customers.

Branches could also be used to inform and educate customers about other, more efficient channels, to advise on and sell new financial instruments like consumer loans, insurance products, mutual fund products, etc.

There is a growing realization among Indian banks that it no longer pays to have a "transaction-based" operating model. There are active efforts to develop a relationship-oriented model of operations focusing on customer-centric services. The biggest challenge our banks face today is to establish customer intimacy without which all other efforts towards operational excellence are meaningless. The banks need to ensure through their services that the customers come back to them. This is because a major chunk of income for most of the banks comes from existing customers, rather than from new customers.

CUSTOMER RELATIONSHIP MANAGEMENT

In literature, many definitions were given to describe CRM. The main difference among these definitions is technological and relationship aspects of CRM. Some authors from marketing background emphasize technological side of CRM while the others consider IT perspective of CRM. From marketing aspect, CRM is defined by [Couldwell 1998] as " a combination of business process and technology that seeks to understand a company's customers from the perspective of who they are, what they do, and what they are like". Technological definition of CRM was given as "the market place of the future is undergoing a technology-driven metamorphosis"

Consequently, IT and marketing departments must work closely to implement CRM efficiently. Meanwhile, implementation of CRM in banking sector was considered by [Mihelis et al. 2001]. They focused on the evaluation of the critical satisfaction dimensions and the determination of customer groups with distinctive preferences and expectations in the private bank sector.

Specifically the customer relationships of new technology-based firms have been studied. They were interested in total sales activities, both volume-related and non-volume related. They also developed a modification of the standard data envelope analysis (DEA) structure using goal programming concepts that yields both a sales and service measures. [Beckett-Camarata et al. 1998] have noted that managing relationships with their customers (especially with employees, channel partners and strategic alliance partners) was critical to the firm's long-term success. It was also emphasized that Customer relationship management based on social exchange and equity significantly assists the firm in developing collaborative, cooperative and profitable long-term relationships. [Yuan and Chang 2001] have presented a mixed-initiative synthesized learning approach for better understanding of customers and the provision of clues for improving customer relationships based on different sources of web customer data.

CRM has been in India for over years now. But its penetration in the Industry in general and that in the financial services market in particular has been rather uninspiring. The surprising aspect that came out from the study was that though the banks were aware of the CRMs' benefits but were skeptical about its applicability to their organization. In this competitive world order, companies strive to attain a competitive edge vis-à-vis their competitors. A firm can gain competitive advantage by:

- Becoming a low cost player
- Achieving operational efficiency
- By cultivating customer loyalty

For obvious reasons of margins involved, the last option is most profitable for any firm. Furthermore, the low cost and operational efficiency can provide competitive edge only in the short to medium. Once someone comes up with matched/ better proposition the customers don't think twice before switching over. In this backdrop, it's no wonder that companies, large and small, strive to turn themselves into customer-driven enterprise. A loyal and happy customer is difficult for competition to wean away even if there are some cost differentials etc. But, fostering a sense of relatedness in customers is at best a daunting task. The customers have become more and more informed and, as an obvious extension, much more demanding regarding what he expects. As a means of satisfying the ever-increasing customer expectation and as a tool for retaining existing customers and appropriating new customers, the CRM philosophy was conceived. It is not a tool or a technology but a way of thinking that has developed and which keeps customer at the forefront of every strategy/action.

CRM is a comprehensive approach that aligns business strategy, corporate culture and organization and supporting information technology, so that the customer relationship proves mutually beneficial to both customer and enterprise. Through widespread implementation of sales, customer service, marketing, field support and other customer touching functions, CRM integrates people, process and technology to maximize relationships with all customers. The ultimate objective is to enhance the customer experience whenever there is interaction with him at one of numerous possible touch-points. This enhanced customer experience translates into happy and loyal customer and thereby, into a greater wallet share.

CRM OBJECTIVES IN BANKING SECTOR

The idea of CRM is that it helps businesses use technology and human resources gain insight into the behavior of customers and the value of those customers. If it works as hoped, a business can: provide better customer service, make call centers more efficient, cross sell products more effectively, help sales staff close deals faster, simplify marketing and sales processes, discover new customers, and increase customer revenues. It doesn't happen by simply buying software and installing it. For CRM to be truly effective an organization must first decide what kind of customer information it is looking for and it must decide what it intends to do with that information. For example, many financial institutions keep track of customers' life stages in order to market appropriate banking products like mortgages to them at the right time to fit their needs. Next, the organization must look into all of the different ways information about customers comes into a business, where and how this data is stored and how it is currently used.

One company, for instance, may interact with customers in a myriad of different ways including mail campaigns, Web sites, brick-and-mortar stores, call centers, mobile sales force staff and marketing and advertising efforts. Solid CRM systems link up each of these points. This collected data flows between operational systems (like sales and inventory systems) and analytical systems that can help sort through these records for patterns. Company analysts can then comb through the data to obtain a holistic view of each customer and pinpoint areas where better services are needed. In CRM projects, following data should be collected to run process engine: 1) Responses to campaigns, 2) Shipping and fulfillment dates, 3)Sales and purchase data, 4) Account information, 5) Web registration data, 6) Service and support records, 7) Demographic data, 8) Web sales data.

BENEFITS THAT BANKS CAN LOOK FORWARD TO FROM CRM

- Real-time forecasting for true sales pipeline visibility and more accurate decisions owing to the ability to predict what all products the customers are expected to purchase over a period of time.

- Providing an integrated view of customers or prospects across companies and channels, this makes cross selling and up selling easier. Research shows the more products a customer buys from a firm, the less likely that person is to leave it. Cross selling to existing customers produces incremental revenue at little cost, increases customer loyalty and improves underwriting accuracy.
- Increased productivity of managerial executives, sales and customer service staff.
- Reduced training costs.
- Streamlining of the business process across different functions aligned to the best practices.
- Giving customers the ability to transact/interact through multiple channels (phone etc).
- Turn around Time (TAT) for closing leads, opening accounts and closing service requests can be drastically improved.
- Campaign definition and performance tracking on a periodic basis (for different financial programs/ promotions).

THE CRM SOLUTION

Customer relationship management (CRM) solutions, if implemented and integrated correctly, can help significantly in improving customer satisfaction levels. Data warehousing can help in providing better transaction experiences for customers over different transaction channels. This is because data warehousing helps bring all the transactions coming from different channels under the same roof. Data mining helps banks analyze and measure customer transaction patterns and behavior. This can help a lot in improving service levels and finding new business opportunities.

It must be noted, however, that customer-centric banking also involves many risks. The banking industry world over is being thrust into a wild new world of privacy controversy.

The banks need to set up serious governance systems for privacy risk management. It must be remembered that customer privacy issues threaten to compromise the use of information technology which is at the very center of e-commerce and customer relationship management-two areas which are crucial for banks' future. The critical issue for banks is that they will not be able to safeguard customer privacy completely without undermining the most exciting innovations in banking.

These innovations promise huge benefits, both for customers and providers. But to capture them, financial services companies and their customers will have to make some critical tradeoffs. When the stakes are so high, nothing can be left to chance, which is why banks must immediately begin developing comprehensive approaches to the privacy issue. The customer centric business models based on the applications of information technology are sustainable only if the banks protect client confidentiality in the process - which is the basic foundation of banking business.

Today, many businesses such as banks, insurance companies, and other service providers realize the importance of Customer Relationship Management (CRM) and its potential to help them acquire new customers retain existing ones and maximize their lifetime value. At this point, close relationship with customers will require a strong coordination between IT and marketing departments to provide a long-term retention of selected customers.

CRM IN THE NEW AGE BANKING SCENARIO

Banks today do much more than lend and borrow money. They sell financial products; pay utility bills; file tax returns; and even get the PAN (Permanent Account Number issued by the Commissioner of Income Tax) card made for their customers.

The new-age private sector banks can be said to be the forerunners in offering such customer-oriented service. Concepts such as anywhere banking, 12-hour banking and transactions through ATMs (automatic teller machines), which were introduced by them, have revolutionised the banking practices in India. Today, many of the routine banking operations, such as cash transactions and checking the statement of account can be done through ATMs. Telephone or Internet banking is also slowly catching on.

The ATMs are themselves turning into quasi banks, as they offer value-added services in addition to plain vanilla cash withdrawal and deposit. Services such as mobile recharge facility, utility bill payments, insurance premium payments and payment of donations to temples are growing. Banking holidays are, therefore, no longer to be feared. The convenience of seven-days-a-week, 24-hours-a-day banking has attracted consumers.

In fact, banks are taking transactions to the doorstep of the customers with mobile ATMs. During the recent monsoon havoc in Mumbai, ICICI Bank provided a mobile ATM van in suburban Kalyan.

Banks are even taking loans to the customers. Another new concept introduced by private sector banks is 12-hour banking. Some of these private and public sectors banks even offer 24-hour banking at their branches located at strategic places like airports. Plastic money has changed the way people look at money. If credit and debit cards have made cash redundant, co-branded cards are changing the customers' spending patterns and lifestyle. The benefits from these cards range from earning frequent flyer miles and free talk time to waiver on fuel surcharge. Most credit cards also offer health and life insurance cover. Many banks have now waived the annual fee on credit cards. While their competitors may dismiss this as a marketing ploy and say it is one way to cover other hidden costs, customers do not stand to lose.

Banks are on their way to becoming a one-stop shop for selling products such as mutual funds, insurance and RBI bonds and offer service such as payment of utility bills and equity trading. Citibank has a dedicated helpline that offers support services, including home maintenance, purchase of movie or train or air tickets.

Cross-selling also helps banks personalise products for their customers. For instance, banks give loans against insurance, or link deposit schemes to insurance, depending on customer.

Wealth management or private banking is another new concept which is becoming popular. It includes all financial services (banking, investment, tax management, legal solutions and transmission of wealth to the next generation), from 'cradle to grave'. As part of wealth management, ABN Amro even offers advice about art as an investment.

Relationship Management in banking sector and the need for Customer Relationship Management to increase customer value by using some analytical methods in CRM applications. CRM is a sound business strategy to identify the bank's most profitable customers and prospects, and devotes time and attention to expanding account relationships with those customers through individualized marketing, repricing, discretionary decision making, and customized service-all delivered through the various sales channels that the bank uses.

SECTION–II

FINANCIAL MARKET

7

CAPITAL MARKETS, MONEY MARKETS AND DERIVATIVE MARKETS IN INDIA

Akinchan Buddhodev Sinha

Economic prosperity is a must, growth of GDP and foreign trade is an essential ingredient for any economy in order to become numero uno in the globe. But all these are only possible when there is sound financial system to cater to long term and short term needs of finance and as we are very well conversant with the risks that every business organization is prone to and in order to minimize them as it may not be possible to completely eradicate them, there is a need for a mechanism which can help in the attainment of this objective.

As we can see that India is on a fast track of growth and in order to maintain this momentum it is essential to develop a conducive environment which can provide a fillip to the ongoing investment activities and all these above mentioned markets are the so called pillars on which the economic development of our country rests.

In this paper we will be discussing on these three markets and rules governing them and the role they are going to play in the future towards building an India which will be recognized for its sound financial system.

CAPITAL MARKETS

Let us first see the present scenario of capital markets in India. In calendar year of 2008, Indian stock market have sailed through rough seas. From the highs of 21,000 in January 2008, the BSE sensex fell to a low about 12,500 in July 2008. In this process, there is a complete erosion of profits accumulated since April 07. In late 07 and January 08, the market moved northwards due to high growth in GDP and sound corporate performance. There was a surge in FIIs inflows in late CY07 assisted the market to move upwards. This euphoria led to the Indian market outperforming its Asian peers by about 15% in December 07-January 08. Everything was going good so far but our stock markets took off their eyes from the factors which attacked the global bourses. As a result of rising crude prices, the subprime crises in the US and depreciation of the dollar vis-à-vis major currencies including the Japanese yen. These global turbulence resulted in withdrawal of liquidity from the Indian market, resulting in a steep fall. Further, domestic factors like spiraling inflation, hike in interest rates, increasing fiscal deficit and prospects of an economic slow down took over.

Now, discussed about the present phase of the capital market let us go deeper and see its other facets. As we are more or less familiar with the concept of capital market but still let us have a brief discussion on it. It is the market for securities where companies and governments can raise long term funds. Selling stock and bonds are two options to raise capital. Therefore bond and stock markets are the two components of capital markets.

The capital markets consist of the primary market, where new issues are distributed to investors , and the secondary market, where existing securities are traded.

So when we talk about Indian Capital Market, it is comprised of Indian Equity Markets and Indian Debt Markets. The Indian Equity Market depends mainly on monsoons, global funds flowing into equities and performance of various companies. Indian equity market is mainly dominated by two kings namely, National Stock Exchange of India ltd (NSE) &

Bombay Stock Exchange (BSE). The benchmark indices of the two exchanges-NIFTY of NSE and Sensex of BSE are closely monitored. The two exchanges also have an F&O (Futures and Options) segment for trading in equity derivatives including the indices. The key players in the Indian equity markets are Mutual Funds, Financial Institutions and FIIs representing mainly Venture Capital Funds and Private Equity Funds.

Inspite of the volatility, Indian equity market is considered as a lucrative market. Indian stocks does not only satisfy the profit appetite for long term and medium term investors but also for the position traders, short-term swing traders and also very short term intra day traders. As on December 30th 2007, market capitalization (BSE 500) at US$ 1638 billion was 150 per cent of GDP, matching well with other emerging economies of the globe and selected matured markets.

Some of the positive developments that have taken place recently regarding stock markets will go a long way in making the capital raising process easier for the companies. The timeline for rights issues have been reduced. The issues will now be completed in 43 days as against the earlier timeline of 109 days. Other developments being pricing norms for QIPs have changed. It is currently done at the average share price of the last two weeks. The norms for QIPs were changed to the average share price of two weeks as against the current six months. Another important development pertaining to capital market is the introduction of the concept of ASBA (Applications Supported by Blocked Account) by SEBI in rights issues on a pilot basis. This is a sequel to the introduction of making applications through ASBA in a book built public issues. ASBA is a component of the market regulator's reform process for primary market and co-exists with current practice of IPO subscription by cheques. Currently, the facility is available only for retail investors bidding at the cut-off price.

Investors have to submit ASBA, physically or electronically, to the banks where their accounts are maintained. Banks then block the application money till the basis of allotment is finalized or till withdrawal or rejection of the applications, as the case may be. In case of IPOs, ASBA also does away with the refund process, besides reducing the time between an issue and its listing, since the listing happens only after refunds are done. Examples of companies opting for ASBA regarding their rights issue are Tata Motors and Sadhana Nitro Chem.

A key player of Indian capital market is FIIs. They are very important source of investments. If we have a look at the data of past few years of investments in the Indian securities market, we can observe that the boom and fall in the market to a big extent is determined by FIIs, i.e. when there is hike in the quantum of investments by FIIs there is a boom and when there is a withdrawal of investments by them the market enters the bearish phase. They are quite active while trading in the Indian securities market. The past boom in the stock markets in 2001-02, 2003-04 and 2005-06 have been attributed to FIIs. But market regulators sees them with a word of caution and worry. However, the bottom line is that FIIs are blessing in disguise for the Indian financial system. Another element which caused uproar in the capital market was Participatory Notes (PNs). They have always created controversies and debate in the financial market circle. The participatory notes were responsible for largest fall in witnessed ever in the Indian stock markets. Participatory notes have been in news for all the wrong reasons and now and then, Indian regulators i.e. SEBI and RBI have been issuing notices or warnings to all the parties associated with these instruments. PNs became a matter of dislike for market regulators to such an extent that they proposed a ban on them in order to insulate Indian capital markets from its ill effects.

India's capital markets have experienced sweeping changes since the beginning of the last decade. Its market infrastructure has advanced while corporate governance has progressed faster than in many other emerging market economies. But in contrast to several developed countries and Asian economies, India's capital markets are still shallow, implying that further reforms are required to make India a world-class financial centre.

After talking on the equity market let us have a view on the other wheel of the capital market i.e. the debt market. In

India the various forms of debt instruments dealt are Bonds, Debentures, Commercial Papers, Certificates of Deposit, Government Securities (G Secs) etc. The Government Securities market is the oldest and the largest component of Indian debt market in terms of market capitalization, trading volumes and outstanding securities. The Reserve Bank of India have permitted Primary Dealers, Banks and Financial Institutions in India to do transactions in debt instruments among themselves or with non-bank clients.

Normally, it has been observed that retail investors have a tendency to invest in equity markets as it fetches them higher capital gains when stock markets have a bull run but now debt market have also become a center of attraction for such investors and particularly they are showing interest towards G-secs.

The kinds of bonds that are traded in India are PSU bonds, Corporate bonds and even certain government securities like Oil bonds, Food bonds, Fertilizer bonds etc. PSU bonds in India, are mostly sold on private placement basis to the targeted investors at market determined interest rates. Often the assistance of investment bankers are sought as arrangers to this issue. At nearly 40% of GDP, the size of India's government bond segment is comparable to many other emerging market economies. Its corporate bonds market however remains small and is dwarfed by those of United States, South Korea and Malaysia.

In annual statement on Development and Regulatory Policies for the year 2008-09 states the significant steps taken by Reserve Bank of India to further broaden and deepen the Government Securities Market in consultation with market participants. Let us have a view on some of its excerpts. First let us take the case of Floating Rate Bonds, status, the Mid-term review of October 2007 had indicated that a new issuance structure for floating rate bonds (FRBs) is being built into the Negotiated Dealing System (NDS) auction format being developed by the Clearing Corporation of India Limited (CCIL). The CCIL is currently developing the primary auction module for the dated Government securities which would cover all kinds of instruments, including FRBs.

Under Ways and Means Advances to the Government of India, status, the Reserve bank in consultation with the Government of India, has retained the extant arrangements for the Ways and Means Advances (WMA) for the fiscal year 2008-09. As per the arrangements, the WMA limits would continue to be fixed on a half-yearly basis and are placed at Rs20,000 crore for the first half and Rs6000 crore for the second half of 2008-09. The applicable interest rate on WMAs and overdrafts would continue to be linked to the repo rate, as hitherto. The Reserve Bank however retains the flexibility to revise the limits in consultation with the Government of India, taking into consideration the prevailing circumstances.

A discussion without the US economic slowdown is completely devoid of interest when it comes for analyzing its impact on Indian capital market. Experts believe that the ongoing financial crisis in the United States and its repercussions on developed market worldwide will result in lower capital inflows into emerging markets like India. At the same time they called for the government to make it easier for Indian companies to borrow overseas by incorporating flexibility in the restrictions that have been clamped in the past in order to curtail the menace of inflation. This will, in turn, lead to a slowing in investment growth in the months ahead. As lending gets tighter and investment flows dry, corporate India will experience difficulty in raising funds through equity and debt. Shubhada Rao, chief economist, Yes Bank , said the developments come as a huge concern. "The risk of a financial contagion would exist. If they (Merill Lynch or Lehman Brothers) were commercial banks, the risks would have heightened," she said, adding that Indian companies would find going harder to raise funds. "The pain is going to linger on. We could see a reversal of portfolio inflows. The time has come for policy action to ease restrictions.

MONEY MARKET

The money market is the mechanism which deals with the lending and borrowing of short term funds. As far as Indian Money Market is concerned it is heavily dependent on real interest rate that is the interest rate that is inflation adjusted. Though the money market is free from the regime of interest rate ceilings, structural barriers and other institutional factors can be held responsible for creating disturbances in the Indian Money Market. Apart from the call market rates, the other interest rates in the Indian Money Market usually do not in the short run. The money market instruments which are dealt in India are as follows:

(a) Call/Notice/Term money
(b) Repo/Reverse Repo
(c) Inter Corporate Deposits
(d) Commercial Paper
(e) Certificate of Deposit
(f) T-bills
(g) Interbank participation note

Indian money market consists of Organized, Unorganized and Co-operative Sectors.

Organized structure comprises of the following: Reserve Bank of India, DFHI(Discount and Finance House of India), Commercial banks which again have both public sector and private banks. Public sector banks falling under this category are, SBI and its subsidiaries, cooperative banks and nationalized banks and institutions falling under the purview of private banks are Indian and Foreign banks. Then comes Development Banks like: IDBI, IFCI, ICICI, NABARD, EXIM, LIG, GIC, UTI, etc.

The components of Unorganized sector of money market are: Indigenous Bankers, Money Lenders, Chits, Nidhis.

Lastly Co-operative Sector consists of State Cooperative and State Land development banks. State Cooperative have three constituents i.e. Central cooperative banks, Primary Agri credit societies and Primary urban banks. State Land development banks is consisted of Central land development banks and Primary land development banks.

As money market plays a pivotal role in easing the financial system from liquidity crunch, RBI recently have decided to come out with a package of moves aimed at removing tight short-term liquidity position in the banking system, while protecting the rupee from the disease of depreciation. The RBI has announced measures that will allow banks to pledge one per cent of their net time and demand liabilities additionally with RBI through repo window to meet their liquidity needs. This will facilitate in raising more funds by banks through the repo window instead of money markets, where call rates have shot up recently to levels as high as 16 per cent. The second liquidity adjustment facility, which was introduced to inject more liquidity in system on every reporting Friday(every week), will also opened up daily to pump additional liquidity in the current scenario.

Black clouds hovered on India's money market when call money stood at 6-6.1% on Tuesday, 11th March, unchanged from Monday's close. The central bank main short term lending rate stood at 7.75%. At that time JP Morgan's economists opined that liquidity shortfall could be around Rs70,000 crore in March, and they also forecasted that existing inefficiencies in the banking system could see a peak shortage of upto 1,00,000 crore.

According to the Market Review of August, 2008 published by SBI Mutual Fund, it states that money market rates remained range bound with an easing bias amidst continued tight liquidity in the system. The money market rates eased in the first half of the month due to fall in global crude prices but then increased in the light of tightness in liquidity and hardening of crude prices. The month ended with improvement in liquidity bringing down the money market rates. However, according to Emkay Global Financial Services Report published on October 4th 2008, stated that Indian Money Market have experienced unprecedented tightening of liquidity over last month. The average daily repo injection over last three weeks has been in excess of Rs. 600 billion (Rs. 822 billion for week ended October 3rd, 2008), highest ever in last eight years.

DERIVATIVE MARKETS

As financial markets are extremely volatile and hence an element of risk always hovers around it which can create trouble for the financial agents. Therefore in order to reduce this risk, derivatives acts as an antibiotics. Derivatives are products whose values are derived from one or more basic variables called bases. These bases can be underlying assets (for instance forex, equity etc.), bases or reference rates.

As far as India is concerned, the first move towards derivatives trading in India was the promulgation of the Securities Laws(Amendment) Ordinance, 1995, which withdrew the prohibition on options in securities. The market for derivatives, however, did not take off, as there was no regulatory framework to govern trading of derivatives. SEBI set up a 24-member committee under the chairmanship of Dr. L.C.Gupta, on November 18, 1996 to develop appropriate regulatory framework for derivatives trading in India.

Different types of derivatives are, Forwards, Futures, Options, Warrants, Leaps, Baskets, Swaps and Swaptions.

Derivative trading in India takes place either on a separate and independent Derivative Exchange or on a separate segment of an Existing Stock Exchange. Derivative Exchange/ Segment function as a Self-Regulatory Organization (SRO) and SEBI acts as the oversight regulator. The clearing and settlement of all trades on the Derivative Exchange/Segment would have to be through a Clearing Corporation/House, which is independent in governance and membership from the Derivative Exchange/Segment.

If we look at commodity derivatives, India's commodity future trade is set to grow more than 40% to Rs57 trillion in the March 2009, despite curbs on eight commodities, 'said the chairman of the Forward Markets Commission. Earlier in 2007, India banned futures trade in rice, wheat, and two varieties of pulses for their role in inflation. Traders have switched from the banned items to other related commodities and bourses have successfully launched a few new commodities to fill the void. In one of the major developments, National Stock Exchange of India started exchange-traded currency futures on 29th August, while others including the biggest commodity exchange, Multi-Commodity Exchange of India, plan to enter the fray soon. Global majors like Goldman Sachs, Citigroup besides bourses like Intercontinental Exchange Corporation and NYSE Euronext hold stakes in Indian commodity exchanges. The other major happenings in derivative market is that after the National Stock Exchange (NSE) and Bombay Stock Exchange (BSE), India's largest commodity bourse, the Multi-Commodity Exchange (MCX) is getting ready to launch futures trading in currency derivatives. MCX informed in an invitation that it will launch exchange- traded rupee futures on Oct 6. The currency future trading will be through MCX stock exchange, the new company that MCX has recently floated.

But there are some dark sides of derivative market also, especially with respect to commodity derivative market and it is CTT (Commodities Transaction Tax). According to The Federal of Indian Commodity Exchanges (FICE), an apex national body of India's major commodity bourses , says the CTT that government has proposed would kill the futures market in the country. In a recent memorandum submitted by FICE to Finance Minister has called for the immediate withdrawal of CTT. One of the argument mentioned in the memorandum which supports its withdrawal is that as commodities derivatives market (CDM) is at an initial stage and it is a market having only single product i.e.only futures, no options, no index futures, no intangible futures and single user only i.e. traders and corporates. No banks, mutual funds, FIs, FIIs are its participants, so levying of CTT may result in its growth being axed.

FINANCIAL TALKS ON INDIAN FINANCIAL MARKET

Any form of financial crisis definitely have its impact on the financial markets of a country but as per the Global Financial Stability report, released by the International Monetary Fund stated that Indian financial sector is likely to manage the risks thrown up by the current financial crisis. IMF pointed out that corporates in India have borrowed dollars and swapped the resulting debt into yen, increasing the gap between borrowing and lending rates, but leaving a large open exposure. Inspite of such acts, IMF's opined that risk arising to the Indian financial sector arising from these transactions are at manageable levels.

India have been ranked at the 31st position in the World Economic Forum's (WEF) first Financial Development Index, topped by the US and UK, on the back of robust performance of its financial markets and non-banking institutions. While India produced solid results in terms of its financial markets particularly foreign exchange and derivatives, its banks appear hamstrung by lack of size, low efficiency and poor information disclosure, the financial development report said, adding despite the lacunae the banking system is stable due to sizable capital buffers. India came in at 31st in terms of its overall ranking, while China is at the 24th position. The other BRIC peers Brazil and Russia are at the 40th and 36th position respectively.

CONCLUSION

The Indian financial sector has remained relatively sheltered from the ongoing volatility in the global markets. "The firms in the financial services space don't have any substantial linkage to the subprime losses in the US except for some banks, which is too low to have any bearing impact. The lack of linkages means they are comparatively insulated against volatility in global markets," says DK Agarwal, Chairman and Managing Director of SMC Wealth Management Services. If we take a closer view of the capital market it is still in its evolving stage as only about 2% of Indian population of 1.1 billion invest in capital markets. Of this, individuals invest only 5% of their total savings into stock markets- an indication of the kind of potential Indian financial services have. The sharp increase in India's stock markets since 2003 reflects its improving macroeconomic fundamentals. The next growth opportunities, believe analysts, will come from online trading, internet banking, currency derivatives and commodity derivatives in this space. Thus the future of Indian financial market seems to be bright and full of energy which will definitely give fillip to the investment activities as well as creating conducive environment for both short and long-term investors.

REFERENCES

http://economictimes.indiatimes.com/Money__You/Current_volatile_market_situation/articleshow/3561132.cms

All about India's Derivatives Markets (*By Namita Jain)*

MCX Stock Exchange to Launch Currency Futures (2008-10-04 09:35:00).

Stock Market May Undergo Correction in Short Term (25 Aug., 2008, 0418 hrs IST).

Indian Derivatives Market (Asani Sarkar).

Deutsche Bank Research-India's Capital Markets, Unlocking the Door to Future Growth.

Livemint.com (*The Wall Street Journal*)

India Money Market.

RBI Steps in to Increase Liquidity (*Business Line*, Thursday, Sep 18th, 2008).

Market Review–August 200811)

Part II. Annual Statement on Developmental and Regulatory Policies for the Year 2008-09.

The Detailed Structure of Indian Money Market *(http://www.indianofficer.com/forums/indian-economy-wiki/1652-structure-indian-money-market.html)*

http://www.business-standard.com/india/story page. php ? autono=334535

http://www.livemint.com/2008/03/11114451/Indian-money-market-liquidity.html

India Witnesses Unforeseen Liquidity Tightening: Emkay, Published on Sat Oct, 2008.

Whether Participatory Notes Be Abolished? *Amar Karndhir & Amit Bhaskar.*

SEBI Extends ASBA to Rights Issues 26 Sep., 2008, 0154 hrs IST, ET *Bureau.*

http://www.financialexpress.com/news/India-likely-to-manage-financial-crisis-says-IMF/294397/

http://www.business-standard.com/india/story page. php ? autono=333986

8

THE CHANGING FACE OF INDIAN FINANCIAL MARKET

Arun Tiwari

INTRODUCTION

The Indian economy is witnessing a mini revolution in commodity derivatives and risk management. Commodity options trading and cash settlement of commodity futures had been banned since 1952 and until 2002 commodity derivatives market was virtually non-existent, except some negligible activity on an OTC basis. Now in September 2005, the country has 3 national level electronic exchanges and 21 regional exchanges for trading commodity derivatives. As many as eighty (80) commodities have been allowed for derivatives trading.

HISTORY

The history of organized commodity derivatives in India goes back to the nineteenth century when the Cotton Trade Association started futures trading in 1875, barely about a decade after the commodity derivatives started in Chicago. Over time the derivatives market developed in several other commodities in India. Following cotton, derivatives trading started in oilseeds in Bombay (1900), raw jute and jute goods in Calcutta (1912), wheat in Hapur (1913) and in Bullion in Bombay (1920). However, many feared that derivatives fuelled unnecessary speculation in essential commodities, and were detrimental to the healthy functioning of the markets for the underlying commodities, and hence to the farmers. With a view to restricting speculative activity in cotton market, the Government of Bombay prohibited options business in cotton in 1939. Later in 1943, forward trading was prohibited in oilseeds and some other commodities including food-grains, spices, vegetable oils, sugar and cloth.

After Independence, the Parliament passed Forward Contracts (Regulation) Act, 1952 which regulated forward contracts in commodities all over India. The Act applies to goods, which are defined as any movable property other than security, currency and actionable claims. The Act prohibited options trading in goods along with cash settlements of forward trades, rendering a crushing blow to the commodity derivatives market. Under the Act, only those associations/ exchanges, which are granted recognition by the Government, are allowed to organize forward trading in regulated commodities. The Act envisages three-tier regulation: (i) The Exchange which organizes forward trading in commodities can regulate trading on a day-to-day basis; (ii) the Forward Markets Commission provides regulatory oversight under the powers delegated to it by the central Government, and (iii) the Central Government - Department of Consumer Affairs, Ministry of Consumer Affairs, Food and Public Distribution-is the ultimate regulatory authority. The already shaken commodity derivatives market got a crushing blow when in 1960s, following several years of severe draughts that forced many farmers to default on forward contracts (and even caused some suicides), forward trading was banned in many commodities considered primary or essential. As a result, commodities derivative markets dismantled and went underground where to some extent they continued as OTC contracts at negligible volumes. Much later, in 1970s and 1980s the Government relaxed forward trading rules for some commodities, but the market could never regain the lost volumes.

CHANGE IN GOVERNMENT POLICY

After the Indian economy embarked upon the process of liberalization and globalization in 1990, the Government set up a Committee in 1993 to examine the role of futures trading. The Committee (headed by Prof. K.N. Kabra) recommended allowing futures trading in 17 commodity groups. It also recommended strengthening of the Forward Markets Commission, and certain amendments to Forward Contracts (Regulation) Act 1952, particularly allowing options trading in goods and registration of brokers with Forward Markets Commission. The Government accepted most of these recommendations and a future trading was permitted in all recommended commodities. Commodity futures trading in India remained in a state of hibernation for nearly four decades, mainly due to doubts about the benefits of derivatives. Finally a realization that derivatives do perform a role in risk management led the government to change its stance. The policy changes favoring commodity derivatives were also facilitated by the enhanced role assigned to free market forces under the new liberalization policy of the Government. Indeed, it was a timely decision too, since internationally the commodity cycle is on the upswing and the next decade is being touted as the decade of commodities.

Why are Commodity Derivatives Required?

India is among the top-5 producers of most of the commodities, in addition to being a major consumer of bullion and energy products. Agriculture contributes about 22% to the GDP of the Indian economy. It employees around 57% of the labor force on a total of 163 million hectares of land. Agriculture sector is an important factor in achieving a GDP growth of 8-10%. All this indicates that India can be promoted as a major center for trading of commodity derivatives.

It is unfortunate that the policies of FMC during the most of 1950s to 1980s suppressed the very markets it was supposed to encourage and nurture to grow with times. It was a mistake other emerging economies of the world would want to avoid. However, it is not in India alone that derivatives were suspected of creating too much speculation that would be to the detriment of the healthy growth of the markets and the farmers. Such suspicions might normally arise due to a misunderstanding of the characteristics and role of derivative product. It is important to understand why commodity derivatives are required and the role they can play in risk management. It is common knowledge that prices of commodities, metals, shares and currencies fluctuate over time. The possibility of adverse price changes in future creates risk for businesses.

Derivatives are used to reduce or eliminate price risk arising from unforeseen price changes. A derivative is a financial contract whose price depends on, or is derived from, the price of another asset.

Two important derivatives are futures and options:

(i) Commodity Futures Contracts: A futures contract is an agreement for buying or selling a Commodity for a predetermined delivery price at a specific future time. Futures are standardized contracts that are traded on organized futures exchanges that ensure performance of the contracts and thus remove the default risk. The commodity futures have existed since the Chicago Board of Trade (CBOT, www.cbot.com) was established in 1848 to bring farmers and merchants together. The major function of futures markets is to transfer price risk from hedgers to speculators. For example, suppose a farmer is expecting his crop of wheat to be ready in two months time, but is worried that the price of wheat may decline in this period. In order to minimize his risk, he can enter into a futures contract to sell his crop in two months' time at a price determined now. This way he is able to hedge his risk arising from a possible adverse change in the price of his commodity.

(ii) Commodity Options contracts: Like futures, options are also financial instruments used for hedging and speculation. The commodity option holder has the right, but not the obligation, to buy (or sell) a specific quantity of a commodity at a specified price on or before a specified date. Option contracts involve two parties–the seller of the option writes the option in favour of the buyer (holder) who pays a certain

premium to the seller as a price for the option. There are two types of commodity options: a 'call' option gives the holder a right to buy a commodity at an agreed price, while a 'put' option gives the holder a right to sell a commodity at an agreed price on or before a specified date (called expiry date). The option holder will exercise the option only if it is beneficial to him; otherwise he will let the option lapse. For example, suppose a farmer buys a put option to sell 100 Quintals of wheat at a price of $25 per quintal and pays a 'premium' of $0.5 per quintal (or a total of $50). If the price of wheat declines to say $20 before expiry, the farmer will exercise his option and sell his wheat at the agreed price of $25 per quintal. However, if the market price of wheat increases to say $30 per quintal, it would be advantageous for the farmer to sell it directly in the open market at the spot price, rather than exercise his option to sell at $25 per quintal. Futures and options trading therefore helps in hedging the price risk and also provide investment opportunity to speculators who are willing to assume risk for a possible return. Further, futures trading and the ensuing discovery of price can help farmers in deciding which crops to grow. They can also help in building a competitive edge and enable businesses to smoothen their earnings because non hedging of the risk would increase the volatility of their quarterly earnings. Thus futures and options markets perform important functions that cannot be ignored in modern business environment. At the same time, it is true that too much speculative activity in essential commodities would destabilize the markets and therefore, these markets are normally regulated as per the laws of the country.

MODERN COMMODITY EXCHANGES

To make up for the loss of growth and development during the four decades of restrictive government policies, FMC and the Government encouraged setting up of the commodity exchanges using the most modern systems and practices in the world. Some of the main regulatory measures imposed by the FMC include daily mark to market system of margins, creation of trade guarantee fund, back-office computerization for the existing single commodity Exchanges, online trading for the new Exchanges, demutualization for the new Exchanges, and one-third representation of independent Directors on the Boards of existing Exchanges etc.

Responding positively to the favorable policy changes, several Nation-wide Multi-Commodity Exchanges (NMCE) have been set up since 2002, using modern practices such as electronic trading and clearing. Selected Information about the two most important commodity exchanges in India [Multi-Commodity Exchange of India Limited (MCX), and National Multi-Commodity & Derivatives]

Top 10 Commodities

The Index Maintenance Committee, comprising senior officials from the Indian Statistical Institute (ISI), Credit Analysis & Research Ltd and MCX, announced changes in the composition and weightage of India's first real-time composite commodity futures index-MCX-COMDEX. The index is calculated and displayed on a real-time basis on MCX Trader Work Stations and at various other display centers.

MCX-COMDEX captures diversified sectors encompassing futures contracts drawn on metals, energy and agricultural commodities that are traded on MCX. The index was initially designed and developed by the Research and Development Department of MCX in association with Indian Statistical Institute (ISI), Kolkata, and launched in June 2005.

Before the changes, the COMDEX was composed of wheat, urad, soya oil, rubber, guarseed, kapaskhali in agri; gold, silver, copper in metals; and crude oil in energy. In order to synchronize index with changing economic dynamics and increased trading activities on the exchange, the Index Committee has decided to revamp its composition and weights.

In the process, group weights in the composite index have been modified from equal weights of sub-indices to 40 percent each in the case of MCX Metal Index and MCX Energy Index and 20 percent in the case of MCX Agri Index. Thus each sector has been given due weightage to represent its significance in the physical and futures markets.

The new composition of commodities and their weights in the MCX-COMDEX are:

Commodity

Final Wts. Group Wts.

MCX-METAL

(1) Gold -16.6%, 40%

(2) Silver -10.6%

(3) Copper -7.0%

(4) Aluminum -2.0%

(5) Nickel -2.0%

(6) Zinc -2.0%

MCX-ENERGY

(7) Crude Oil -31.8%, 40%

(8) Natural Gas -8.2%

MCX-AGRI

(9) Ref. Soy Oil -3.1%, 20%

(10) Mentha Oil -4.5%

(11) Potatoes -3.3%

(12) Kapaskhalli -2.0%

(13) Cardamoms -2.0%

(14) Chana -3.1%

(15) Guar seed -2.0%

The new composition comes on the back of continuous research, intensive analysis and interaction with economists, statisticians and market players to position MCX-COMDEX as an effective barometer of economic trends in the country. It also enables the Comdex to retain its characteristics as an attractive tradable index in the longer term.

With its component weight ages being adjusted to reflect their physical market shares, COMDEX with its underlying futures prices of commodities could function as the augury of future price trends. It could thereby provide enough leeway for country's economic managers to take appropriate corrective action if not in advance at least on time.

A precise relationship if established between balance sheet parameters and COMDEX would serve to help corporates with extensive exposure to component commodities take advance remedial measures while charting their growth path and add value for investors.

Investors who own stocks of companies having exposure to primary commodities could use the COMDEX as a guide to hedge their risk in the commodity exchange, thereby bringing stability to the financial markets and strengthening linkages.

Headquartered in the financial capital of India, Mumbai, MCX (www.mcxindia.com) is an independent, demutualised nationwide electronic multi commodity futures exchange set up by Financial Technologies with permanent recognition from Government of India for facilitating online trading, clearing & settlement operations for futures market across the country. The exchange started operations in November 2003 and presently is the top commodity exchange in the country with 70% market share of the total commodity derivatives trading volume in the country. Among the top ten commodity derivatives exchanges in the world, MCX ranks among the top three bullion, energy and copper exchanges in the world in terms of contracts traded. The average daily turnover of MCX is about US$2.2 billion

Apart from being accredited with ISO 9001:2000 for quality management, it is the world's first and only multi-commodity exchange to have achieved ISO 27001:2005 certification, the global benchmark for information security management systems.

MCX offers futures trading in 58 commodities, defined in terms of the type of contracts offered, from various market segments including bullion, energy, ferrous and non-ferrous metals, oils and oil seeds, cereals, pulses, plantations, spices, plastics and fibers. The exchange strives to be at the forefront of developments in the commodities futures industry and has forged eleven strategic alliances across the world, including with Tokyo Commodity Exchange, Chicago Climate Exchange,

London Metal Exchange, New York Mercantile Exchange, New York Board of Trade and Bursa Malaysia Derivatives, Berhad.

Financial Technologies India Ltd, a leading provider of transaction automation technologies for Equities, Derivatives, Forex and Commodity markets, is the majority shareholder of MCX. Other key stakeholders include Fidelity International, State Bank of India & its subsidiaries, National Stock Exchange (NSE) and National Bank for Agriculture & Rural Development (NABARD).

The above does indicate that he commodity derivatives market has a bright future in India. The Volume and value of trade in commodity derivatives could in fact take a quantum jump as bullion, crude oil and other high value commodities being added with each passing day get more actively traded in the coming months. It is also being speculated by market operators that finally the commodity derivatives market would out-pace and overtake the market for stock derivatives

In addition to the above mentioned commodities the news is that future trading of carbon credit and future trading of foreign currency will start shortly in MCX this will widen the scope of trade area and the scope of income for investors.

Hedge Fund

The term hedge fund is used to indicate a 'hedge' against investment deterioration. Hedge fund can be defined as a managed portfolio that has targeted a specific return goal regardless of market conditions. Hedge funds specialize in gaining maximum returns for minimum risk. Hedge funds use a wide variety of different investing strategies to achieve this goal and generally these strategies are managed and executed by a portfolio manager. Strategies that can be used by the portfolio manager of a hedge fund include short selling, arbitrage, hedging and leverage. The portfolio manager uses these options to remain flexible and weather the various storms of the market.

Short selling means borrowing a security (or commodity futures contract) from a broker and selling it, with the understanding that it must later be bought back (hopefully at a lower price) and returned to the broker. Short selling (or "selling short") is a technique used by investors who try to profit from the falling price of a stock.

Arbitrage means attempting to profit by exploiting price differences of identical or similar financial instruments, on different markets or in different forms.

Hedging is the practice of offsetting the price risk inherent in any cash market position by taking an equal but opposite position in the futures market. A long hedge involves buying futures contracts to protect against possible increase in prices of commodities. A short hedge involves selling futures contracts to protect against possible decline in prices of commodities.

Leverage is the use of borrowed funds at a fixed rate of interest in an effort to boost the rate of return from an investment. Increased leverage causes the risk and return on an investment to also increase.

Benefits include:

- Hedging the price risk associated with futures contractual commitments.
- Efficient price discovery prevents seasonal price volatility.
- Facilitate informed lending.
- Provide trading limit finance to traders in commodities exchanges.
- Greater flexibility, certainty and transparency in procuring commodities aids bank lending.
- Hedged positions of producers and processors reduce the risk of default faced by banks.

Future Trading

Futures trading is an agreement between a buyer and a seller obligating the seller to deliver a specified asset of specified quality and quantity to the buyer on a specified date at a specified place and the buyer, in turn, is obligated to pay to the seller a pre-negotiated price in exchange of the delivery. In futures trading the contracting parties negotiate on, not only the price at which the commodity is to be delivered on a future date but also on what quality and quantity to be deliver and at what place.

Futures trading perform two important functions: price discovery and hedging of price risk in a commodity. Presently, future trading is permitted in 41 commodities in India. These include pepper (domestic and international), turmeric, gur, castorseed, hessian, jute, sacking, cotton, potato, castoroil (international), soyabean (oil and cake), kapas, RBD palmolein, sugar and tea.

Derivative Trading

Derivatives are contracts that are based on or derived from some underlying asset, reference rate, or index. The underlying asset can be securities, commodities, bullion, currency, livestock or anything else.

With Securities Laws (Second Amendment) Act 1999, Derivatives has been included in the definition of Securities. As per the Act a Derivative includes:

- A security derived from a debt instrument, share, loan, whether secured or unsecured, risk instrument or contract for differences or any other form of security;
- A contract which derives its value from the prices, or index of prices, of underlying securities;

Derivative trading implies a forward, future, option or any other hybrid contract of pre determined fixed duration, linked for the purpose of contract fulfillment to the value of a specified real or financial asset or to an index of securities.

Derivative trading in India can take place either on a separate and independent Derivative Exchange or on a separate segment of an existing Stock Exchange. Derivative Exchange/Segment function as a Self-Regulatory Organization (SRO) and SEBI acts as the oversight regulator.

UNRESOLVED ISSUES AND FUTURE PROSPECTS

Even though the commodity derivatives market has made good progress in the last few years, the real issues facing the future of the market have not been resolved. Agreed, the number of commodities allowed for derivative trading have increased, the volume and the value of business has zoomed, but the objectives of setting up commodity derivative exchanges may not be achieved and the growth rates witnessed may not be sustainable unless these real issues are sorted out as soon as possible. Some of the main unresolved issues are discussed below.

(a) Commodity Options: Trading in commodity options contracts has been banned since 1952. The market for commodity derivatives cannot be called complete without the presence of this important derivative. Both futures and options are necessary for the healthy growth of the market. While futures contracts help a participant (say a farmer) to hedge against downside price movements, it does not allow him to reap the benefits of an increase in prices. No doubt there is an immediate need to bring about the necessary legal and regulatory changes to introduce commodity options trading in the country. The matter is said to be under the active Consideration of the Government and the options trading may be introduced in the near future.

(b) The Warehousing and Standardization: For commodity derivatives market to work efficiently, it is necessary to have a sophisticated, cost-effective, reliable and convenient warehousing system in the country. The Habibullah (2003) task force admitted, "A sophisticated Warehousing industry has yet to come about". Further, independent labs or quality testing centers should be set up in each region to certify the quality, grade and quantity of commodities so that they are appropriately standardized and there are no shocks waiting for the ultimate buyer who takes the physical delivery. Warehouses also need to be conveniently located. Central Warehousing Corporation of India (CWC: www.fieo.com) is operating 500 Warehouses across the country with a storage capacity of 10.4 million tonnes. This is obviously not adequate for a vast country. To resolve the problem, a Gramin Bhandaran Yojana (Rural Warehousing Plan) has been introduced to construct new and expand the existing rural godowns. Large scale privatization of state warehouses is also being examined.

(c) Cash Versus Physical Settlement: It is probably due to the inefficiencies in the present warehousing system that only about 1% to 5% of the total commodity derivatives trade in the country are settled in physical delivery. Therefore the warehousing problem obviously has to be handled on a war footing, as a good delivery system is the backbone of any commodity trade particularly difficult problem in cash settlement of commodity derivative contracts is that at present, under the Forward Contracts (Regulation) Act 1952, cash settlement of outstanding contracts at maturity is not allowed. In other words, all outstanding contracts at maturity should be settled in physical delivery. To avoid this, participants square off their positions before maturity. So, in practice, most contracts are settled in cash but before maturity. There is a need to modify the law to bring it closer to the widespread practice and save the participants from unnecessary hassles.

(d) The Regulator: As the market activity pick-up and the volumes rise, the market will definitely need a strong and independent regular, similar to the Securities and Exchange Board of India (SEBI) that regulates the securities markets. Unlike SEBI which is an independent body, the Forwards Markets Commission (FMC) is under the Department of Consumer Affairs (Ministry of Consumer Affairs, Food and Public Distribution) and depends on it for funds. It is imperative that the Government should grant more powers to the FMC to ensure an orderly development of the commodity markets. The SEBI and FMC also need to work closely with each other due to the inter-relationship between the two markets.

(e) Lack of Economy of Scale: There are too many (3 national level and 21 regional) commodity exchanges. Though over 80 commodities are allowed for derivatives trading, in practice derivatives are popular for only a few commodities. Again, most of the trade takes place only on a few exchanges. All this splits volumes and makes some exchanges unviable. This problem can possibly be addressed by consolidating some exchanges. Also, the question of convergence of securities and

commodities derivatives markets has been debated for a long time now. The Government of India has announced its intention to integrate the two markets. It is felt that convergence of these derivative markets would bring in economies of scale and scope without having to duplicate the efforts, thereby giving a boost to the growth of commodity derivatives market. It would also help in resolving some of the issues concerning regulation of the derivative markets. However, this would necessitate complete coordination among various regulating authorities such as Reserve Bank of India, Forward Markets commission, the Securities and Exchange Board of India, and the Department of Company affairs etc.

f. Tax and Legal bottlenecks: There are at present restrictions on the movement of certain goods from one state to another. These need to be removed so that a truly national market could develop for commodities and derivatives. Also, regulatory changes are required to bring about uniformity in octroi and sales taxes etc. VAT has been introduced in the country in 2005, but has not yet been uniformly implemented by all states.

CONCLUSION

India is one of the top producers of a large number of commodities, and also has a long history of trading in commodities and related derivatives. The commodities derivatives market has seen ups and downs, but seem to have finally arrived now. The market has made enormous progress in terms of technology, transparency and the trading activity. Interestingly, this has happened only after the Government protection was removed from a number of commodities, and market forces were allowed to play their role. This should act as a major lesson for the policy makers in developing countries, that pricing and price risk management should be left to the market forces rather than trying to achieve these through administered price mechanisms. The management of price risk is going to assume even greater importance in future with the promotion of free trade and removal of trade barriers in the world. All this augurs well for the commodity derivatives markets.

ANNEXURE

Bombay Stock Exchange

The *BSE Sensex or Bombay Stock Exchange Sensitive Index* is a *value-weighted index* composed of 30 stocks with the base April 1979 = 100. It consists of the 30 largest and most actively traded stocks, representative of various sectors, on the *Bombay Stock Exchange*. These companies account for around one-fifth of the market capitalization of the BSE.

The base value of the sensex is *100* on *April 1, 1979*, and the base year of BSE-SENSEX is *1978-79*.

At irregular intervals, the Bombay Stock Exchange (BSE) authorities review and modify its composition to make sure it reflects current market conditions.

The index has increased by over ten times from June 1990 to the present. Using information from April 1979 onwards, the long-run rate of return on the BSE Sensex works out to be 18.6% per annum, which translates to roughly 9% per annum after compensating for *inflation*.

Sensex Milestones

Here is a timeline on the rise and rise of the Sensex through Indian stock market history.

- *1000, July 25, 1990*-On *July 25*, 1990, the Sensex touched the four-digit figure for the first time and closed at 1,001 in the wake of a good monsoon and excellent corporate results.
- *2000, January 15, 1992*-On *January 15, 1992*, the Sensex crossed the 2,000-mark and closed at 2,020 followed by the liberal economic policy initiatives undertaken by the then finance minister and current Prime Minister Dr Manmohan Singh.
- *3000, February 29, 1992*-On *February 29, 1992*, the Sensex surged past the 3000 mark in the wake of the market-friendly Budget announced by the then Finance Minister, Dr Manmohan Singh.
- *4000, March 30, 1992*-On *March 30, 1992*, the Sensex crossed the 4,000-mark and closed at 4,091 on the

expectations of a liberal export-import policy. It was then that the Harshad Mehta scam hit the markets and Sensex witnessed unabated selling.

- *5000, October 11, 1999*-On *October 8, 1999,* the Sensex crossed the 5,000-mark as the BJP-led coalition won the majority in the 13th Lok Sabha election.
- *6000, February 11, 2000* - On *February 11, 2000,* the infotech boom helped the Sensex to cross the 6,000-mark and hit and all time high of 6,006.
- *7000, June 21, 2005*-On *June 20, 2005,* the news of the settlement between the Ambani brothers boosted investor sentiments and the scrips of RIL, Reliance Energy, Reliance Capital and IPCL made huge gains. This helped the Sensex crossed 7,000 points for the first time.
- *8000, September 8, 2005*-On *September 8, 2005,* the Bombay Stock Exchange's benchmark 30-share index — the Sensex — crossed the 8000 level following brisk buying by foreign and domestic funds in early trading.
- *9000, December 9, 2005* - The Sensex on *November 28, 2005* crossed 9000 to touch 9000.32 points during mid-session at the Bombay Stock Exchange on the back of frantic buying spree by foreign institutional investors and well supported by local operators as well as retail investors.
- *10,000, February 7, 2006*-The Sensex on February *6, 2006* touched 10,003 points during mid-session. The Sensex finally closed above the 10K-mark on February 7, 2006.
- *11,000, March 27, 2006*-The Sensex on *March 21, 2006* crossed 11,000 and touched a peak of 11,001 points during mid-session at the Bombay Stock Exchange for the first time. However, it was on March 27, 2006 that the Sensex first closed at over 11,000 points.
- *12,000, April 20, 2006* - The Sensex on *April 20, 2006* crossed 12,000 and touched a peak of 12,004 points during mid-session at the Bombay Stock Exchange for the first time.

- *13,000, October 30, 2006*-The Sensex on *October 30, 2006* crossed 13,000 and still riding high at the Bombay Stock Exchange for the first time. It took 135 days to reach 13,000 from 12,000. And 124 days to reach 13,000 from 12,500. On 30 October 2006 it touched a peak of 13,039.36 & closed at 13,024.26.
- *14,000, December 5, 2006*-The Sensex on *December 5, 2006* crossed 14,000 and touched a peak of 14028 at 9.58 AM(IST) while opening for the day December 5, 2006.
- *15,000, July 6, 2007*-The Sensex on *July 6, 2007* crossed another milestone and reached a magic figure of 15,000. it took almost 7 month and 1 day to touch such a historic milestone.
- *16,000, September 19, 2007*-The Sensex on *September 19, 2007* crossed the 16,000 mark and reached a historic peak of 16322 while closing. The bull hits because of the rate cut of 50 bit/s in the discount rate by the Fed chief Ben Bernanke in US.
- *17,000, September 26, 2007*-The Sensex on *September 26, 2007* crossed the 17,000 mark for the first time, creating a record for the second fastest 1000 point gain in just 5 trading sessions. It failed however to sustain the momentum and closed below 17000. The Sensex closed above 17000 for the first time on the following day. Reliance group has been the main contributor in this bull run, contributing 256 points. This also helped Mukesh Ambani's net worth to grow to over $50 billion or Rs.2 trillion. It was also during this record bull run that the Sensex for the first time zoomed ahead of the *Nikkei* of Japan.
- *18,000, October 9, 2007*-The Sensex crossed the 18k mark for the first time on October 9, 2007. The journey from 17k to 18k took just 8 trading sessions which is the third fastest 1000 point rise in the history of the sensex. The sensex closed at 18,280 at the end of day. This 788 point gain on 9 October was the second biggest single day absolute gains.

- *19,000, October 15, 2007*-The Sensex crossed the 19k mark for the first time on *October 15, 2007*. It took just 4 days to reach from 18k to 19k. This is the fastest 1000 points rally ever and also the 640 point rally was the second highest single day rally in absolute terms. This made it a record 3000 point rally in 17 trading sessions overall.
- *20,000, October 29, 2007*-The Sensex crossed the 20k mark for the first time with a massive 734.5 point gain but closed below the 20k mark. It took 11 days to reach from 19k to 20k. The journey of the last 10,000 points was covered in just 869 sessions as against 7,297 sessions taken to touch the 10,000 mark from 1,000 levels. In 2007 alone, there were six 1,000-point rallies for the Sensex.
- *21,000, January 8,2008*–The Sensex opened with a huge positive gap of 157 points at 20,970, and rallied past the 21,000-mark to a fresh all-time high of 21,078.

Sensex Falls

The top ten single-day falls of the Sensex have occurred on the following dates:

(1) January 21, 2008	—	1,408.35 points
(2) October 24, 2008	—	1,071.65 points
(3) March 17, 2008	—	951.03 points
(4) January 22, 2008	—	857 points
(5) February 11, 2008	—	833.98 points
(6) May 18, 2006	—	826 points
(7) March 13, 2008	—	770.63 points
(8) December 17, 2007	—	769.48 points
(9) March 31, 2007	—	726.85 points
(10) October 17, 2007	—	717.43 points
(11) January 18, 2007	—	687.82 points
(12) November 21, 2007	—	678.18 points
(13) August 16, 2007	—	642.70 points
(14) June 27, 2008	—	620.00 points

There was a blood bath in almost all the stock markets of the world due to Global Economic Crisis a lot of money was eroded from the market and R.B.I had to pump more money through the of reducing C.R.R & Repo Rate. The sentiments are still not positive and this phase is expected to go on for few more months before things get better.

We can also see that the parties ruling the country also affect the stock market as we can recollect that when the *Left Parties* supported the *Congress* to form the government the sensex plunged down as the *Lefties* are against market driven economy & when the withdrew their support from government & then also govt. won the trust vote this event was by stock market as it ended in green.

People investing in stock market should be well versed with the fundamentals of the market and should be ready to take some risk in order to enjoy high return as the principle remains same that *"High Risk High Return"*.

Investors should believe on their knowledge & experts suggestion and should not go rat race to either sell or buy stocks to avoid the notional losses that they can suffer as the recent example of *"Reliance Power IPO"* in which many people lost money due to lack of knowledge.

This proves that volatility which prevails in the market hurts the retail investors to a great extent the recent Bearish Market sentiment has resulted in huge loss of money to investors and at the same time Commodities Trading has not performed so badly, thus we can say that *"it is good to invest in Commodities Market with a fair knowledge than to invest in Stock Market Beleaving on Grapevine"*.

9

THE STOCK MARKET CONUNDRUM: 1995-2008 AND BEYOND

Indrani Parida & Biraj Kumar Mohanty

India has the third largest investor base in the world after the USA and Japan with over 20 million shareholders. Over 9,000 companies are listed on the stock exchanges, which are serviced by approximately 7,500 stockbrokers. The Indian capital market is significant in terms of the degree of development, volume of trading and its tremendous growth potential. India's market capitalization was one among the highest in the emerging markets. Total market capitalization of the BSE as on July 31, 1997 was Rs 5,573.07 billion growing by 18 per cent over a period of twelve years and as of August 2007 was over Rs 43 lakh crores.

India has emerged as the world's 10th largest equity market after it added several companies to the billion dollar club in terms of capitalization, taking the total to 81 companies.

This was the Indian story of Secondary Market till January 2008, when due to global economic slowdown the security market continuously plummeted to give nightmare to several investors and traders. The fall of SENSEX from 21000 index points in January 2008 to 9000 in November 2008 led to soul searching by the analysts and the planners at different level. Besides continuously reducing the CRR, Repo Rate, Reverse

Repo Rate, Bank Rate, the Finance Ministry also tried to have monthly review of banks to increase the off take of credit. As it seems now nothing has worked out. Squarely the blame is on the Foreign Institutional Investors (FII), who has withdrawn the money from our stock market to revamp their balance sheets. Although from the surface it seems FIIs are the villains in the show, some also suggested that correction like this was overdue. At this juncture, we need to examine the basics:

(1) First of all is it the fall out of FII withdrawal?

(2) Is the crash a short term phenomenon?

(3) Does the Indian Economy have the resilience of bouncing back?

(4) Where do you stand in the present global scenario?

Although lot of deliberation centers around these four factors in the subsequent discussion ,we focus primarily on the FII factor and its impact.

FII INVESTMENT IN INDIA

Investment in the capital market by FIIs first started during late 1992 and it was formalized in 1995 through Securities and Exchange Board of India (Foreign Institutional Investors) Regulations 1995. The act defines FII as an institution established or incorporated outside India which proposes to make investment in Indian Securities. The institution can be a Pension Fund, Mutual Fund, Investment Trust, Reinsurance Company, Asset Management Company Endowment, University Fund or Charitable Trust. They may have to register themselves directly or they may have a sub account if they will have to invest on behalf of another entity.

SEBI also led down a framework of investment for the FIIs. The purchase of equity shares of each company by a Foreign Institutional Investor investing on his own account shall not exceed ten per cent and in case of individual sub accounts it should not exceed five per cent of the total issued capital of the company in which such investment is made. Moreover, FIIs are also allowed to invest in both primary and secondary market through the stock exchanges in India. Overall investment limit in this mechanism is 24 per cent of paid up capital of any company and 20 per cent of the paid up capital of an Indian Bank. This scheme is called the Portfolio Investment Scheme.

On the available platform, growing economy and untapped potential for investment, FIIs found it quite encouraging to invest in Indian Capital Market. They parked their money at different opportune moments and in the year 2007 their involvement in Indian Capital Market was the maximum. In August 2008 when the exposure of FIIs in Indian Market was one among its highest, Government of India smelt rat in the dealing of FIIs. It was found out that lot of transactions in the market by FIIs were supported by Participatory Notes (PN).

It is pertinent to discuss the mechanism and fallacy of PNs in equity investment.

(1) Every individual FII interested to invest in India must be registered. But few outside parties who did not want to be registered took the via media of the FIIs to invest. They were popularly known as unregistered sub accounts.

(2) The sub accounts were not also investing their own money. They were collecting money from the High net worth individuals (HNI) or from different University Funds or Trusts.

(3) In fact the money supposed to be given to the FIIs by the sub accounts for purchase of shares was in terms of an undertaking to pay i.e. PN.

(4) Besides the PNs were invested in the derivative instruments which implies that giving an undertaking for a small volume of money, huge volume of transactions were being clinched.

(5) Due to the involvement of second party transaction, document money, derivative trading, the volume of transaction was huge, leading to huge volatility in the market.

PNs could have a cascading effect. If the HNI or investment firms want to close their deal in turn sub accounts will call back their money leading to cancellation of the PNs and squaring off of the future transactions. Future transactions can influence the spot market resulting in the market crash. Usually the money withdrawn from the market is in bulk.

It was believed that the FIIs had better risk taking ability because of the huge volume of fund involved. But later on it was proved otherwise. The huge volume of money involved leads to huge loss which is experienced now through the sub prime crisis.

Realizing bubble of this virtual instrument based on Indian Securities by foreign unknown players, SEBI tried to ban the PNs. In August 2007 the exposure of the PNs were Rs. 3.53 trillion and was about 51.6% of the net assets owned by the FIIs in India. FIIs owned nearly 30% of the share in Indian Market. It was decided that within 18 months all the PNs should be squared off and no fresh PNs should be issued. But in October 2008 again the curb on participatory note was lifted when economy slowed down due to sluggish market sentiment and SEBI thought it fit to give fillip to the market through PNs.

FII and Decline of Market

The second argument involved in the process is whether it is a short term phenomenon. The slump and ever descending market over last one year proves that in medium term also the shots are called by the FIIs. We have tried to examine the impact of FIIs investment in the growth of our market in long term through statistical data pertaining to 13 years (1995-2008). Here we examine two parameters i.e. FII investment and Growth rate of the country and their influence on SENSEX. As we understand that growth rate of a country leads to internal well being of the economy starting from production, performance of different sectors, economic and fiscal policy, inflation rate, foreign exchange reserve etc, we can consider it as indicator of economic health of a country. On visual observation of the graphs of these three parameters it is obvious that FII investment has a bigger influence on SENSEX than the economic health of the country.

This is further affirmed by finding out a correlation between

(1) Growth rate with Growth of SENSEX and

(2) Growth of FII investment against SENSEX

Growth rate is a relative figure which relates the GDP of current year to the previous year. So to bring commonality, we have also found out relative growth in SENSEX and FII s net buying and it is represented in the fifth and sixth column of Table 1.

Table 1

Year	*SENSEX (Closing Price of 31st March)*	*FII Net Buying in Billion Dollar*	*GDP Growth Rate in Percentage*	*Growth of SENSEX (Y2-Y1)/ Y1*	*Growth of FII Buying (Y2-Y1)/Y1*
1995-96	3366.61	2.01	7.3	0.00	-0.04
1996-97	3360.89	1.93	7.5	0.16	-0.49
1997-98	3892.97	0.98	5	-0.04	-1.40
1998-99	3739.96	-0.39	6.8	0.34	-6.49
1999-00	5001.28	2.14	6.4	-0.28	-0.14
2000-01	3604.38	1.85	5.2	-0.04	-0.18
2001-02	3469.35	1.51	5.4	-0.12	-0.74
2002-03	3048.72	0.4	3.8	0.83	26.25
2003-04	5590.6	10.9	8.5	0.16	-0.20
2004-05	6492.82	8.7	7.5	0.74	0.14
2005-06	11279.96	9.9	9.4	0.16	-0.68
2006-07	13072.1	3.2	9.6	0.20	5.34
2007-08	15644.44	20.3	9	-0.31	-1.55
2008-09 (Upto October 2008)	10809.12	-11.1	8		

Source: SENSEX- http://www.bseindia.com/histdata/hindices.asp
FII Net Buying: www.eximbankindia.com
GDP Growth rate: Economic Survey 2007-08;, RBI Monthly Bulletin, Annual Report & Weekly Statistical Supplement;

Correlation between GDP growth rate and growth of SENSEX	-0.17
Correlation between Incremental FII investment and growth of SENSEX	0.57

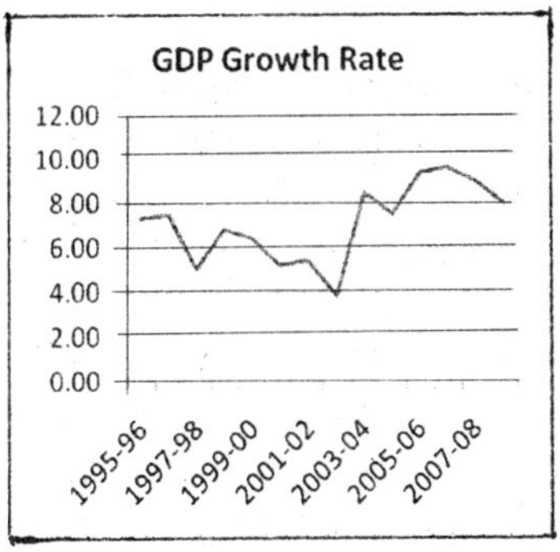

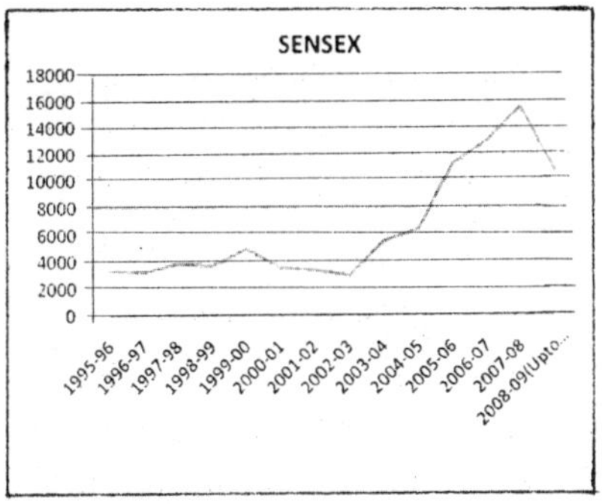

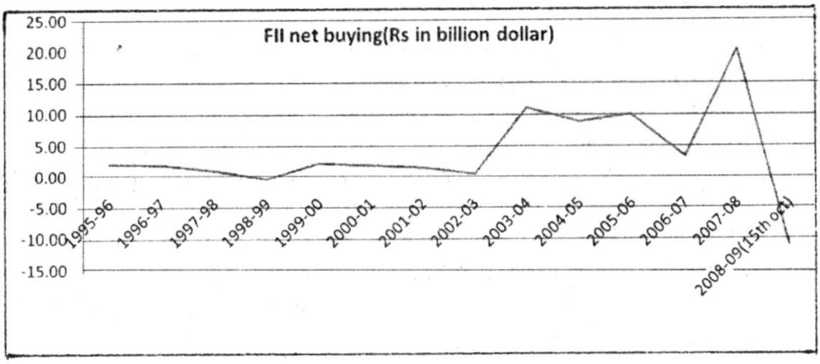

If we examine the same three parameters in short run we are bound to find still a better correlation between the FII investment and the rise of SENSEX. In short run several other factors may also contribute for the volatility in the market. We may get few conclusions from the above analysis.

(1) A 30% holding in the stock market held by the FIIs can have tremendous impact on the market. Whereas rest 70% holding by Indian Financial Institutes and Indian Public can not affect the market so much. This explains the fact that FIIs are traders rather than investors.

(2) It also reaffirms the lack of depth in Indian Market. Although Indian Public has high saving potential they are not investment savvy. They are prone to panic selling and induced buying.

(3) Looking into the kind of over dependence our country has on FII investment, we cannot buy the argument

that foreign investment is the only panacea to a growing capital market.

(4) FIIs invested heavily in the market during 2007 and through their brisk trading took SENSEX to a new height. They exit the market by booking huge profit. In the process the Indian individual and institutional investors suffered.

Government Initiative

It is understood that withdrawal of FII investment from India was extraneous and primarily due to the global meltdown. But during the up and down of market Indian Government has been taking various reform measures for attracting offshore FII investment inside the country.

- Government of India has increased the cumulative debt investment limit from US $3.2 billion to US $ 6 billion for FII investment in Government Securities and $1.5 billion dollar in corporate debt.(SEBI Notification dt June 20th 2008)
- Restriction of issuance of PNs were removed. (Cir No.IMD/FII & C/31/2008 October 07, 2008).
- There are lot of concessions on the registration of FIIs and sub accounts in India by including new entities under the purview of FII.
- SEBI in consultation with Government of India removed the restriction on of 70:30 ratio of FII investment in equity and debt respectively. FIIs can now invest in equity and debt as per their choice.(RBI/ 2008-09/240A. P. (DIR Series) Circular No. 25 October 17, 2008)

Now situation has changed. In 2000, when the SENSEX dropped about 20%, 74 FIIs fled the Indian equity market and the number of such investors in India dropped from 556 to 482. The next year, when the SENSEX dropped close to 18%, only seven new FIIs entered the market. But now when the market is going down with every passing day, there is net increase of 375 registered FIIs during September to November

2008. The new additions constitute additional 120 Institutions and 358 sub accounts. This seems that the FIIs are thinking in long term and want to enter the market when the prices are low. It is expected that Indian Market is going to revive in the coming year and its P/E ratio will be comparable with matured markets maintaining a balanced growth. With a big customer base of 111 crore population this country will have huge domestic requirement in the years to come. Moreover being a developing economy, Indian Economy will grow at a steady rate. Resilience of the Indian economy with its controlled and cautious approach provides the right opportunity for long term investment. So it is expected that in the years to come FII investment in India is bound to go up.

CONCLUSION

But this medium term catastrophe in Indian Capital Market is doing a great harm to our economy. The meltdown in the market should be viewed as an opportunity and our planners and law markers should see that

(1) Only serious kinds of investors are encouraged in our stock market. There should be some kind of cap on FII investment on the time frame of investment.

(2) Besides Indian economic system should be so vibrant, composed and regulated that it should be second to none.

Besides other reform and regulatory measures taken by the Government, these two steps will make our country attractive in terms of investment both for FDI and FII. Otherwise gullible investor in our country will be affected a lot on the volatility of the market, where the FIIs can trap the investors and churn out the hard earned money of Indian public by manipulating the market.

REFERENCE

Business Line Thursday Oct. 18 2007, D Sampatkumar What are Participatory Notes ?

http://www.ibef.org/economy/foreigninvestors.aspx

http://www.bseindia.com/histdata/hindices.asp

www.eximbankindia.com

Economic Survey 2007-08;

RBI Monthly Bulletin, Annual Report & Weekly Statistical Supplement;

SEBI.gov. in

10

A STUDY ON "EFFECT OF FDI'S AND FII'S ON INDIAN FINANCIAL MARKET"

Abhijit Dutta & Pradip Banerjee

INTRODUCTION

Among the different forms of capital flows, academics and policymakers talk about foreign direct investment (FDI) the most. This is because of several benefits of FDI and its importance in the world economy vis-à-vis other forms of capital flows. In the past fifteen years, FDI has been the dominant form of capital flow in the global economy, even for developing countries. So, now lets look at the meaning of FDI. Foreign direct investment can broadly be defined as a long term capital inflow into a country other than aid, portfolio investment or a repayable debt. In other words, it is usually a long term investment in equity by an entity that is outside the host country. This investment is deployed to earn a return over a long period of time by way of dividend. An additional objective of the investment is often to obtain a significant or controlling interest in the management of the firm or company in which such an investment is made.

The FDI relationship, consists of a parent enterprise and a foreign affiliate which together form a *transnational corporation (TNC)*. In order to qualify as FDI, the investment must afford the parent enterprise *control* over its foreign affiliate. Some of the factors that affect foreign direct investment are as follows: Availability of infrastructure in all areas (transport, hospitality, telecom, power), Capital account convertibility so that all capital and payments can flow easily in and out of the economy, acceptance of International Standards including accounting standards, stability of policies (entry, exit, labour etc) over a definite time horizon so that definite plans can be made, transparency of processes, policies and decision making and reduction of government decision making lead time, Improvement in the enforcement of intellectual property rights (since Indian laws in this area are already among the best in the world).

In the years after the Second World War global FDI was dominated by the United States, as much of the world recovered from the destruction wrought by the conflict. The U.S. accounted for around three-quarters of new FDI (including reinvested profits) between 1945 and 1960. Since that time FDI has spread to become a truly global phenomenon, no longer the exclusive preserve of OECD countries. FDI has grown in importance in the global economy with FDI stocks now constituting over 20% of global GDP. In the last few years, the emerging market countries such as China and India have become the most favoured destinations for FDI and investor confidence in these countries has soared. As per the FDI Confidence Index compiled by A.T. Kearney for 2005, China and India hold the first and second position respectively, whereas United States has slipped to the third position.

HISTORY OF FDI IN INDIA (1900S-2000)

The history of FDI in India has evolved through a six time periods, viz., 1900s-1918, 1919-1942, 1943-1961, 1962-1977, 1978-1990, and 1991-2000.

During the first phase (1900s-1918), there were hardly any restrictions on the nature and type of FDI. The foreign investments could flow 'freely' into India. However, except U.K., most of the countries neither had the need nor the will to invest in India. Foreign Investment to India was mainly through the Managing Agents from U.K.

It was in the second phase (1919-1942) that FDI in India actually originated. The introduction of import duties during this period 'stimulated' many British companies to invest in the Indian manufacturing sector to protect their businesses in India. Although, the Japanese companies increased their share of trade with India, U.K. remained to be the dominant investor in India during this period.

The third phase (1943-1961) saw a huge increase in the flow of FDI into India. During this period the Indian companies and GOI realized the need to import technology and finance from foreign companies and encouraged the same. This led to 'ambitious' investments by many companies from countries like U.K. and USA.

The fourth phase (1962-1977) marked the Indian Government's regulatory regime that imposed severe restrictions to control foreign exchange, type of FDI and ownership of foreign companies in India. These restrictions led to a 'controlled' flow of FDI in India and nearly eighty foreign companies also divested from India during this period.

The fifth phase (1978-1990) saw a new direction in the history of FDI in India with liberalization in imports and exports of the country. Although, the amount of FDI increased by over 13 times during this period, foreign companies invested 'cautiously' during this period with a wait and watch attitude.

And, in the final phase (1991-2000), the liberalization process in India was accelerated under the behest of IMF and World Bank. There have been very high growths in the amount of inward FDI and the number of joint ventures in India. More importantly, FDI has flown from across the world resulting in a globalized structure of FDI in India.

The table below summarizes the periods, the drivers of change, the driving forces, the major sources of direct investments, the nature of investments and the phases of evolution of present globalization of FDI in India.

Table 1
History of FDI in India: 1900s-2000

Characteristics/ Period	*Drivers of Change*	*Driving Forces*	*Major Sources of Investments*	*Nature of Investments*	*Stages of Evolution*
1900s-1918	U.K.	No restriction in FDI	U.K.	Trading & Finance	Free Flow Phase
1919-1942	U.K., Japan and Local Textile companies	Import duties were introduced	U.K. and Japan	Trading, Finance & Manufacturing	Stimulated Phase
1943-1961	Govt. of India	Demand for foreign technology & capital in manufacturing sector	U.K. and U.S.A.	Manufacturing, Sales & Services	Ambitious StagePhase
1962-1977	Govt. of India	MRTP, 1970, FERA, 1973, And Investments in public sector companies	U.S.A., Germany and U.K.	Manufacturing	Controlled Phase
1978-1990	Govt. of India, WTO and Local companies	Liberalization of imports and exports	U.S.A. and Germany	Manufacturing	Cautious Phase
1991-2000	IMF, World Bank, WTO and Local Business Houses.	Acceleration of liberalization and Globalization of FDI	Globalized	Manufacturing, Trade & Financial Service	Globalized Phase

FOREIGN INSTITUTIONAL INVESTMENT IN INDIA: AN OVERVIEW

India opened its stock markets to foreign investors in September 1992 and has, since 1993, received considerable amount of portfolio investment from foreigners in the form of Foreign Institutional Investor's (FII) investment in equities. This has become one of the main channels of international portfolio investment in India for foreigners. In order to trade in Indian equity markets, foreign corporations need to register with the SEBI as Foreign Institutional Investors (FII). SEBI's definition of FII's presently includes foreign pension funds, mutual funds, charitable/endowment/university funds etc. as well as asset management companies and other money managers operating on their behalf.

The trickle of FII flows to India that began in January 1993 and has gradually expanded to an average monthly inflow of close to Rs. 1900 crore during the first six months of 2001. By June 2001, over 500 FII's were registered with SEBI. The total amount of FII investment in India was accumulated to a formidable sum of over Rs. 50,000 Crores during that time. In December 2007 the number of registered FII's has gone up to 1200 and they have invested another 60,000 crore in last five years. In terms of market capitalization too, the share of FII's has steadily climbed to about 9% of the total market capitalization of BSE.

The sources of these FII flows are varied. The FII's registered with SEBI come from as many as 28 countries (including money management companies operating in India on behalf of foreign investors). US-based institutions accounted for slightly over 41%, those from the UK constitute about 20% with other Western European countries hosting another 17% of the FII's . It is, however, instructive to bear in mind. The closed-end country fund, "The India Fund" launched in June 1986 provided a channel for portfolio investment in India before the stock market liberalization in 1992. Global Depository Receipts, American Depository Receipts, Foreign Currency Convertible Bonds and Foreign Currency Bonds issued by Indian companies and traded in foreign exchanges provide other routes for portfolio investment in India by foreign investors.

INVESTMENT LIMITS FOR FII

An FII or a Sub-Account can hold upto 10% of paid up equity capital of any company. The total investments made by all the foreign corporates and foreign individuals shall not exceed 5% of total issued capital of that company within the aggregate limit for FII portfolio investments. The total investments by FII and Sub-Accounts in any Indian Company cannot exceed 24% of its total paid up capital.

However, in certain companies, which have passed a Special Resolution in this regard, the total FII investment can be made upto 49% of the paid up capital. This limit of 24%/ 49% is exclusively available for investments by FII only.

It may further be noted that this limit of 24% does not include investments made by FII outside the Portfolio investments route i.e., through the direct investment approval process. Investments made offshore through purchases of GDR, ADR and convertibles are also excluded.

IMPACT OF FDI ON COMMODITY MARKET

India is not China. Although owing to their mammoth population and the poverty in which they have been mired since long, the two countries are often talked in the same breath. However, the fact remains that India is not a patch on China, so long as broad economic parameters are considered or ground realities observed. The yellow country has made stellar progress on all the fronts, particularly in attracting the FDI, and has registered an unprecedented growth in exports, besides making phenomenal investments in infrastructure.

India has been trying to learn, but has a lot to pick up. Take for example the foreign direct investment. India attracted a mere 5.33 billion US dollars of FDI in 2004 compared to 4.26 billion US dollars in 2003. China, on the other hand, managed to attract the same amount every month totaling 60.63 billion US dollars in 2004. The same difference is reflected in two countries' bilateral trade. Last year India's exports to China grew by 28.3 per cent to 6.7 billion US dollars while the country's imports from China witnessed a hefty 58.7 per cent increase to touch 5.5 billion US dollars.

This doesn't mean India is not consuming more. No doubt Indian consumption of commodities is rising. More cars are being registered than ever before, more DVD players and Plasma tvs are percolating in. Besides, the country is importing record quantities of oil, and its import of edible oils, pulses, as well as a host of other agro commodities. Yet the fact remains that as of today, India's commodity consumption is far less than that of China.

However, India is not all that silent in commodity trading. The country already has three full fledged commodity exchanges, and there are more in the pipeline. Although these exchanges are barely three years old, their volumes have surged from Rs. 45 billion in FY 2002 to Rs. 21342.710 billion in FY 2006-an amazing growth by any yardstick. Of this, one exchange, Multi Commodity Exchange or MCX, has already notched up daily turnover in excess of 2.5 billion dollars. Of this the lion's share belonged to precious metals, with gold grabbing about 1.2 billion dollars and silver about 0.7 billion. The same exchange has already affected record deliveries of silver and it has very consistent turnover in gold futures contracts.

STEPS INITIATED TO INTEGRATE STOCK, COMMODITY MARKETS

Among the clutch of proposals to broaden and deepen the capital markets as well as to strengthen the regulatory regime enunciated by the Finance Minister in his budget, initiation of steps to integrate the commodities markets and the securities markets is by far the most important one.

In most of the developed economies, equity markets, forex markets, bond markets and commodity markets are integrated, and funds flow from one market to the other depending on the risk-reward profile.

There is also unification of the regulator in some countries. For instance, the UK has a "super regulator" overseeing all the markets; however, the US has separate regulators overseeing stock and commodity markets.

While the equity and forex markets in our country have matured over a period of time, commodity markets are at a nascent stage. Most of the restrictions on physical trade were removed only recently; and the adoption of futures trading as a price risk management tool is yet to take-off.

To be effective, any proposal for integration of securities and commodities markets must start from the top. There is need to shift policy making, administrative control of the commodities-futures market and its regulator from the Ministry of Consumer Affairs to the Ministry of Finance.

MoF is the administrative ministry for the equity market with Securities and Exchange Board of India (SEBI) as the regulator and the forex market with Reserve Bank of India (RBI) as the regulator.

The commodities market regulator— Forward Markets Commission (FMC) — should be brought under the MoF for an effective integration of policymaking.

Once policy making for the markets is under a single ministry, the next question would be the future of SEBI and FMC. Should they be merged into a single entity or should both be allowed to have their separate identity? There are risks in creating one super regulatory organisation given the extant nature of the markets, a perceived bias towards equity market and lack of expertise in regulating the commodity market. The future of small, regional, single-commodity exchanges have also to be kept in mind.

However, without reforming the markets and creating a strong regulator with appropriate powers and perceived authority to deal with exigent situations, it will be difficult for Indian bourses to attract large investment.

IMPACT OF FII ON CAPITAL MARKET

India has a long tradition of functioning capital markets. The Bombay stock exchange is over a hundred years old and the volume of activity has increased in the recent years. The process of reform of capital markets started in 1992 and aimed at removing direct government control and replacing it by a regulatory framework based on transparency and disclosure. The first step was taken in 1992 when SEBI was elevated to a full-fledged capital market regulator.

An important policy initiative in 1993 was the opening of capital markets for foreign institutional investors and allowing Indian companies to raise capital abroad. FII registrations in the country have gone up significantly over the years. The number of registered FIIs has gone up from 823 in December 2005 to 972 in October 2006. FII inflow to India grew manifold from US $0.18 million (net, monthly) in January 1993 to about US $400 million within a year's time and it also had made $10.7

billion worth of investment (Rs 47,181 crore) in calendar 2005. The FIIs have been rewarded well by attractive valuations and increasing returns. The depository and share dematerialization systems have been introduced to enhance the efficiency of the transaction cycle.

The SEBI FII Regulations and RBI policies are amended and modified from time to time in response to the gradual maturing of the Indian financial market and changes taking place in the global economic scenario. A number of significant reforms have been implemented in the spot equity and related exchange traded derivatives markets since the early 1990s. For instance, spot prices are mostly market-determined, trading volumes in the derivatives market exceed those in spot markets and market practices such as speed of settlement and dematerialization are close to international best practices.

The magnitudes of FDI [foreign direct investment] and FII flows are tending to be large and volatility has perhaps increased. The impact of such flows on the stock markets is discernible, but perhaps less evident at this juncture in corporate ownership and control. There is scope for enhancing the quality of flows through a review of policies relating to eligibility for registration as FIIs, and an assessment of the risks involved in flows through hedge funds, participatory notes, sub-accounts, etc. Strict adherence to the 'know your investor' principle, especially in regard to flows from tax havens, including beneficial ownership, would enhance quality.

IMPACT OF FDI ON INSURANCE SECTOR: A CLOSE LOOK

THE Finance Minister, while presenting the first Budget of the UPA government, has proposed to raise the FDI cap in three sectors. Elaborating upon the decision he said, "The NCMP declares that FDI will continue to be encouraged and actively sought, particularly in areas of infrastructure, high technology and exports. Three sectors of the economy fully meet this description. They are telecommunications, civil aviation and insurance." The specific proposal for the insurance sector is to raise the FDI cap from 26 to 49 per cent. There were many criticisms and also that this move is unjustifiable on several grounds.

PRIVATE PLAYERS, FOREIGN EQUITY & PROFITABILITY

The Union government opened up the insurance sector for private participation in 1999, also allowing the private companies to have foreign equity up to 26 per cent. Following the opening up of the insurance sector, 12 private sector companies have entered the life insurance business. Apart from the HDFC, which has foreign equity of 18.6 per cent, all the other private companies have foreign equity of 26 per cent. In general insurance 8 private companies have entered, 6 of which have foreign equity of 26 per cent. Among the private players in general insurance, Reliance and Cholamandalam do not have any foreign equity. The following table gives an aggregate picture of the current scenario of the insurance sector in India. (A full list of private companies in life and non-life insurance is given in the Appendix).

Table 2

Type of Business	*Nos of Public Sector Companies*	*Nos of Private Sector Companies*	*Total Companies*
Life Insurance	01	12	13
General Insurance	06	08	14
Re insurance	01	0	01
Total	08	20	28

Source: Reserve Bank of India, Handbook of Statistics

According to the Annual Report of the IRDA, 9 out of the 12 private companies in life insurance suffered losses in 2002-03. The aggregate loss of the private life insurers amounted to Rs. 386.33 crore in contrast to the Rs. 9620 crore surplus (after tax) earned by the LIC. In general insurance, 4 out of the 8 private insurers suffered losses in 2002-03, with the Reliance, a company with no foreign equity, emerging as the most profitable player. In fact the 6 private players with foreign equity made an aggregate loss of Rs. 294 lakhs. On the other hand the public sector insurers in general insurance made an after tax profits of Rs. 625.70 crore.

Not only are the public sector insurance companies more profitable than the private ones, the private insurer which is most profitable (Reliance) is one which has no foreign equity. If profitability is taken to be an important indicator of efficiency, it is clear that the case for further hike in the FDI cap in the insurance sector cannot be made on efficiency grounds.

QUESTIONABLE REPUTATION OF THE FOREIGN PARTNERS

The record of some of the foreign companies who have started operating in India is being questioned abroad. A recent article published in *The Economist* (May 4, 2004) on 'AIG's Accounting Lessons' (AIG is Tata's partner in India) came with the screaming headline which said it all: "The world's largest insurance company shows how to polish profits statement". The Prudential Financial Services (ICICI's partner in India) is facing an enquiry by the securities and insurance regulators in the US based upon allegations of having falsified documents and forged signatures and asking their clients to sign blank forms (*New York Times*, May 31, 2003 and *Wall Street Journal*, May 31, 2003). This follows a payment of 2.6 billion dollar made by Prudential to settle a class-action lawsuit attacking abusive life insurance sales practices in 1997 and a 65 million dollar fine from state insurance regulators in 1996. It is evident that the questionable activities of these insurance companies are not deterred by state imposed penalties and litigations.

The financial health of many of the foreign insurance companies operating in India is also a cause of serious concern. *The Economist* (April 1, 2004) reports the sorry plight of Standard Life of UK (HDFC's partner in India), which is unable to remain afloat without the possibility of raising money in debt or equity markets. AMP closed its life operations for new business in June 2003. Royal Sun Alliance also shut down their profitable businesses in 2002. A recent report by Mercer Oliver Wyman, a consultancy, found that European life insurance companies are short of capital by a whopping 60 billion euros. The reason for the short fall in capitalization, among other things, is due to European Unions' new regulation on solvency called 'Solvency 2' that will be enforced across Europe from 2005 through 2007. According to the Mercer Oliver Wyman Report the German, Swiss, French and British insurers suffer from severe capital inadequacy, which is a result of undertaking risky investments in equity and debt instruments in the past.

Several issues of *Sigma*, a reputed Swiss journal on insurance, have reported that the US and Europe based insurance companies are faced with gloomy growth prospects in the advanced country markets, with several companies experiencing negative growth in the recent past. Moreover, tighter capital adequacy norms and other regulations that are currently being imposed in the advanced countries are forcing these insurance companies to seek less regulated markets in developing countries to undertake their high-risk ventures. Raising the FDI cap in India at this juncture would expose our financial markets to the dubious and speculative activities of the foreign insurance companies at a time when the virtues of regulating such activities are being rediscovered in the advanced countries.

COMPETITION IN THE INSURANCE SECTOR

Even after the liberalisation of the insurance sector, the public sector insurance companies have continued to dominate the insurance market, enjoying over 90 per cent of the market share. In fact, the LIC, which is the only public sector life insurer, enjoys over 98 per cent of the market share in Life insurance.

Table 3
Market Share of Life and Non-Life Insurance Sectors
(As per cent of total premium underwritten by insurers)

Insurance Sector	*2001-02*	*2002-03*
Life Insurance, Private Sector	0.54	1.99
Life Insurance, Public sector	99.46	98.01
General Insurance, Private Sector	3.68	8.64
General Insurance, Public Sector	96.32	91.36

Source: *IRDA Annual Report, 2002-03.*

Given the huge market share enjoyed by the public sector companies, the argument, which is often made by advocates of greater liberalisation, that the entry of private players would bring down the cost of insurance due to enhanced competition, does not seem to be convincing. The price making capacity of the market leaders in the public sector is likely to remain intact for the time being. The foreign insurance companies do have the reputation of charging less premium compared to the risks involved and promising abnormally high returns, in order to grab greater market share. Such competition, however, although capable of bringing down the 'cost' of insurance for a while, has often led to gigantic frauds and bankruptcies.

Moreover, as is the case in other markets, the initial flurry of entries into the Indian insurance market would invariably be followed by a phase of mergers and acquisitions that would lead to cartelisation, precluding the possibility of competition driving down the costs in the medium run. In the long run, other forms of non-price competition like aggressive advertisement wars are likely to lead to increasing costs, eventually harming the interests of the consumers. These phenomena in the insurance market have been observed in several advanced countries. If the public sector companies start imitating the strategies of the foreign insurance companies in order to defend their market shares, it would be at the cost of undermining their important social objectives, which they have been fulfilling so impeccably till date.

IMPLICATIONS FOR RESOURCE MOBILISATION

A major role played by the insurance sector is to mobilise national savings and channelise them into investments in different sectors of the economy. However, no significant change seems to have occurred as far as mobilising savings by the insurance sector is concerned, following the liberalisation of the insurance sector in 1999. Data from the RBI show that the trend of the savings in life insurance by the households to GDP ratio, while showing a clear upward trend through the 1990s signifying increasing business for the insurance sector, does not show any structural break after 1999. It can be inferred therefore that the foreign capital which flowed in after the opening up of the insurance sector has not been accompanied by any technological innovation in the insurance business, which would have created greater dynamism in savings mobilisation.

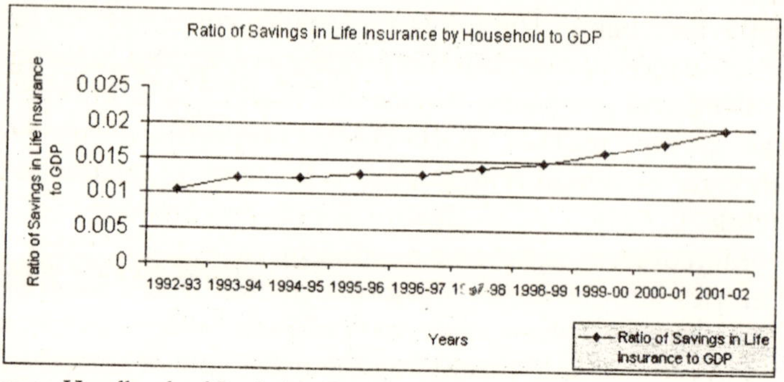

Source: Handbook of Statistics, Reserve Bank of India

Figure 1

Far from expanding the market for the insurance sector, the business activities of the private companies are limited in urban areas, where a fairly good market network of the public sector insurance companies already exists. The glaring evidence for this is the composition of agents operating in the insurance sector. According to the IRDA *Annual Report* the number of insurance agents in urban and rural India was in 100:76 ratio in the public sector companies, in 2001-02. For the private insurance companies this ratio was 100:1.4. Due to their urban-biased operational activity, the private insurance companies can neither increase the insurance base of the economy significantly, nor lead to substantial employment generation. Given this scenario, further increase in foreign participation is only going to lead to intensified competition for the urban insurance markets, rather than leading to a growth in overall savings.

While the proposals for hike in FDI were placed, the arguments advanced were that FDI will continue to be encouraged and actively sought, particularly in areas of infrastructure, high technology and exports.

ARE THESE ARGUMENTS TENABLE?

No new technology or product is brought into the country: The issue of foreign equity is often linked with induction of new technology and products. The private insurance companies have nothing to offer in this respect. In the insurance sector, there is no technology needed to be brought in from other countries, leave alone high technology. The mortality rates and other principles of insurance are based on the Indian conditions, because the policyholders are from this country. The products of LIC are being renamed by the private insurance companies and are sold as their own products. Hence, foreign expertise is also not involved in this sector.

So there is no justification even on this count. It was also argued that competition will expand market and the foreign insurers will bring better products. This has simply not happened. The size of the market has remained by and large the same and from this market the private companies are picking up the creamy sections in the metros seriously eroding the ability of public sector to cross subsidise its products in the rural areas.

Flow of funds for infrastructure is a myth. Life insurance is all about mobilising the savings for long term investment in social and infrastructure sectors. It was also argued that opening up of insurance market would enable huge flow of funds into infrastructure. The record of private companies on this is dismal. More than fifty per cent of the policies they sell are unit-linked insurance where the decision on investment of savings element in insurance is taken by the policyholders. In fact as per a press report, ninety five per cent of policies sold by Birla Sun Life and over 80 per cent of policies sold by ICICI Prudential were unit-linked policies during 2003-04. Under these schemes, nearly 50 per cent of the funds are invested in equities thus limiting the fund availability for infrastructural investments. As against this, the LIC has invested Rs 40, 000 crore as at 31.3.2003 in power generation, road transport, water supply, housing and other social sector activities.

The Law Commission of India released a consultation paper on June 16, 2003 on the revision of the Insurance Act,

1938. The consultation paper proposes a suitable amendment to Section of 27C of Insurance Act allowing insurers especially carrying on general insurance business to invest funds outside India. So, once the law is amended to allow insurers to invest funds abroad, the exports that these private companies would generate, would be the export of savings of the people.

Raising the FDI cap also does not seem justifiable as far as channelising savings into investments are concerned. The life insurance sector invested a total of Rs 31335.89 crore in the infrastructure sector in 2002-03. Out of this the contribution of the LIC was Rs. 30998.16 crore, which was 98.92 per cent of the total investment in infrastructure by the entire life insurance sector. The figures provided by the IRDA Reports further suggest that the share of the public sector life and non-life insurance companies in investment in infrastructure is greater than their market share. Despite the FDI cap being set at 26 per cent, the investment from the insurance sector to the infrastructure sector was predominantly from the public sector companies. Therefore, the argument that raising the FDI cap in the insurance sector would help in mobilising resources for infrastructure does not hold. On the other hand, greater foreign control is more likely to lead to a decline in the share of investment of the private insurance companies into the infrastructure sector, given the record of the foreign insurance companies in siphoning resources for speculative financial ventures.

It is also worth mentioning that the only insurance company involved in insuring Indian exports is the Export Credit Guarantee Corporation of India (ECGC), which provides insurance cover to export credit. The ECGC has been in existence since 1957. It is functioning under the United India Insurance Co. No private player with foreign partnership has ventured into this area. Moreover, the LIC and other public sector units are the only ones to undertake overseas operations, as reported by the Annual Reports of the IRDA. Foreign participation has also not helped in marketing Indian insurance products abroad.

So to be in brief Governments of the advanced countries like the US continue to apply pressure on developing countries to open up their insurance sectors. China, for instance was pressurised to open up its insurance sector, in return of its entry into the WTO. However, the existing regulations on foreign capital in the insurance sector in China has been a source of continuing debate in the US-China Economic and Security Review Commission, where the Chinese side has resisted attempts to force further deregulation.

The unilateral move to further liberalise the insurance sector in India is unjustifiable. Events over the decade of the 1990s have borne out the fact that financial liberalisation does not contribute positively to investment and economic growth. Countries which enthusiastically opened up their financial sectors in order to attract capital inflows often experienced enhanced volatility in their financial markets and speculative attacks on their currency. Further opening up of the insurance sector to foreign capital, which serves as a vital financial intermediary of the national economy, is therefore not warranted.

REASONS FOR PRESENT FII INFLOWS

There has been a tremendous focus on emerging markets in the last six months or so which may be due the following reasons:

- Cheap stocks in emerging markets including India. Indian stocks look comparatively cheaper with a price to earning multiple of 15.
- Average return in emerging markets is more attractive since in developed markets returns have almost saturated for the time being.
- Excess liquidity in developed markets which is giving a boost to emerging markets.
- Excess liquidity in developed economies is due to cheap money policy of most Central banks. This implies cutting interest rates in recent months to support growth and development in Europe and the USA, also Japan is pumping in money to drag it's economy out of recession.

- Low interest rates and expansion in money supply creates a liquidity in the system which is far in excess of the needs of the domestic stock markets and cannot be absorbed by them.
- Fund managers do not want to experience another Black Monday (in October'87) when stock markets in the USA crashed. So to hedge their risks adequately they allocate a portion of their funds in the emerging markets.
- All major economies are in a phase of increasing but still slow growth, so demand for money from the real sector is not very high, this money is available for inflows in financial assets.

We have seen some of the reasons why there is an increase in FII inflows but everybody knew that FII's are highly volatile than FDI and here are some of the reasons for such volatile flows:

Firstly, in as much as an increase in investment by FIIs triggers a sharp price increase, it would provide additional incentives for FII investment and in the *first* instance encourage further purchases, so that there is a tendency for any correction of price increases unwarranted by price earnings ratios to be delayed. And when the correction begins it would have to be led by an FII pull-out and can take the form of an extremely sharp decline in prices.

Secondly, as and when FII's are attracted to the market by expectations of a price increase that tend to be automatically realised, the inflow of foreign capital can result in an appreciation of the rupee vis-à-vis the dollar (say). This increases the return earned in foreign exchange, when rupee assets are sold and the revenue converted into dollars. As a result, the investments turn even more attractive triggering an investment spiral that would imply a sharper fall when any correction begins.

Thirdly, the growing realisation by the FII's of the power they wield in what are shallow markets, encourages speculative investment aimed at pushing the market up and choosing an appropriate moment to exit. This implicit manipulation of the market if resorted to often enough would obviously imply a substantial increase in volatility.

Finally, in volatile markets, domestic speculators too attempt to manipulate markets in periods of unusually high prices. Thus, most recently, the SEBI is supposed to have issued show cause notices to four as-yet-unnamed entities, relating to their activities on around Black Monday, May 17, 2004, when the Sensex recorded a steep decline to a low of 4505.

FACTS ABOUT FDI

Inflows of foreign direct investment (FDI) into India (equity capital components only) during the first four months of the current financial year 2006-07 (April-July), was US $ 2.9 billion compared to US$ 1.5 billion in the same period of 2005-06, showing a record increase of nearly 92%. FDI inflows (equity capital components only) during the month of July 2006 surged by a record 259%, having increased to US $ 1163 million from US $ 324 million in July 2005. This was indicated by Shri Kamal Nath, Union Minister of Commerce & Industry, at a news briefing here today.

What is significant is that FDI inflows into the manufacturing sector and sectors impacting the manufacturing sector continue to show a record growth. FDI equity inflows into manufacturing alone in April-July 2006-07 is estimated at US $ 668.41 million, Shri Kamal Nath said while pointing out that some of the services sector like design and engineering, air/sea transport, ports, construction activities etc. have a bearing on the growth of the manufacturing sector. The FDI policy rationalisation and liberalisation measures have resulted in the increased inflows into such sectors as well, he said.

According to the details available upto July 2006, the 10 sectors attracting highest FDI into India since 1991 are: electrical equipments (including computer software & electronics); services sector (financial & non-financial); telecommunications (radio paging, cellular mobile, basic telephone services); transportation industry; fuels (power + oil refinery); chemicals (other than fertilisers); food processing industries; drugs & pharmaceuticals; cement and gypsum products; and metallurgical industries.

The 10 top investing countries are: Mauritius, USA, Japan, Netherlands, UK, Germany, Singapore, France, South Korea and Switzerland. The single largest inflow received in the current financial year to the tune of US$ 380 million has been brought in by Barclays Bank PLC, Singapore in the financial service sector. This has been received in the month of July 2006. Other major investors include Global Communication Services Holdings, Mauritius in Aircel Ltd. (Telecom services); SIERO Investment Holding, Mauritius in Orange Realty P Ltd. (Real Estate); Flextronics (Computer Software); Aspen Pharmacare Holdings Ltd., South Africa (Drugs & Pharma).

According to the Reserve Bank of India (RBI)'s revised data as per international practices, (i.e., including equity plus reinvested earnings and other capital) cumulative total FDI inflows into India from August 1991 to June 2006 were US$ 50.1 billion.

ANALYSIS

A large number of observers in India, including the mass media, believe that FII flows "cause" Indian equity returns. Does really FII flows cause equity returns? This can be very much observed with the help of the following analysis. For the purpose of the analysis FII flows and Market Returns (BSE Sensex) will be compared from April 2005 to September 2006. The data is being collected from RBI bulletin and Prowess data base. The data is represented in the following table.

Table 4

Month	*Avg. FII Flows (Net) ($ Million)*	*Average Sensex Closing Values*	*Sensex Returns*
Mar-05		6679.18	
Apr-05	-350	6379.29	-0.0448992
May-05	-503	6482.66	0.016204
Jun-05	1288	6925.86	0.068367
Jul-05	1645	7336.7	0.05931971
Aug-05	1139	7726.03	0.05306609
Sep-05	1008	8272.32	0.07070772
Oct-05	-469	8220.45	-0.0062703
Nov-05	-17	8552.09	0.04034329

Contd...

Month	*Avg. FII Flows (Net) ($ Million)*	*Average Sensex Closing Values*	*Sensex Returns*
Dec-05	2122	9162.07	0.07132525
Jan-06	1386	9539.67	0.04121339
Feb-06	1692	10090.08	0.05769696
Mar-06	684	10857.03	0.0760103
Apr-06	3276	11741.74	0.08148729
May-06	-3906	11599.16	-0.012143
Jun-06	-1157	9934.75	-0.143494
Jul-06	-595	10557.15	0.06264878
Aug-06	1212	11305.04	0.07084204
Sep-06	1064	12035.69	0.06463047

Sensex Returns: To calculate Sensex returns, firstly the closing values of Sensex of each month is taken into consideration. Secondly average is taken for each month and thirdly return is calculated with the help of the formula:

Today's Value–Yesterday's Value

Yesterday's Value

Correlations

		Fill	*Sensex Returns*
FII	Pearson Correlation	1,000	.627**
	Sig. (2-tailed)		.005
	N	19	18
Sensex Returns	Pearson Correlation	.627**	1.000
	Sig. (2-tailed)		
	N	18	18

**.Correlation is significant at the 0.01 level (2-tailed).

If we look at the result it is very much evident that there is a correlation between the FII flows and Market Returns. There is a correlaton of .627 between the two variables which means that for every 1% change in the market returns there will be a .627% change in the fII flows. This is one of the reasons for a high degree of volatility of the FII flows. So, if India wants to attract the FII's it should give better returns compared to other markets.

CONCLUSION

On the whole this report is a detailed study about the FDI and FII and their impact on the Indian Financial Market. This report also deals why India is able to attract FDI's and FII's and also the factors that could effect the FDI flows. An analysis is also conducted to know whether there is a relation between the FII flows and the Market Returns and from the analysis it is evident that there is a relation between the two variables. The report also compares the driving forces for the FDI flows into the country from 1900 to 2000. Anybody going through this report could add to their knowledge about the FDI's and FII's. Last but not the least I believe that India would occupy the 1st position in attracting the foreign investments with its openness policies towards the foreign investments.

REFERENCES

Foreign Direct Investment in Developing Countries: What Economists (Don't) Know and What Policymakers Should (Not) Do! - Peter Nunnenkamp, Kiel Institute of World Economics, Germany.

People's Democracy(*Weekly Organ of the Communist Party of India (Marxist)*, Vol. XXVIII, No. 38, September 19, 2004.

The Economics of Foreign Direct Investment Incentives, Magnus Blomström & Ari Kokko, Working Paper 168, January 2003.

FII Flows to India: Nature and Causes-Rajesh Chakrabarti, Georgia Institute of Technology, USA.

Financial Liberalization in India: An Assessment of its Nature and Outcomes-C.P. Chandrasekhar and Parthapratim Pal.

Government of India, Ministry of Commerce & Industry, Department of Industrial Policy & Promotion, (FC Section), PRESS NOTE NO. 4 (2006 Series),

Are Indian Capital Markets (Debt + Equity) on the Threshold of Explosive Growth?(2005) - Apurv Parashar, IIM Bangalore.

A Gap Analysis of FIIs Investments–An Estimation of FIIs Investments Avenues in Indian Equity Market- Prof. Lakshmi Sharma, Assistant Professor, T A Pai Management Institute, Manipal, Karnataka.

Can India work? – India's economic reforms' *Economist*, 10 June 2004 (Delhi)

Website

www.rbi.gov.in

http://www.philipsandco.com/indianlaw.html

www.indiamart.com

www.epw.org.in

www.indobase.com

http://www.financialsense.com/fsu/editorials/kakani/2006/0509.htm

www.pd.cpim.org

http://www.thehindubusinessline.com/cgi-bin/bl.pl?subclass=310

http://dipp.nic.in

http://siadipp.nic.in/publicat/most_frq.htm

http://dipp.nic.in/manual/manual_0403.pdf

http://www.ccindia.com/faq_show.asp?cat name=India%20 Entry % 20Strategy & catid=CCI_C01 & contentid=67

http://www.kesardass.org/doing_b1.html

http://www.munothfinancial.com/fii_intro.html

www.india_resource.tripod.com/fdi.html

Appendix
Trends in FII Investment

Period	*Gross Purchases (Rs. Mn.)*	*Gross Sales (Rs. Mn.)*	*Net Investment (Rs. Mn.)*	*Net Investment* (US $ mn.)*	*Cumulative Net Invetment* (US $ mn.)*
1993-94	55,925	4,663	51,262	1,634	1,638
1994-95	76,310	28,348	47,963	1,528	3,167
1995-96	96,935	27,517	69,420	2,036	5,202
1996-97	155,539	69,794	85,745	2,432	7,634
1997-98	186,947	127,372	59,575	1,649	9,284
1998-99	161,150	176,994	-15,844	-386	8,898

Contd.

Period	*Gross Purchases (Rs. Mn.)*	*Gross Sales (Rs. Mn.)*	*Net Investment (Rs. Mn.)*	*Net Investment* (US $ mn.)*	*Cumulative Net Invetment* (US $ mn.)*
1999-2000	568,555	467,335	101,219	2,339	11,237
2000-01	740,506	641,164	99,340	2,160	13,396
2001-02	499,200	411,650	87,552	1,846	15,242
2002-03	470,601	443,710	26,889	562	15,804
2003-04	1,448,575	990,940	457,645	9,949	25,754

* Net investment at US $ mn. at monthly exchange rate
Source: SEBI Bulletin, October 2004.

FII and MF Activity and Sensex Response

Period	*FII Activity (US $ M)*	*MF Activity (US $ M)*	*Total (US $ M)*	*Change in Sensex*
CY 2003	6940	93	7033	+86.3%
CY 2004	8958	-261	8697	+23.1%
CY 2005	10896	3089	13985	+42.2%
CY 2006	7994	3442	11435	+53.3%
CY 2007	17235	3121	20357	+68.5%
Cum till CY 2007	52023	9484	61,507	742.1%

CY = Calendar year.

11

"ANALYZING THE IMPACT OF MACROECONOMIC VARIABLES ON EQUITY INVESTORS"

Sumeet Gupta & Amiya K. Mohapatra

India is a growing economy. It grows by leaps and bounds day by day. Emergence of liberalization, privatization and globalization has brought forth the need to have analysis of Macro Economic Variables. India is flourishing with the improved economic conditions and increasing foreign direct investment. Indian capital market is also bouncing at high arena. Traditionally, India has been a country of conservative, risk averse investors lived in era of Safe and Secured investments like post office schemes like *NSC's, PPF and KVP* etc. The rates on the interest bearing investment like fixed deposit and RBI Bonds were also very attractive. The traditional investment plans worked wonderfully for investors till the time the government had a stiff control on business and borrowing/lending rates. When India made the migration to a market driven economy and floating exchange rate in the 1990's, it marked the beginning of the end for the era of high guaranteed returns on traditional plan and ushered in the more dynamic 'market linked era'.

Equity investing is an interesting and challenging area. By buying even a single share, you are buying a percentage of the ownership of the company or business and therefore the fundamental approach is to be geared towards valuing the company. There are various variables which affect the equity market like budget, Inflation, Exchange Rate Movement etc. Indian equity market will be counted in most emerging market. Indian economy is growing at 9% approx with this equity market also shows growth. Macroeconomic variables have different effect on the equity market. There is a quotation "every action has reaction". In the same manner if there is any action in the variable it will directly or indirectly affect the equity market.

STATEMENT OF THE PROBLEM

Equity market is very much volatile market which is used for hedging as well as speculation. There are number of macroeconomic variable affecting the equity market. It becomes essential to throw some light upon the macro economic variables affecting the Equity market. This paper is a brief study for the relationship between macroeconomic variable and equity investors. It is essential to obtain quantitative estimates of the links between macroeconomic variable changes and stock prices. The paper starts with the depth study of these macroeconomic factors which influence the equity investor decision. The objective of in depth study was to mainly understand about these macroeconomic variables and analysis of these variables

OBJECTIVES OF THE STUDY

- To analyze the impact and incidence of Macro Economic Variables on Equity Investors.
- To analyze the relationship between Macro Economic Variables and Equity Investors using Test of Independence and Factor Analysis.
- To suggest measure for equity investor based on the finding of the study.

Methodology

The preset study is an empirical study basically based on the Primary data but secondary data have also been collected from various published and unpublished sources as per the requirements of the study.

Sampling Technique: Random Sampling has been applied to collect the data from the Equity Investors.

Sample Size: The survey was conducted on *150 Equity Investors* belonging to Jaipur City of Rajasthan.

Area Coverage: Jaipur City, Rajasthan.

FINDINGS AND RESULTS OF THE STUDY

Findings of the study have been given with the help of following graphs:

Tax Slab

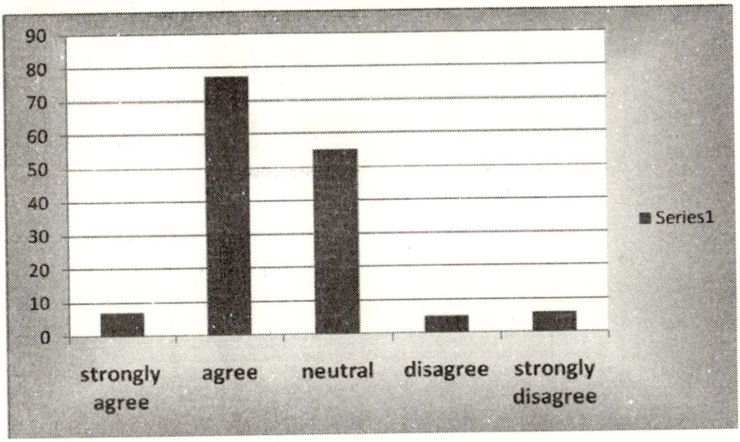

Chart 1

Table 1

strongly agree	7
agree	77
neutral	55
disagree	5
strongly disagree	6

This chart shows that more than half of the investors from the sample taken believe that increase in tax slab will affect the investment in equity market trade in derivatives with an objective of getting liquidity. Though 15% of the investors give weightage to earning potential of the derivatives before trading yet most of them feel they can trade more with less amounts in the derivatives as compared to the cash market. Hence they go for liquidity as their first priority to enter into derivatives market.

Restrictions on P Note Imposed by SEBI

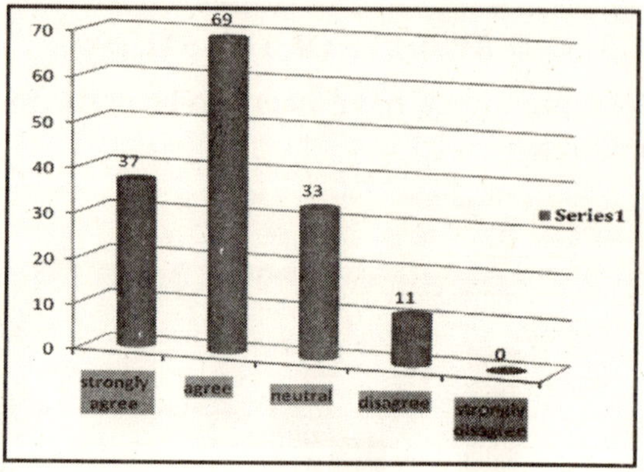

Chart 2

Table 2

strongly agree	37
agree	69
neutral	33
disagree	11
strongly disagree	0
	150

It can be seen from the above chart that most of the people feels that restriction on p- note imposed by the SEBI during November will affect the investment in equity market. 51% investor says that restriction on p-note will affect the equity market as people from other country invest in the Indian equity market if they get some problem while investing ,so they prefer to invest in other country.

Effect of Fluctuations in Exchange Rate

This chart shows that near to half of the investors from the sample taken believe that fluctuation in exchange rate will affect the investment in equity market .This is because that many company listed in the stock exchange deals in the foreign country so as the exchange rate change it also affect the earning of the earning and if the value of rupee increases then FII's will have to invest more money in the equity.

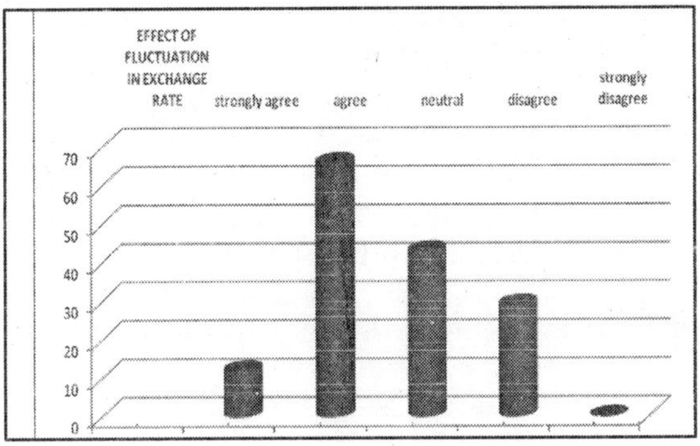

Chart 3

Table 3

strongly agree	12
agree	66
neutral	43
disagree	29
strongly disagree	0
	150

Effect of Recession on Economy

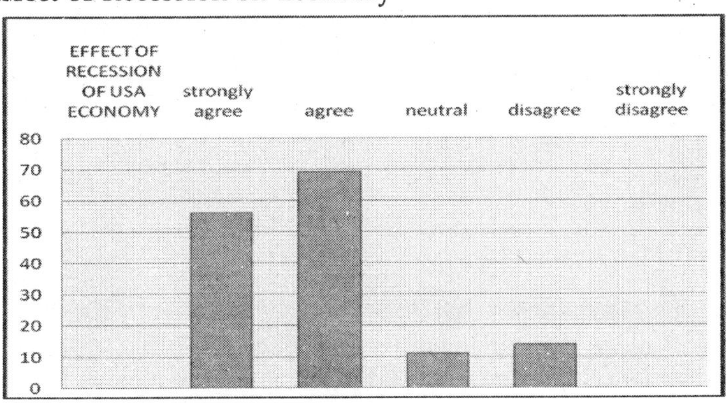

Chart 4

Table 4

strongly agree	56
agree	69
neutral	11
disagree	14
strongly disagree	0
	150

It can be seen from the above chart that most of the people feels that recession in the US economy will affect the equity investor. 8 % respondent strongly agrees that it will and 44% agree that it will affect the Indian equity market.

FII's Investment

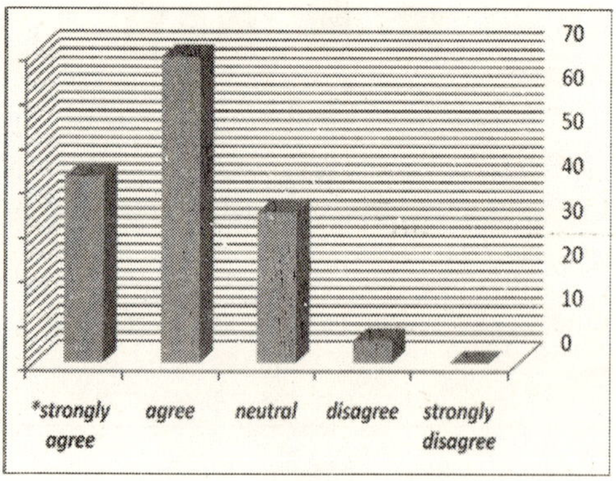

Chart 5

Table 5

*strongly agree	42
Agree	69
neutral	34
disagree	5
strongly disagree	0
	150

As this chart shows that 38% strongly feels that FII's play a major role in the Indian equity market and 46% feels that FII's investment will bring the volatility in the share market. As the FII's invest in the market suddenly the market start went up, and if they sell the market will come into green.

Change in Interest Rate

It can be seen that 46 % investor from the sample taken feels that change in interest rate will affect the equity market. And 28% investor believes that change in interest rate will not affect the equity investment decision.

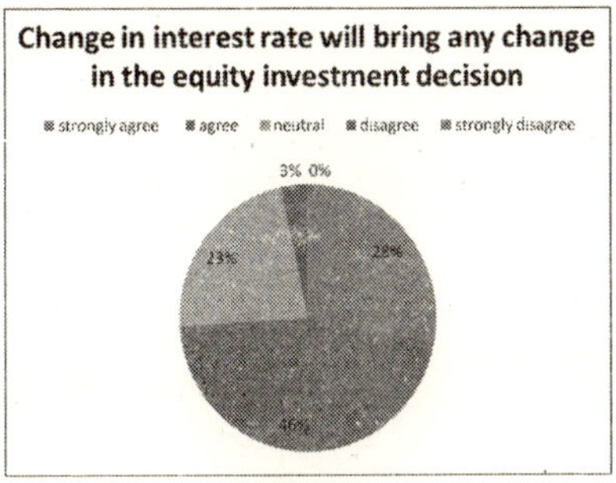

Chart 6

Economic Growth

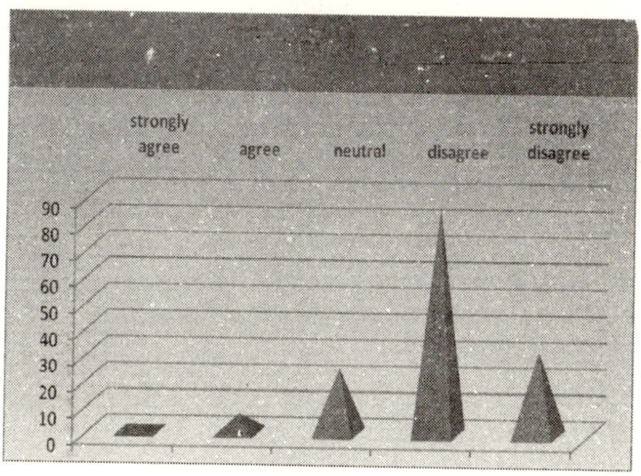

Chart 7

Table 6

strongly agree	0
agree	7
neutral	25
disagree	86
strongly disagree	32
	150

This chart shows that more than half of the investors from the sample taken believe that when the economy growing at approx 8% will definitely lead the stock market to grow. around 64% respondent feel that as Indian economy grows the share market will also grow.

Increase in CRR Rate

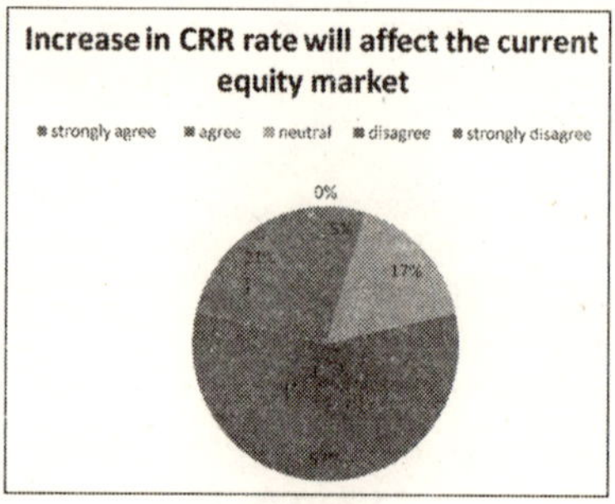

Chart 8

Table 7

strongly agree	55
agree	82
neutral	12
disagree	1
strongly disagree	0
	150

As the chart shows that increase in CRR rate will not affect the current equity market situation. 57% respondent disagrees that CRR will affect the equity market and 24% strongly disagree this statement. Only 5% respondent feel that increase of CRR to 8 basis point will affect the current market.

Impact of Budget

Table 8

strongly agree	0
agree	25
neutral	27
disagree	72
strongly disagree	26
	150

The above table is for the analysis of how many investors feels that Budget will affect the equity investment. 55% respondent agrees that budget will affect the equity investment and 36% respondent strongly agree that announcement made during the budget hour will affect the equity investment. But 1% disagree this statement

Impact of Global Cues

Table 9

strongly agree	41
agree	61
neutral	36
disagree	12
strongly disagree	0
	150

This shows that 48% respondent believes that Global cues will not affect the equity investment. 17% respondent strongly disagrees that global market will not influence the Indian equity market. 17% respondent feels that global market influence the equity investment in India.

Increase in Short Term Capital Gain Tax

These can be infer from the chart that increase in short term capital gain tax rate from 10 to 15% will affect investment in equity as 41 % respondent agree that it will affect. 27% respondent disagrees that increase in tax rate will affect the equity market.

Table 10

strongly agree	27
Agree	72
Neutral	33
disagree	18
strongly disagree	0
	150

Decrease in the Index of Industrial Production

As this chart shows that 18% respondents are strongly and 48 % are agreed that Decrease in the index of industrial production rate will influence the equity investment. If the production rate of the industry decrease it will affect the equity market negatively.12%respondent disagree that IIP does not influence the market.

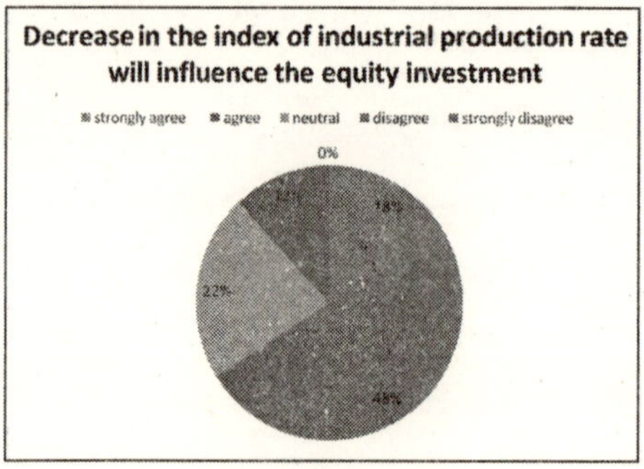

Chart 9

US Fed Rate Cut

13% respondents are strongly agreed that cutting the Fed rate by US will influence the Indian equity market. 40% respondents believe that it will influence the market. 13% respondent feels that reducing the Fed rate by US will not bring any stability in the Indian equity market.

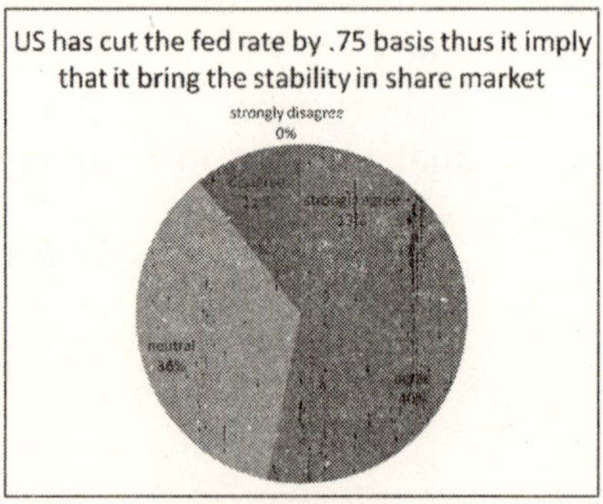

Chart 10

Bill Passed by Central Govt.

This chart shows that 25% respondent believe that if the government passed any bill about a particular sector will influence the price of share from the particular sector. 48%

respondent agrees that it will affect the market while only 4% respondent disagrees that it will not affect the equity prices of particular sector.

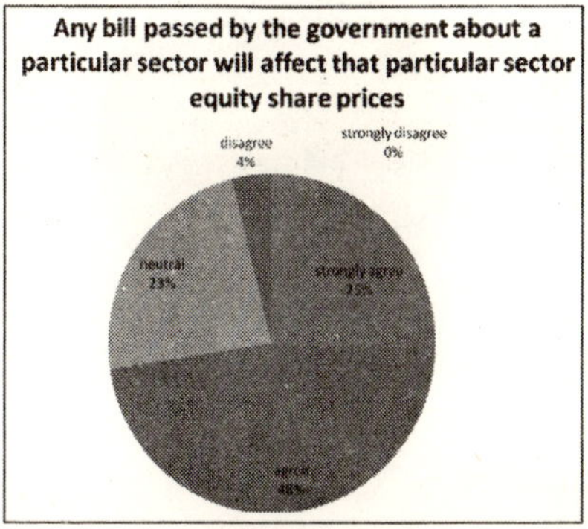

Chart 11

Inflation Rate

19 % respondent strongly agrees that increase in the inflation rate will distress the equity market. 63% respondents agree that high inflation has negative effect on the equity market.

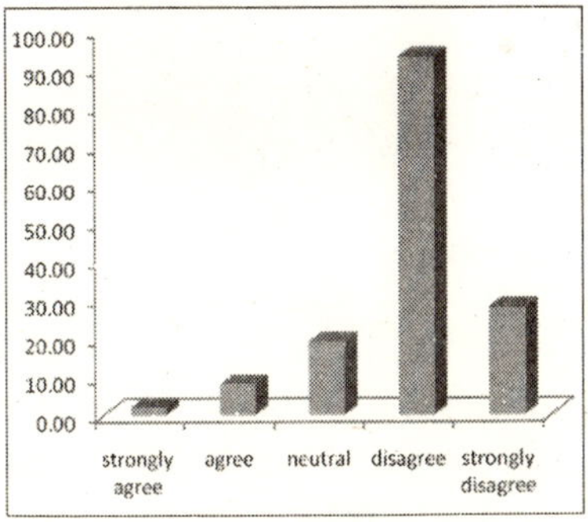

Chart 12

Economic Policy

Every country has their own economic policy which influences whole economy. 62% respondent disagrees that economic policy will influence the share market. 16 % respondent believes that economic policy will not influence the Indian equity market.

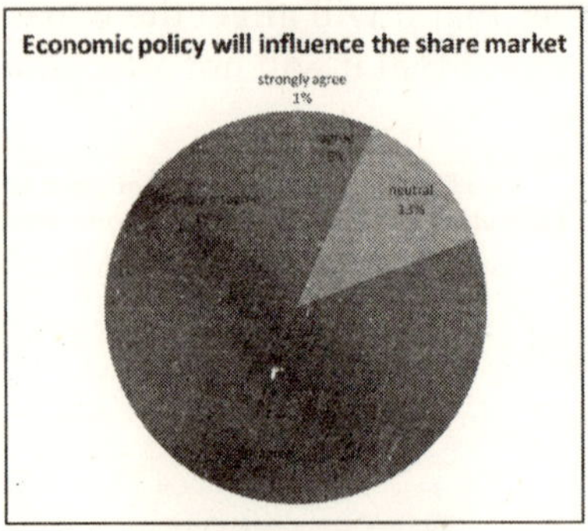

Chart 13

Paucity of Liquidity

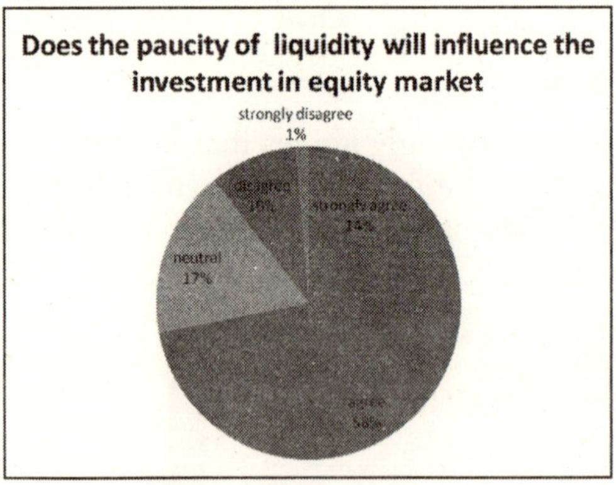

Chart 14

The above chart shows the analysis of how many investor feels that lack of liquidity will affect the investment in equity market.14% respondent strongly agree that paucity of liquidity influence the investment in the equity market.58% respondent agree that it influence the investment decision while only 10% respondent believes that it won't influence their decision.

Instability in Foreign Country

If there is instability in the foreign country it will disturb the Indian equity market. 9% respondent strongly favors this argument. And 55% respondent favors this statement.

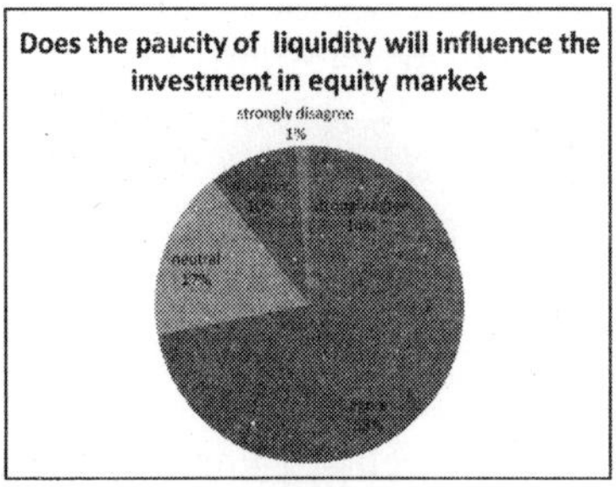

Chart 15

Market Volatility

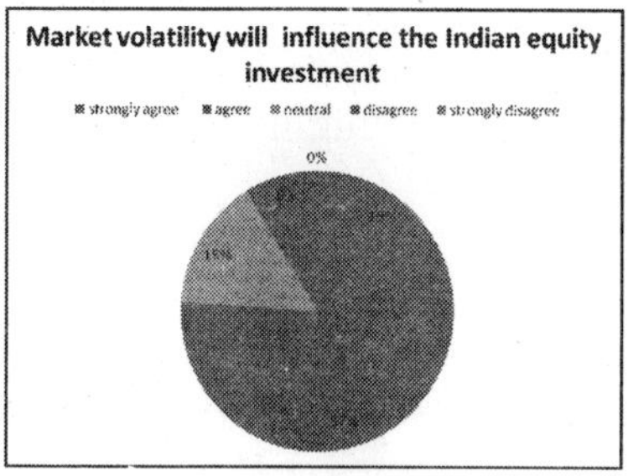

Chart 16

The above chart shows that 57% respondent believes that market volatility will influence the Indian equity market.19% strongly believes that market volatility will influence this investment in equity decision.

Security Transaction Tax

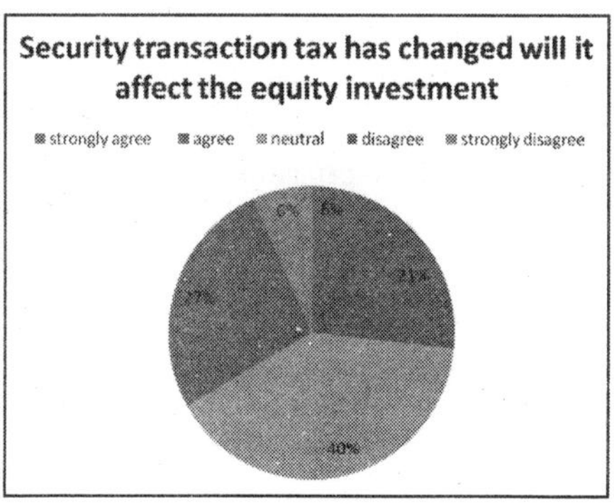

Chart 17

The above graph shows that as the norms of STT have changed it will affect the equity investment. Respondent has mixed reply about this norm. 27 % respondent believes that it does not affect the equity investment.

FACTOR ANALYSIS

Factor analysis is a class of procedures primarily used for data reduction and summarization. In factor analysis relationships among sets of many interrelated variables are examined and represented in terms of a few underlying factors. Using the data from a large scale factor analysis applies an advanced form of correlation analysis to the responses to a no of statements. The purpose of this analysis is to determine if the responses to several of the statement are highly correlated.

Correlation matrix

Exhibit 1.1 shows a portion of the correlation matrix. These data represent correlation matrix among the 20 variable. As from the above table it shows variable are not very much correlated .In this matrix there is a triangular correlation among each other variable which is one (1).Apart from these variable there is a less correlation among the other variable which is visible through exhibit 1.1. variable less than 4 shows that variable are less correlated. That means these variable only supports each other variable. The influence of one variable on other is very little. Negative variable sign shows that variables do not affect other variable. From Table 11 it can be seen that ,which variable is most correlated to whom.

Variable (1) increase in tax slab is correlated with v8 (increase in CRR rate), v9 (budget) and v12 (decrease in IIP) this mean these variable are correlated and influence each other while v2 (curbs on p-note), v19 (market volatility), increase in inflation rate are negatively correlated which mean that these variable do not influence each other .

Variable 2 curbs on promissory note is more correlated with variable v4 (recession in US economy), v5 (FII's investment), which value is 0.377, 0.160 respectively, that means these variable are correlated and influence each other

Table 11
Correlation Matrix

	Increase in Tax Slab	*Curbs _on _Promis-sionary _ote*	*Fluctuation _in_ Exchange _Rate*	*Recession _in_ US_ Economy*	*FII_ Invest-ment*	*Change _in_ Interest_ Rate*	*GDP_ Approx_ 8*	*Increase_ in_CRR _Rate*	*Budget*
increase in tax slab	1	-0.192	0.078	-0.085	-0.172	-0.02	0.17	0.322	0.304
curbs_on_promissionary_note	-0.192	1	-0.119	0.377	0.16	0.053	-0.192	-0.173	-0.142
fluctuation_in_exchange_rate	0.078	-0.119	1	0.198	0.051	0.167	0.239	0.08	-0.069
recession_in_US_economy	-0.085	0.377	0.198	1	-0.181	0.136	-0.071	-0.053	-0.071
FII_investment	-0.172	0.16	0.051	-0.181	1	-0.019	-0.085	-0.12	-0.087
change_in_interest_rate	-0.02	0.053	0.167	0.136	-0.019	1	-0.103	0.023	0.494
GDP_approx_8	0.17	-0.192	0.239	-0.071	-0.085	-0.103	1	-0.046	0.184
increase_in_CRR_rate	0.322	-0.173	0.08	-0.053	-0.12	0.023	-0.046	1	-0.028
Budget	0.304	-0.142	-0.069	-0.071	-0.087	0.494	0.184	-0.028	1
Global_cues	0.098	-0.12	0.137	-0.006	-0.072	0.281	0.073	-0.022	0.331
increase_in_short_term_tax	0.013	-0.188	0.405	-0.274	0.063	0.058	0.499	-0.233	0.141
decrease_in_index_of_ industrial_production	0.368	-0.202	0.032	-0.155	-0.186	0.087	0.259	-0.04	0.396
Cut_in_FED_rate	-0.131	-0.358	0.292	-0.038	-0.068	0.142	0.518	-0.087	0.184
Bill_passed_by_the_Government	0.027	-0.038	0.325	0.181	-0.132	0.293	0.21	-0.107	0.446
Increase_in_inflation_rate	-0.066	0.048	0.109	0.247	0.109	0.084	-0.003	-0.161	0.101
Economic_policy	-0.072	-0.429	0.062	0.037	-0.129	0.164	0.159	0.096	0.117
Pacucity_in_liquidity	-0.029	-0.393	-0.052	-0.319	-0.055	0.119	0.317	-0.071	0.088
Instability_in_Foreign_market	0.122	-0.018	0.071	0.133	-0.05	0.331	0.099	0.264	0.384
Market_volatility	0.169	-0.39	0.415	0.058	-0.163	-0.031	0.065	0.186	0.003
Change_in_security_transacton_ tax_norm	-0.047	-0.027	-0.046	-0.179	0.027	0.116	0.335	-0.142	0.103

to affect the equity market. It has a single value with same variable which is one and negative correlated with v1 (increase in tax slab), v3 (fluctuation in exchange rate), v7(GDP), v8 (increase in CRR rate), v9(budget), v10 (global cues), v11 (increase in STCG), v12 (decrease in IIP), v13 (cut in Fed rate), v16 (economic policy), v17 (paucity in liquidity), v19 (market volatility). That means these variables do not influence variable.

V3 (Fluctuation in exchange rate) is more correlated with v1 (increase in tax slab), v4(recession in US economy), v5 (FII's investment), v6 (change in interest rate), v7(GDP), v8 (increase in CRR rate), global cues), v11 (increase in STCG), v12 (decrease in IIP), v13 (cut in Fed rate), v16 (economic policy), v19 (market volatility), , v18 (instability in foreign country), v15 (increase in inflation). These above mention variable are correlated and influence each other. It has a single value with same variable which is one and negative correlated with v2 (curbs on p- note), v10 (budget). It shows that these variables are not correlated.

V4 (recession in US economy) is more correlated to v2 (curbs on p-note) and v15 (increase in inflation) which value is 0.377, 0.247respectively, that mean these variable are associated with these variable and influence each other with the equity market. It has a single value with same variable which is one and negative correlated with v11 (increase in STCG), v17 (paucity in liquidity). The analysis shows that these variables do not influence each other.

V5 (FII's investment) is more correlated to v2 (curbs on p-note) and v15 (increase in inflation) which value is 0.160, 0.109 respectively, that mean these variable are associated with these variable and influence each other with the equity market. It has a single value with same variable which is one and negative correlated with v1 (increase in tax slab), v12 (decrease in IIP). The analysis shows that these variables do not influence each other.

V6 (change in interest rate), is more correlated to, v10 (budget), v18 (instability in foreign country) and v14 (bill passed by the government) that mean these variable are associated with these variable and influence each other with the equity market. It has a single value with same variable which is one and it is negative correlated with few variables.

V7 (GDP) is more correlated to, v11 (increase in STCG), v13 (cut in Fed rate), and v17 (paucity in liquidity) that mean these variable are associated with these variable and influence each other with the equity market. It has a single value with same variable which is one and it is negatively correlated with few variables.

V8 (Increase in CRR rate) is more correlated with increase in tax slab. And negatively correlated with, v11 (increase in STCG).

V9 (budget) is more correlated with v6 (change in interest rate), v1 (increase in tax slab), v12 (decrease in IIP) and v14 (bill passed by the government) this mean that these factor are associated with this variable and influence the equity market. It has a single value with same variable which is one and it is negative correlated with few variables.

V10 (Global cues) is more correlated with v12 (decrease in IIP) and v14 (bill passed by the government). It has a single value with same variable which is one and it is negative correlated with few variables.

V11 (increase in STCG) is more correlated with , v3 (fluctuation in exchange rate), v7(GDP), v13 (cut in Fed rate), and v17 (paucity in liquidity) that mean these variable are associated with these variable and influence each other with the equity market. It has a single value with same variable which is one and negative correlated with V4 (recession in US economy). That means these variable are less correlated

V12 (Decrease in index of industry production) is more correlated V10 (Global cues), v14 (bill passed by the government). It has a single value with same variable which is one and it is negative correlated with few variables.

V13 (Cut in Fed rate) is more correlated with v7(GDP), (increase in STCG), and v14 (bill passed by the government) this mean that these factor are associated with this variable and influence the equity market. It has a single value with same variable which is one and it is negatively correlated with v2 (curbs on p-note).

V14 (Bill passed by the government) is correlated with v10 (budget), V10 (Global cues), V12 (Decrease in index of industry production) and V13 (Cut in Fed rate). And it is negatively correlated with v20 (change in STT norm).

V15 (Increase in Inflation rate) is correlated with v4 (recession in US economy) with the value of 0.247 and these variable is negative correlated with economic policy.

V16 (Economic policy) is correlated with v19 (market volatility). It has a single value with same variable which is one and it is negatively correlated with v2 (curbs on p-note imposed by SEBI).

V17 (paucity of liquidity) is correlated with (increase in STCG) and v14(cut in Fed rate) that means these variable are associated with each other. It has a single value with same variable which is one and it is negatively correlated with v2 (curbs on p-note imposed by SEBI).

V18 (Instability in foreign market) is correlated with v9 (budget), v14 (any bill passed by government). It is negative correlated with many variable but the values are less than 0

V19 (market volatility) is correlated with v3 (fluctuation in exchange rate) and v15 (change in Economic policy) and negative correlated with v2 (curbs on p-note).

V20 (change in the norms of security transaction tax) is correlated with v7 (GDP), only and less correlated with other variable.

Table 12

KMO and Bartlett's Test

Kaiser-Meyer-Olkin Measure of Sampling Adequacy.		.512
Bartlett's Test of Sphericity	Approx. Chi-Square	1.208E3
	df	190
	Sig.	.000

This table shows two tests that indicate the suitability of your data for structure detection.

The *Kaiser-Meyer-Olkin* Measure of Sampling Adequacy is a statistic that indicates the proportion of variance in the variables that might be caused by underlying factors. High values (close to 1.0) generally indicate that a factor analysis may be useful with your data. The value of KMO test is .512 which shows it is suitable for the factor analysis.

Bartlett's test of sphericity tests the hypothesis that the correlation matrix is an identity matrix, which would indicate that the variables are unrelated and therefore unsuitable for structure detection. Small values (less than 0.05) of the significance level indicate that a factor analysis may be useful with your data. As the value of significance level is .000 which shows that is useful for factor analysis.

Table 13
Communalities

	Initial	*Extraction*
increase in tax slab	1.000	.797
curbs_on_promissionary_note	1.000	.709
fluctuation_in_exchange_rate	1.000	.836
recession_in_US_economy	1.000	.767
FII_investment	1.000	.770
change_in_interest_rate	1.000	.648
GDP_approx_8	1.000	.781
increase_in_CRR_rate	1.000	.652
Budget	1.000	.728
Global_cues	1.000	.739
increase_in_short_term_tax	1.000	.770
decrease_in_index_of_industrial_production	1.000	.838
Cut_in_FED_rate	1.000	.694
Bill_passed_by_the_Government	1.000	.831
Increase_in_inflation_rate	1.000	.826
Economic_policy	1.000	.819
Pacucity_in_liquidity	1.000	.716
Instability_in_Foreign_market	1.000	.730
Market_volatility	1.000	.774

Communalities indicate the amount of variance in given explained by the all factor variable that is accounted for. Initial communalities are estimates of the variance in each variable accounted for by all components or factors. For principal components extraction, this is always equal to 1.0 for correlation analyses. Extraction communalities are estimates of the variance in each variable accounted for by the components the table shows the communalities among 20 variables. It is extracted from value 1. If a variable has value

Table 14
Total Variance Explained

	Initial Eigenvalues			*Extraction Sums of Squared Loadings*			*Rotation Sums of Squared Loadings*		
Component	*Total*	*% of Variance*	*Cumulative %*	*Total*	*% of Variance*	*Cumulative %*	*Total*	*% of Variance*	*Cumulative %*
1	3.929	19.644	19.644	3.929	19.644	19.644	2.667	13.334	13.334
2	2.419	12.097	31.741	2.419	12.097	31.741	2.243	11.216	24.550
3	2.073	10.367	42.108	2.073	10.367	42.108	2.015	10.074	34.624
4	1.749	8.746	50.855	1.749	8.746	50.855	2.006	10.028	44.652
5	1.448	7.238	58.093	1.448	7.238	58.093	1.837	9.186	53.838
6	1.224	6.121	64.214	1.224	6.121	64.214	1.584	7.921	61.758
7	1.182	5.912	70.126	1.182	5.912	70.126	1.482	7.409	69.168
8	1.102	5.509	75.635	1.102	5.509	75.635	1.293	6.467	75.635
9	.882	4.412	80.047						
10	.715	3.577	83.624						
11	.658	3.292	86.916						
12	.526	2.629	89.545						
13	.508	2.538	92.083						
14	.404	2.019	94.102						
15	.289	1.446	95.548						
16	.252	1.260	96.808						
17	.232	1.161	97.970						
18	.157	.785	98.755						
19	.145	.724	99.478						
20	.104	.522	100.000						

Extraction Method: Principal Component Analysis.

more than 8 it means that among 1 that value is extracted which influence the equity.

TOTAL VARIANCE

The variance explained by the initial solution, extracted components, and rotated components. This first section of the table shows the Initial Eigen values (the Eigenvalues represent the total variance explained by each factor). A factor's Eigenvalues may be computed as the sum of its squared factor loadings for all the variable The Total column gives the Eigen values or amount of variance in the original variables accounted for each component. The % of Variance column gives the ratio, expressed as a percentage, of the variance accounted by each component to the total variance in all of the variables. The Cumulative % column gives the percentage of variance accounted for the first components. For the initial solution, there are as many components as variables, and in a correlations analysis, the sum of the Eigenvalues equals the number of components.

The initial Eigen values" and "Extraction Sums of Squared Loadings" columns are the same, except the latter only lists factors which have actually been extracted in the solution. The second section of the table shows the extracted components. The "rotation Sums of Squared Loadings" gives the Eigen value after rotation improves the interpretability of the factor. The total % of Variance explains the same but rotation changes the eigen value for each of the extracted factor.

Scree Plot

A scree plot is a plot of the eigen value against the no of factors in order of extraction. The shape of a plot is used to determine the number of factor. Typically, the plot has a distinct break between the steep slope of factor, with large eigen value and gradual trailing off associated with rest of the factors. The scree plot is used to determine the optimal number of components. The eigen value of each component in the initial solution is plotted. The components on the shallow slope contribute little to the solution. Through this plot it can be interpreted that 8 factor are extracted.

Table 15

GDP_approx_8	.576	-.307			-.136	.368	.311	-.308
increase_in_CRR_rate		.344	-.520	-.136	.121	.430		.204
Budget	.537	.316	.242	-.483	.214			
Global_cues	.592	.253	.167	-.139	-.189	-.347	-.280	.205
increase_in_short_term_tax	.648	-.500	.141	.133	-.128		.136	.145
decrease_in_index_of_industrial_production	.645		.104	-.420	-.420	-.103	-.217	
Cut_in_FED_rate	.696	-.191		.314			.111	-.222
Bill_passed_by_the_Government	.568	.507	.274		-.206	-.253	.212	-.136
Increase_in_inflation_rate	.164		.547	.227		.345	-.523	.227
Economic_policy	.418		-.277	.374	.518		-.394	
Pacucity_in_liquidity	.502	-.455	-.239	-.116	.303	-.228	.138	-.152
Instability_in_Foreign_market	.257	.526		-.116	.461	.194	.345	
Market_volatility	.344	.335	-.534	.396	-.193	-.165	-.123	.146
Change_in_security_transaction_tax_norm	.256	-.596	.300	-.156	.104	.364	-.152	

Extraction Method: Principal Component Analysis.
a. 8 components extracted.

Table 16
The Component Matrix

Cut_in_FED_rate	.652	.164	.166	.283	.222	-.260		-.131
Bill_passed_by_the_Government	.128	.539	.435	-.106	.477	-.167	-.137	-.221
Increase_in_inflation_rate		.115					.892	
Economic_policy			.202	.823			.246	-.130
Pacucity_in_liquidity	.547	.103		.420	-.292	-.158	-.317	.110
Instability_in_Foreign_market		-.111	.803		.116	.185	-.107	-.110
Market_volatility	-.107	.209	-.119	.556	.575	.144	-.183	-.103
Change_in_security_transacton_tax_norm	.559				-.390		.454	.160
Extraction Method: Principal Component Analysis.								
Rotation Method: Varimax with Kaiser Normalization.								
a. Rotation converged in 10 iterations.								
recession_in_US_economy	-.216	-.159	.162	-.222	.392	-.172	.367	-.549
FII_investment		-.135		-.169	.117	-.142		.823
change_in_interest_rate		.172	.749			-.111	.160	.122
GDP_approx_8	.841				.138	.141		-.179
increase_in_CRR_rate	-.161	-.221	.170	.235	.108	.687		
Budget	.138	.469	.651		-.173	.178		
Global_cues		.796	.177	.193	.142		.106	
increase_in_short_term_tax	.751	.254		.123	.120		.147	.283
decrease_in_index_of_industrial_production	.296	.836				.189		

The "Component Matrix" above, gives the factor loadings. This is the central output for factor analysis. The factor loadings, also called component loadings, are the correlation coefficients

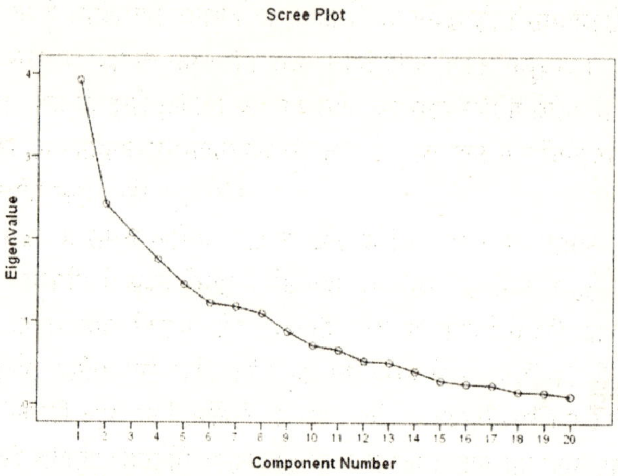

between the variables (rows) and factors (columns). Factor loadings, are the basis for computing a label to the different factors. Loadings above .6 are usually considered "high" and those below 4 are "low".

Interpretation

The Table 16 gives the rotated solution. Normally the rotated solution will be significantly easier to interpret.

Variable 1(increase in tax slab) is strongly associated with factor 6 and moderate associated with factor 2.

Variable 2 (curbs on P- note) is less associated with factor 7 and negative influenced with factor 1,2,4.6. That means this variable do not influence the equity market.

Variable 3 (fluctuation in exchange rate) is strongly associated with factor 5 and moderately associated with factor 1, 7 and 8.

Variable 4 (Recession in the US Economy) is less associated with factor 7, 3, 5 and negative associated with factor 1,2,4.6,8. That means this variable do not influence the equity market.

Variable 5 (FII's Investment) is strongly associated with factor 8 and negative associated with factor 2, 4, 6.

Variable 6 (change in Interest rate) is strongly associated with factor 3 and moderately associated with factor 2, 7, 8.

Variable 7 (India GDP is growing at 8 approx) is strongly associated with factor 1, and negative associated 8.

Variable 8 (Increase in CRR rate) is strongly associated with 6, and negative associated with factor 1, 2.

Variable 9 (Announcement in the Budget) is associated with factor 3 and moderately associated with factor 1, 2, 6.

Variable 10 (Global Cues) is strongly associated with factor 2 and moderately associated with 3, 4, 5, 7.

Variable 11 (Increase in short term capital gain tax) is strongly associated with factor 1 and moderately associated with 2, 4, 5, 7, 8.

Variable 12 (Decrease in Index of Industrial production) is strongly associated with factor 1 and moderately associated with factor 2, 3, 4, 5.

Variable 13(Cut in Fed rate) is strongly associated with factor 1 and negative associated with factor 6, and 8.

Variable 14 (Any Bill passed by the Government) is associated with factor 2, 3, 5 and negative associated with 4, 6, 7, 8.

Variable 15 (Increase in Inflation Rate) is strongly associated with factor 7.

Variable 16 (Economic policy) is strongly associated with factor 4 and negative associated with factor 8.

Variable 17 (paucity of liquidity) is strongly associated with factor 1, 4 and negative associated with factor 5, 6, 7.

Variable 18 (Instability in Foreign Market) is strongly associated with factor 3 and moderately associated with 5, 6.

Variable 19 (market volatility) is strongly associated with 4, 5 and negative associated with factor 1, 3, 7, 8.

Variable 20 (Change in security transaction tax rate) is associated with factor 1, 7, and 8.

Component Score Coefficient Matrix

For each case and each component, the component score is computed by multiplying the cases standardized variable values component's score coefficients. The resulting 8 component score variables are representative of, and can be used in place of, the twenty original variables with only a 15% loss of information. Use of 8 variables in place of twenty variables is enough. As these 8 variables are representative of all twenty original variables. Although the linear correlation between the components is guaranteed to be 0.

Interpretation

The graph shows that 62%brokers believe that the future of commodity market is at very good level. Only few percentage i.e.4% brokers found the future of commodity market to be at average level. So it can be concluded that the commodity market is growing up in all aspects.

The main findings of the study can be summarized in the following points:

(1) Due to the current market conditions (Sensex movement) many brokers are trying to explore new avenues in commodities market.

(2) Majority of the population in the survey was falling in the bracket of 1-5 yrs time frame in all the three markets be it Futures and options ,Cash , Commodities market .Brokers who were new to the system were the ones who choose commodity markets as their first trade area which shows a positive trend for the commodities market.

(3) It is found that the trading volume is not very high in commodity market because of lack of awareness of this market.

(4) Level of awareness of the brokers about Commodity market is increasing day by day.

(5) It is being found that the most important factor effecting the trading in commodity market is government policies because 48 brokers rated this parameter very highly between 9-10 point. It is the grey area in the development of the Commodity Market.

Table 17
Component Score Coefficient Matrix

	Component							
	1	*2*	*3*	*4*	*5*	*6*	*7*	*8*
increase in tax slab	.033	.098	-.049	-.102	.001	.547	.068	-.018
curbs_on_promissionary_note	.007	-.031	.068	-.369	.051	-.088	.037	-.036
fluctuation_in_exchange_rate	.126	-.083	-.029	-.067	.506	.109	.063	.202
Recession_in_US_economy	-.021	-.105	.041	-.096	.171	-.087	.222	-.408
FII_investment	-.055	-.034	.091	-.060	.166	-.022	.028	.686
Change_in_interest_rate	-.069	.004	.396	.046	-.049	-.074	.071	.157
GDP_approx_8	.421	-.158	.006	-.152	.077	.117	-.069	-.192
increase_in_CRR_rate	-.034	-.171	.107	.104	.056	.442	.035	.058
Budget	.001	.145	.304	-.045	-.159	.091	.011	.014
Global_cues.	-.172	.418	-.027	.094	.024	-.086	.066	.095
increase_in_short_term_tax	.261	.036	-.060	-.024	.091	-.009	.062	.191
Decrease_in_index_of_industrial_production	.018	.412	-.128	-.075	-.083	.092	.023	-.066
Cut_in_FED_rate	.243	-.045	.050	.062	.086	-.177	-.041	-.128
Bill_passed_by_the_Government	.018	.204	.139	-.143	.217	-.159	-.173	-.104
Increase_in_inflation_rate	-.052	.043	-.033	.080	-.005	.040	.627	.008
Economic_policy	-.068	-.111	.081	.478	-.045	-.075	.223	-.082
Pacucity_in_liquidity	.180	-.024	.072	.165	-.184	-.150	-.241	.027
Instability_in_Foreign_market	.053	-.199	.455	-.029	.019	.101	-.095	-.018
Market_volatility	-.130	.101	-.143	.267	.290	.031	-.070	.005
Change_in_security_transacton_tax_norm	.222	-.059	-.022	-.030	-.207	.105	.308	.043

Extraction Method: Principal Component Analysis.

(6) It is being found that most widely used function for the commodity market is arbitraging which is the signal of the development of the commodity market.

(7) It is being observed that because the margin has the negative effect on the development of the Commodity market and the trading is reduced on the same grounds.

(8) It appears that the commodity market is on the path of progress and crossing the targets of trading by leaps and bounds.

SUGGESTIONS AND RECOMMENDATIONS

(1) The awareness of the brokers regarding the trading in the commodity market has to be increased for the development of the commodity market.

(2) The margin is the major impediment in the development of the market. So it is required to squeeze this margin so that commodity market can be developed to a greater extent.

(3) Government. has to frame the policies in such a way that proper growth and all round dimension can be given to this market.

(4) Though Commodity Market is an effective tool but many of the brokers are not using it due to non awareness of the same. Now the responsibility lies with exchanges to make them aware about Commodity trading through publicity, Advertisement and sometimes with personal contacts.

(5) It has been observed even the brokers and traders who know about Commodity Trading are not using this facility due to misconception and lack of trust in the system. These brokers must be convinced to use the same.

(6) Being the agriculture country, trading in grain market is very low in India though it has the great potential. This area has to be taken up for discussion so that commodity market can grow to a greater extent.

CONCLUSION

Over the years commodities markets have been experiencing tremendous progress, which has become the boon for the global economy today. The gifted nature of these markets has made them an attractive investment avenue for investors. Commodity market is the stepping stone for the growing economy like India. Indian markets have recently thrown open a new avenue for retail investors and traders to participate in commodity derivatives. The current market situation is very critical if we analyse in reference with the Sensex and nifty. More and more investors are turning their pathways towards the commodity markets which they are exploring in the today's very volatile market situations. The only left grey area which is to be addressed is the Margin System, Awareness for trading and framing of Govt. Policies is such a way that this market would grow and make Indian Economy strong enough to face challenges confronting it in the dynamic arena.

REFERENCES

www.fmc.gov.in

www.derivativesindia.com

www.cbot.com

Sharan, Vyuptakesh, "International Financial Management", Prentice Hall of India, pp. 28-57.

Cox, J.C. and M. Rubenstein (1985), *Options Markets,* Englewood Chiffs, N.J: Prentice Hall.

Hancock, G.D. (1991), "Futures Options Expirations and Volatility in the Stock Index Future Market", *Journal of Futures Market,* June.

Macketh, J. and L.J. Merville, (1980), "Tests of the Black Scholes and Cox call option Valuation Models", *Journal of Finance,* May.

Avadhani, V.A. (1991), *"Investment & Securities Markets in India"* Himalya Publishing House, New Delhi, Sep.

Sengupta, N. K. (1999), *"Govt. & Business"*, Kanishka Publishers.

Donald, E; Fisher & Ronald, J. Jordan (1999), *"Security Analysis & Portfolio Management"*. Prentice Hall of India.

Balkishan & S.S.Narta *"Securities Markets in India"*, Kanishka Publishers & Distributors.

Rodanto Riccardo *"Volatility ND correlation: In the Pricing of Equity, FX and Interest-Rate Options"*, Wiley Series in Financial Engineering.

Shri Mohammad Tahir, Executive Director, Reserve Bank of India, at the Fourth Annual Conference on (2003), *"Bonds & Derivatives -The Road Ahead" Organized Jointly by FIMMDA and PDAI at Goa on February 1.*

DR. Ayub Mehar (2007), "Stock Market Consequences of Macro Economic Fundamentals", MPRA, Pakistan, November.

http://mpra.ub.uni-muenchen.de/442/

Keki M. Mistry, "The Mortgage-Backed Securities Market in India".

"How will the US Sub-prime Mortgage Crisis Effect the Indian Stock Markets", *The Indian Times,* August 13, 2007.

The Big Stories for Global Equity Market in Next Ten Year.

www.watsonwyatt.com.

"Measures For Improving Common Investor Confidence in Indian Primary Market: A Survey" Final Proposal.

12

INVESTMENT PERFORMANCE OF COMMON STOCKS AND P/B RATIO

Shradhanjali Panda & Munmun Mohanty

INTRODUCTION

These are the days that value and dividend, investors long for .With growing awareness in capital market, investors are trying for various parameters for accessing the performance of stocks in the stock market .Among all the valuation tools P/E Ratio is probably the most widely used one .The P/E Ratio has long been recognized as one of the useful financial indicators for valuing both individual stocks and stock- markets. However as with individual stock, it can be misleading if not also taking into account the growth prospects for a particular economy.

After the publication of the article "The Cross-Section of Expected Stock Returns" by Fama and French, it set off a wide range of academic analysis. According to them "beta" of risk of a port folio did not explain returns as financial theory would dictate. In this paper we have tried to test this hypothesis. Some recent studies have find limitations in P/E Ratio and according to many finance experts P/B Ratio appears to be superior to P/E Ratio. In this study we have examined the validity of this ratio. The research problem for this paper is trying to find out whether the low P/B Ratio stocks generate higher returns than the high P /B ones.

LITERATURE SURVEY

To the several tools for putting a value on a stock, P/B Ratio is considered to be a recent addition. A P/B Ratio represents the market value for every rupee of tangible assets. When a company is established, its value equals the investment made by the owners. A market value of the company's share begins to take shape when its operations show promise of long term returns, such market value being the present value of future dividends under the generally accepted accounting principles (GAAP) based on historical costs. However, the book value remains relatively unchanged at the amount of the original investment plus the reinvestment of undistributed profits. Thus, the change in the value of a company may be considered as a change in the ratio between the market price of its shares and their book value. At unity, the price-to-book-value ratio indicates that the market value and book value are identical. A ratio of greater than one would mean that the company has added value and vice versa for a smaller than one ratio.

According to Keith Anderson and Chris Brooks (March 2005), the price–earning's effect has been a challenge to the idea of efficient markets for many years. The P/E used has always been the ratio of the current price to the previous year's earnings. However, the P/E is partly determined by outside influences, such as the year in which it was measured, the size of the company and the sector in which the company operates.

In 1984 J. W. Wilcox stated in his writing that though P/E Ratio is a great way to evaluate yet the P/B-ROE valuation model seems to be a better model. In 1995, Fama and French showed that a firm's current P/B Ratio is related to its future operating performance. They linked P/B Ratio and earnings of a firm by showing in their figure that the ratio of earnings to book equity (ROE) decreases over a five year period (after measuring the P/B Ratio) for firms with high P/B Ratios and increases over a five year period for firms with low P/B Ratio.

Fairfield (1994) states where the P/E Ratio is a function of expected changes in future profitability at the same time P/B Ratio is a function of expected levels of future profitability.

Fama and French (1991) demonstrate that the ratio of book value to market value explains the differences in returns better than "beta" does and think that book-to-market ratios are proxies for other fundamentals.

For the first time S.Agrawal, Reza Monem and Mohd. Ariff (1996) carried out the cross-sectional and longitudinal analysis for their in Asian market i.e. in Singapore. They examined the theoretical validity of the P/B Ratio as a valuation model and find that the identified fundamental variables which are supposed to determine the value of a firm also explain a significant portion of the variability in its P/B Ratio and therefore the P/B Ratio may be considered to be a valid valuation model.

R. Vaidyanathan (October 2000) attempted in his study to examine whether the P/B Ratio is a good criteria on which investment decisions should be based. He revealed that the annual returns of portfolios formed on the basis of P/B Ratio are not significantly different from each other.

Many critics say that P/E Ratio does not tell you anything about how the market values the stock. For this reason many use P/E Ratio to figure out how much the market is willing to pay for a company's earnings. The most important thing here is last year's P/E would be actual, while current year and forward year P/E would be estimates, but in each case, the "P" in the equation is the current price. So, companies that are not currently profitable (that is, those ones which have negative earnings) don't have a P/E Ratio.

On the other hand, the net worth of a company i.e. its total assets minus total liabilities which is popularly known as the book value of a company shows how much the company would have left over in assets if it went out of business immediately. Since companies are usually expected to grow and generate more profits in the future, most companies end up being worth for more in the marketable place than their book value would suggest. For this reason, book value is of more interest to investors.

RESEARCH METHODOLOGY

Initially the sample is selected from 'A' category shares of National Stock Exchange. As 'A' category shares are actively traded which means they trade on every business day in a year. The meaning of trade is either buying or selling of scrip on a particular day. This active trading accounts for a continuous time series of data where there is no clustering data and there are no unexplained phenomena due to non-trading.

We have considered the time period from 1st March, 2001 to 31st March 2007 i.e. duration of 7 years financial data for this study. Only those shares are which have been traded throughout the period of 2001 to 2007, have been considered. So, out of 200 companies we filtered out 56 companies, basing on this criterion. Thus our dataset restricted to 56 companies

Sources of Data

Share prices used here are taken from nseindia website where all the share price histories are easily available and for the corresponding P/E and P/B Ratios we have taken the help of CMI database.

Methods Used

At first the share price history is taken. After filtering 56 companies we created seven portfolios each consisting eight (8) companies. All the portfolios are equally weighted ones . Average return of each portfolio is also taken into account.

Hypothesis

Our aim here is to test the statement that investment in lower P/B Ratio stocks will give higher return than investment in higher P/B Ratio stocks.

The null hypothesis can be stated here in the form of

$Ho : \mu i = \mu j$ for each pair of portfolios i and j at the 95% confidence level.

Portfolio Construction

For portfolio construction, first we calculated the Price to Book Value ratio of each share at the end of March of each year. After collecting the P/B Ratio of all the shares for seven years we arranged the shares in ascending order according to their P/B Ratio. So We got the series starting from lowest P/B Ratio to ending in highest P/B Ratio. Then out of 56 companies we formed 7 portfolios, each consisting of 8 companies. That means the first portfolio consists of the first 8 shares of lowest P/B Ratio and the last portfolio consists of the highest P/B Ratio. So each year we got 7 portfolios (ranging from low P/B to high P/B) , that is the portfolios are reshuffled or reformed each year in March based on the prevailing P/B Ratio.

Testing for Significance

The annual return for each of these seven portfolios is computed using the seven returns for the entire period (1st March 2001 to 31st March 2007) and then we conducted a t-test to find out the annual return of the portfolios. The t-test was for each pair of portfolios i.e. (1 , 2) , (1 , 3) , ...(1 , 7) , (2 , 1) , (2 , 3)..........(6 , 7).

ANALYSIS OF RESULTS

The results of the paired sample t-test are depicted in table 1 to table 6 for all the different pairs of portfolio combinations. They are as follows:

Table 1
Results of Paired Sample T-test for Portfolio 1

	Portfolio	*Mean*	*S.D*	*Std. Error*	*T*	*2tail Sign*
		Differences		*Mean*		
Pair 1	P1—P2	16.5557	5.5657	2.1036	7.87	0
pair 2	P1—P3	-5.75	8.7977	3.3252	-1.729	0.135
pair 3	P1—P4	11.29	6.1472	2.3234	4.859	0.003
pair 4	P1—P5	-0.15	5.4353	2.0543	-0.073	0.944*
pair 5	P1—P6	6.05	3.703	1.3996	4.323	0.005
pair 6	P1—P7	14.37	5.7501	2.1733	6.612	0.001

* Significant at 5 % level

From the table it is clear that except one value that is for the pair P1-P5, the t-value (.944) is not statistically significant. All the remaining values are significant at 5% level which means the null hypothesis of equality of means between the average return of P1 and all other remaining portfolios except portfolio 5 is summarily rejected.

Table 2
Results of Paired Sample T-test for Portfolio 2

	Portfolio	*Mean*	*S.D*	*Std. Error.*	*T*	*2tail Sign*
	Differences			*Mean*		
Pair 1	P2—P3	-22.3057	12.797	4.8368	-4.612	0.004
Pair 2	P2—P4	-5.2657	5.6855	2.1489	-2.45	0.05
Pair 3	P2—P5	-16.7057	5.35	2.0221	-8.262	0
Pair 4	P2—P6	-10.5057	6.1377	2.3198	-4.529	0.004
Pair 5	P2—P7	-2.1857	4.9854	1.8843	-1.16	0.29

This table shows that all the values are statistically significant at 5% level. This means the null hypothesis is rejected here. So we can say that portfolio 2 with all other portfolios provides values which are significant at 5% level.

Table 3
Results of Paired Sample T-test for Portfolio 3

	Portfolio	*Mean*	*S.D*	*Std. Error*	*T*	*2tail Sign*
	Differences			*Mean*		
Pair 1	P3—P4	17.0400	9.5671	3.616	4.712	0.003
Pair 2	P3—P5	5.6	9.229	3.4882	1.605	0.16*
Pair 3	P3—P6	11.8	8.2097	3.103	3.803	0.009
Pair 4	P3—P7	20.12	10.8078	4.085	4.925	0.003

*significant at 5% level

In this table we can observe that the pair P3—P5 does not prove that the t-value (.16) is statistically significant. Except this pair remaining pairs prove the values are significant at 5% level. So P3 with the combination of all portfolios except P5 rejects the null hypothesis here.

Among the three pairs the pair P4-P7 shows the t-value (0.072) is not statistically significant and rest two pairs reject the null hypothesis as their values are significant at 5% level.

Table 4
Results of Paired Sample T-test for Portfolio 4

	Portfolio	*Mean*	*S.D*	*Std. Error*	*T*	*2tail Sign*
	Differences			*Mean*		
Pair 1	P4—P5	-11.44	1.5976	0.6038	-18.946	0
Pair 2	P4—P6	-5.24	5.2065	1.9679	-2.663	0.037
Pair 3	P4—P7	3.08	3.7287	1.4093	2.185	0.072*

*Significant at 5% level

Table 5
Results of Paired Sample T-test for Portfolio 5

	Portfolio	*Mean*	*S.D*	*Mean*	*T*	*2tail Sign*
	Differences					
Pair 1	P5—P6	6.2	4.5081	1.7039	3.639	0.011
Pair 2	P5—P7	14.52	2.9258	1.1058	13.13	0

This table clearly rejects the null hypothesis of equality of means between the average returns of the pairs as the pairs are statistically significant at 5% level.

Table 6
Results of Paired Sample T-test for Portfolio 6

	Portfolio	*Mean*	*S.D*	*Mean*	*T*	*2tail Sign*
	Differences					
Pair 1	P6—P7	8.32	4.6615	1.7919	4.722	0.003

This last table also rejects the null hypothesis by its value.

CONCLUSION

Out of 21 paired sample t-test, only 3 t – values are found to be insignificant where as the remaining 18 values are statistically significant. In other words 85.2 % of values reject the null hypothesis of equally means, which is a high percentage. This definitely encourages us to consider the P/B Ratio as one of the measure stock picking factors.

The rational behind such an argument may be that the company having low P/B Ratio is undervalued by the market. Hence giving rise to a low MPS (Market Per Share).However before blindly investing in low P/B stocks many other factors like the economic scenario in general , the entry barriers in the industry , the nature of competition , the permanence of the industries along with the company's future growth and profit potential must be studied very thoroughly. As a last word we would like to put emphasis that more thorough and in-depth research is needed in this area before our results can be generalized.

REFERENCES

Agrawal , Surendra P. , Monem , Reza M and Ariff, Mohamed (1996), "Price to Book Value as a Valuation Model: An Empirical Investigation", *Finance India,* Vol. X No 2 , June

Cole , Kevin; Helwege, Jean; Laster David (1996), "Stock Market Valuation Indicators: Is this Time Different ? ", *Financial Analyst Journal* , May.

Fama , Eugene and French K. (1992), "The Cross –Section of Expected Stock Returns", *Journal of Finance,* June.

Fairfield , Patricia M. (1994), "P/E, P/B and the Present Value of Future Dividends", *Financial Analysts Journal,* July.

Vaidyanathan R. , Chava S. (2000), "Stock Returns and Price to Book Value Ratio", Applied Finance, October.

www.investopedia.com

www.wikipedia.org

13

CORPORATE GOVERNANCE AND CAPITAL MARKETS: (A STUDY BASED ON INVESTORS' PERSPECTIVE)

Sai Baba M. D., Sushil Kumar & Abhishek Tiwari

INTRODUCTION

The stakeholders mainly the shareholders of the firm are always concerned about the performance of the firm. Infact to know about how actually a firm is doing they need some supportive evidence. This evidence comes in the form of financial reports, annual reports, corporate governance report, auditors and directors' report, future plans of the firm, and over all the sustainability of the company. The investors judge the performance of the firm on the basis of these reports and statements. As the investors want that their money must be in the safe hands, they are very selective about where and what amount to invest. Thus when it comes to understand the options available for investment they naturally try to acquire the best possible source of information. This service, according to SEBI clause 49 directions, is expected to be provided by the firm itself, to the investors and hence the investors look towards this service to analyze the profitability of their investments. This has been the practice since the very beginning of the business and the practice of selling the rights or shares to the investors. According to SEBI clause 49 of listing agreement and amendments declared on dated 26th August 2003, *"all companies which were required to comply with the requirement of the erstwhile clause 49 i.e. all listed entities having a paid up share capital of Rs 3 Crores and above or net worth of Rs 25 crores or more at any time in the history of the entity, would be required to comply with the requirement of this clause on or before March 31, 2004. The non-mandatory requirement given in Annexure – 1C shall be implemented as per the discretion of the company. However, the disclosures of the adoption/non-adoption of the non-mandatory requirements shall be made in the section on corporate governance of the Annual Report."* But still it is found that even after having such stringent rules being in force there are huge lists of corporate who do not find it necessary to comply with the guidelines.

Corporations are republics. The ultimate authority rests with the voters (Shareholders). These voters elect representatives (directors) who delegate most decisions to bureaucrats (managers). As in any republic, the actual power-sharing relationship depends upon the specific rules of governance. One extreme, which tilts toward a democracy, reserves little power for management and allows shareholders to quickly and easily replace directors. The other extreme, which tilts toward a dictatorship, reserves extensive power for management and places strong restrictions on shareholders' ability to replace directors. Presumably, shareholders accept restrictions of their rights in hopes of maximizing their wealth, but little is known about the ideal balance of power. From a theoretical perspective, there is no obvious answer.

In this work it has been tried to analyze this relationship of the investor and corporate, which has a large effect on the performance of capital market as a whole. Since the investors invest through the route of capital markets only, like NSE, BSE, BGSE etc. there are many options available with the investors to collect the information about the performance of the firms, like SEBI, EDIFAR, corporate sites, other services like money control.com, annual reports service etc. this work focuses to find the answer of following questions:

(1) What is the effect on corporate performance of not the reports to the investors?
(2) What is the relationship between corporate governance and investors perceptions?

In this work the authors have considered the amalgamation of both old and new forms of management. Where cement industry being one of the oldest industries in India enjoys the amalgamation of both old and new forms of management. In the recent past, cement industry has experienced recessions, which badly hit the Indian cement industry. This was the time when the US financial market suffered due to Enron scandal following which Sarbanes and Oxley act was passed which is considered to be most sweeping corporate governance rules passed in past 70 years. In India, SEBI, reflects the contents of the SOX Act and the other country regulations under clause 49 of the listing agreements. On the other hand there are Pharmacy and IT/ITES firms, which are newer comparatively and have a history of nearly 10 years.

Corporate Governance

There is no universal definition of corporate governance, however a study of various definitions listed below indicate the changing nature of the definitions in the contexts in which the businesses operate. We have picked up those which reflect the conceptual changes happening over a period. One can see the transition from shareholder centric to stakeholder centric. Nobel laureate Milton Friedman defined Corporate Governance as the conduct of business in accordance with the shareholders business, which generally is to make as much money as possible, while confirming to the basic rules of the society embodied in law and local customes.

According to James De.Wolfensohn, President of World Bank, "Corporate Governance is about promoting corporate fairness, transparency and accountability".

Cadbury Committee, U.K. has defined Corporate Governance as follows: "it is the system by which the companies are directed and controlled".

It may also be defined as a system of structuring, operating and controlling a company with the following specific aims:

(1) Fulfilling long-term strategic goals of owners.
(2) taking care of the interest of the employees.
(3) A consideration for the environment and local community.
(4) Maintaining excellent relations with customers and suppliers.
(5) Proper compliance with all the applicable legal and regulatory requirements.

Regulations

SEBI and SOX-Era of managing multiple complex regulations

Sarbanes Oxley Act

The Sarbanes-Oxley Act of 2002 (SOX), introduced in the United States of America in the aftermath of Enron, has fundamental governance implications for listed American companies, their foreign subsidiaries and foreign companies that have US listings. It applies to all Securities and Exchange Commission (SEC) registered organizations, irrespective of where their trading activities are geographically based. The SEC is responsible for implementation of SOX. The SEC has mandated US companies to use a recognized internal control framework that has been established by an organization that developed the framework through a due process, including inviting public comments. Emerging best practice recognizes that those organizations that build compliance into their processes, rather than bolting it on afterwards, tend to get more cost-effective, business-orientated results. both in terms of compliances and competitiveness.

In response to the Enron and other corporate failures, the US has passed the Sarbanes-Oxley Act requiring chief executive officers and chief financial officers to certify in the quarterly and annual financial reports that:

(1) the signing officer has reviewed the report;
(2) based on the officer's knowledge, the report does not contain any untrue statement of a material fact or omit to state a material fact necessary in order to make the

statements made, in light of the circumstances under which such statements were made, not misleading;

(3) based on such officer's knowledge, the financial statements, and other financial information included in the report, fairly present in all material respects the financial condition and results of operations of the issuer as of, and for, the periods presented in the report;

(4) the signing officers—

   (a) are responsible for establishing and maintaining internal controls;

   (b) have designed such internal controls to ensure that material information relating to the issuer and its consolidated subsidiaries is made known to such officers by others within those entities, particularly during the period in which the periodic reports are being prepared;

   (c) have evaluated the effectiveness of the issuer's internal controls as of a date within 90 days prior to the report; and

   (d) have presented in the report their conclusions about the effectiveness of their internal controls based on their evaluation as of that date;

(5) the signing officers have disclosed to the issuer's auditors and the audit committee of the board of directors (or persons fulfilling the equivalent function)—

   (a) all significant deficiencies in the design or operation of internal controls which could adversely affect the issuer's ability to record, process, summarize, and report financial data and have identified for the issuer's auditors any material weaknesses in internal controls; and

   (b) any fraud, whether or not material, that involves management or other employees who have a significant role in the issuer's internal controls; and

(6) the signing officers have indicated in the report whether or not there were significant changes in internal controls or in other factors that could significantly affect internal controls subsequent to the date of their evaluation, including any corrective actions with regard to significant deficiencies and material weaknesses.

Corporate Governance-Indian Scenario

Corporate governance in India is a recent phenomenon. Traditionally, it is the "companies Act-1956" that laid down the governance mechanisms. Recently, there have been amendments to the listing *agendas* as:

(1) Report of the committee on regulation of Private companies and Partnerships (Naresh Chandra committee-II, July, 2003.

(2) Report of the SEBI committee on Corporate Governance-Narayana Murthy (SEBI-Feb 2003).

(3) Report of the committee on corporate audit and Governance (Naresh Chandra committee; SEBI-Dec 2002).

(4) Report of the consultative group of Directors of Banks/Financial Institutions (RBI-April 2002).

(5) Report of the Advisory group on Corporate Governance-Standing Committee on Inter-official Financial Standards and Codes (RBI-march, 2001).

(6) Report of the Task Force on Corporate Excellence through Governance (Department of Company Affairs-Nov, 2000).

(7) Report of the committee on Corporate Governance (Kumar Mangalam Birla-SEBI may 1999)

(8) Desirable Corporate Governance: A code (CII-April 1998).

SEBI, as part of its endeavor to improve the standards of corporate governance in line with the needs of the dynamic market, has revising the guidelines periodically.

Regulatory Response in India

There has been some thinking in India on adopting salient features of the Sarbanes-Oxley Act and other US regulatory changes in India. A high level committee appointed to review the corporate governance issues in India has submitted a report recommending many measures similar to that of the Sarbanes-Oxley Act:

(1) Strengthened auditor independence.

(2) Prohibition on provision of non audit services to an audit client.

(3) Compulsory rotation of the audit partner and 50% of the engagement team every five years.

(4) Enhanced disclosure of contingent liabilities.

(5) CEO and CFO certification of annual accounts.

(6) Establishment of an independent Quality Review Board to conduct audit quality reviews (This is closer to the erstwhile Public Oversight Board than to the Public Company Accounting Oversight Board set up under the Sarbanes-Oxley Act in the US.).

(7) Strengthened role of independent directors.

(8) Establishment of a Corporate Serious Fraud Office on the lines of the Serious Fraud Office in the United Kingdom.

The Institute of Chartered Accountants of India has taken some steps to strengthen its auditing standards to address the problem of frauds. It has issued an exposure draft171 stating that "When planning and performing audit procedures and evaluating and reporting the results thereof, the auditor should consider the risk of material misstatements in the financial statements resulting from fraud or error." The Institute has also revised172 its auditing standard on risk assessment requiring the auditor to "assess audit risk and to design audit procedures to ensure that it is reduced to an acceptably low level."

Linkages between Corporate Governance and Capital Market

The capital market reflects and regulates corporate governance standards. Many jurisdictions use securities markets as a tool to improve corporate governance. During our study we found how the Indian securities market has been undergoing a cleansing over the last decade or so and building resilience to corporate scandals. With the objectives of improving market efficiency, enhancing transparency, preventing unfair trade practices and bringing the Indian market up to international standards, a package of reforms consisting of measures to liberalize, regulate and develop the securities market was introduced in the 1990s. The practice of allocating resources among different competing entities by a central authority was discontinued. The issuers–complying with the eligibility criteria— now have the freedom to issue securities at market-determined rates. The secondary market overcame the geographical barriers by moving to screen based trading, which made trading system accessible to everybody anywhere in the Indian sub-continent. Trades enjoy counter-party guarantees. The trading cycle was shortened to a day and trades are settled within two working days, while all deferral products are banned. Physical security certificates have almost disappeared. A variety of derivatives are available. In fact, some reforms such as straight-through process in securities, the clearing corporation as the central counter-party to all the trades on the exchanges, real-time monitoring of brokers' positions and margins, and automatic disabling of brokers' terminals are singular to the Indian securities market. Indian disclosure and accounting standards are as modern, updated, potent and versatile as those of any other market. Today, the Indian securities market stands shoulder to shoulder with most developed markets in North America, Western Europe and East Asia.

Corporate Governance and firm value

The magnitude of the return from our study suggests that the corporate governance rules had an economically significant impact on firm value, and that firms that less compliant with the rules realize a greater value improvement compared to firms that are more compliant with the rules. We find some evidence that the rules associated with board independence and internal controls do not enhance the value of small firms, since small firms that are less compliant with the board independence provisions and small firms that are less compliant with the internal control provisions exhibit lower returns compared to other firms. In general, our results capture only relative costs and benefits between firms that are more compliant and firms that are less compliant with the rules. To the extent that these benefits are substantial, they will increase the positive overall effect of the rules on the society. We see two avenues for future research. First, our analysis captures investors' perceptions in relation to the rules, but does not look at actual improvements in shareholder wealth in the long run. It is important to see whether the rules actually enhance firm performance. Second, our analysis suggests that, compared to their size, small firms suffer larger costs from implementing the rules than large firms. Analyzing these costs and studying their effect on a firm's financial and nonfinancial strategies is an important term in which explains properly the linkages between corporate governance and firm value.

Corporate Governance and Equity Prices

The power-sharing relationship between investors and managers is defined by the rules of corporate governance. There is significant variation in these rules across different firms, resulting in large differences in the balance of power between investors and managers. If corporate governance matters for firm performance *and* this relationship are fully incorporated by the market, then a stock price should quickly adjust to any relevant change in the firm's governance. This is the logic behind the use of event studies to analyze the impact of takeover defenses. If such a reaction occurs, then expected returns on the stock would be unaffected beyond the event window. If, however, governance matters but is not incorporated immediately into stock prices, then realized returns on the stock would differ systematically from equivalent securities.[2] In this section, we analyze whether such a systematic difference exists. One possible explanation is that the performance differences are driven by differences in the riskiness or "style" of the two portfolios. Researchers have identified several equity characteristics that explain differences in realized returns. In addition to differences in exposure to the market factor ("beta"), a firm's market capitalization (or "size"), book-to-market ratio (or other "value" characteristics), and immediate past returns ("momentum") have all been shown to significantly forecast future returns. If the Management Portfolio differs significantly from the Shareholder Portfolio in these characteristics, then these differences may explain at least part of the difference in annualized raw returns.

DATA ANALYSIS: STUDY OF INDIAN COMPANIES

During the data collection, this was resorted to both primary (data from web-sites of the firms) as well as secondary (web-sites like Investors services, Money control etc.) modes, it is seen that many of the firms do not believe in making available their data to the general public. Even after sending continuous reminders only very few of them replied positively, and many didn't even bothered about that, as direct mails were sent to the head offices and/or to the departments dealing with the investor relations. Many of the firms do not even post their investor relations e-mail ID's, on their websites. Many firms do not post their annual reports on their websites, and other agencies hat keep records of these such as SEBI Edifar (the premier institute which keeps eye on the firms who are dealing in the capital market) among other are Business-Beacon, investors services, money control (which gives full fledged services regarding the performance of stocks, companies as well as keeps track of the all the recent as well as past developments of the performing as well as non-performing firms) etc.

The sample space used contains full gamut of the cement companies from major as well as minor cement manufacturers. Out of 158 cement companies that existed in India, only 42 of them have posted their financials at different sources and 32 of them have shown their annual reports and corporate governance reports. Similarly 50 pharmacy companies and 50 IT/ITES firms were selected randomly. And their financials were considered which were very regular in the case of pharmacy and IT/ITES firms but very discontinued and irregular In the case of cement companies. In this study the data collection was resorted to credible limits, so that the credibility of the data is maintained. Since from corporate governance point of view during our study we found that there is lot of variations and factors which gives a good strength to come up with a required inference after concentrating more on Cement industry compare to IT/ITES or Pharmacy industry so at the time of data analysis we give preference to cement industry only because the data collected in case of IT/ITES or Pharmacy where more in approximate figure instead of that the same was more accurate in case of Cement industry.

Some important figures that we would like to bring into notice, is shown in the Table 1 below:

Table 1

Attributes	*Cement Companies*
No. of Comp's in India	158
Annual reports available	42
Financial reports available	42
No. of comp's whose official website not found	78
No. of companies merged	4
No. of comp's closed their operations	3
No of comp's didn't replied on being contacted	35
No of companies whose information is not clear	15

Over a period of two months of our research study our correspondence with companies did not reach to an expected result. Because we could not get the required data or response we were looking for and in such case we tried to complete our study with the best whatever data we got. After considering some valuable parameters like last price, change in price, percentage change in price, net sales, earning per share, total assets, and net profit we come up with a data which shows the selected list of companies which can be considered as a good source to get the required conclusion from our study at the same time to answer the research questions, complete the hypothesis and objective of the research properly. In fact in the following data mentioned below in Table 2 we have also shown the ranking of the company in terms of net sales for the current fiscal year. We have tried to clear that how can a company cannot have a good EPS in that case also when company has a good figure in terms of net sales which shows a poor governance and leads to lower down the value of the firm from investors point of view, the percentage change shows the variation which depends on the governance policy of the company. It also shows how a poor governance policy affect the net profit of the firm even though the company has a good figure in terms of total assets. Where ACC, AMBUJA and ULTRA TECH are leading the market in terms of net sales at the same time SHREE CEMENTS and ULTRA TECH are proved successful in terms of attracting the investors, one of the most important reason behind it is having a good corporate governance policy which is evidently shown following mentioned Table 2.

Following mentioned pie-chart in Figure 1 shows the top ten gainers in terms of net sales percentage according to the current fiscal year. Which is based on the data mentioned in

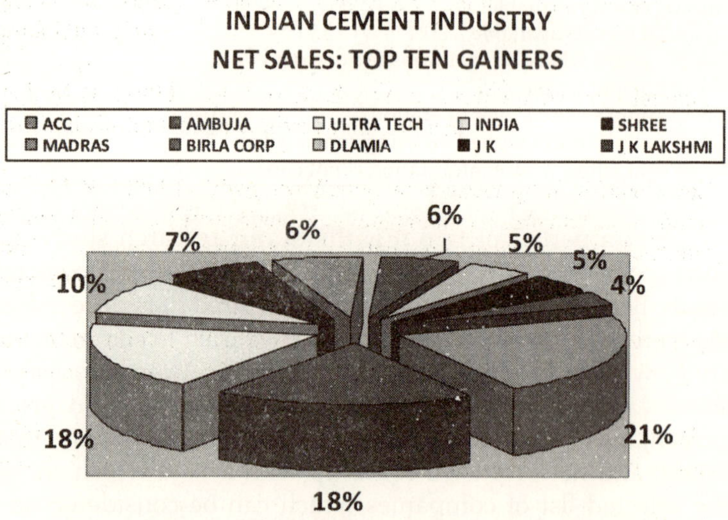

Figure 1 : Indian Cement Industry Net Sales Top Ten Gainers

Table 2

Company Name	Last Price	Change	% Change	Net Sales (Rs. cr)	EPS	Totai Assets	Net Profit (Rs. cr)
ACC	590.4	-8.3	-1.39	6,894.79	72.08	4,449.64	1,438.59
Ambuja Cements	74.3	1.55	2.13	5,671.39	9.23	4,991.67	1,769.10
Ultra Tech Cernent	461.55	-8.65	-1.84	5,512.43	81.39	4,437.49	1,007.61
India Cements	105.6	-2.15	-2	3,044.25	21.15	5,132.61	637.54
Shree Cements	499	2.45	0.49	2,108.21	83.83	1,942.93	260.37
Madras Cements	101.75	-1.2	-1.17	2,005.32	17.72	2,589.49	408.29
Birla Corp Cements	115.1	1.6	1.41	1,724.91	50.37	1,232.48	393.57
Dalmia Cement	143.4	-3.9	-2.65	1,469.12	39.06	2,730.48	347.15
JK Cement	86.9	-3.6	-3.98	1,458.25	35.58	1,562.53	265.17
JK Lakshmi Cements	52.85	-1.45	-2.67	1,111.29	39.38	1,337.30	223.67
Binani Cement	35.45	-0.45	-1.25	963.04	10.8	1,187.91	175.82
Chetinad Cem	484	-0.2	-0.04	933.38	58.36	828.68	163.77
Prism Cement	23	-1.65	-6.69	878.1	8.1	617.77	241.63
OCL India	57.45	-4.25	-6.89	764.41	21.75	1,052.34	116.15
Mysore Cement	19	0	0	593.82	11.3	362.8	97.65
Mangalam Cement	61.45	-2.05	-3.23	509.88	37.83	286.61	113.55
Rain Commoditie	171	-2	-1.16	462.41	16.63	717.64	25.33
Andhra Cements	19.05	-1.35	-6.62	442.27	5.74	372.26	73.96
Saurastra Cemen	19.85	0.85	4.47	409.76	0.23	417.07	22.29
Guj Sidhee Cem	12.49	-1.18	-8.63	398.05	2.12	198.52	52.36
KCP	188	-14.4	-7.11	343	47.84	246.26	66.54
Shree Digvijay	7.75	-0.21	-2.64	254.08	–	129.92	-14.02
Panyam Cements	195.5	0.9	0.46	169.07	27.42	8.34	41.91
Barak Vally Cem	24	-0.25	-1.03	70.31	5.62	104.34	11
Burnpur Cement	11.55	-0.43	-3.59	27.03	–	83.97	1.42

Table 2, it very clearly shows that ACC leads the market with the figure of 21% at the same time DALMIA and J K Cements exists at the same place and like the same BIRLA CORP and MADRAS Cements to gets the same position with a figure of 6%, which can always be considered as one of the important parameter to attract the attention of the investors.

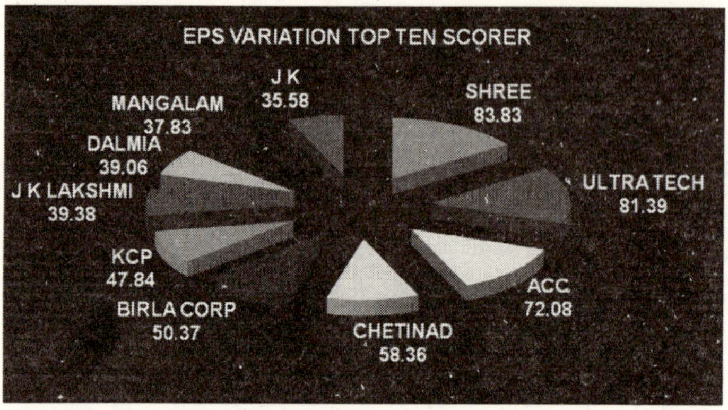

Figure 2 : EPS Variation Top Ten Scorer

Based on Table 2 data in terms of earning per share the above illustration an Figure 2 shows that the EPS variation which is one of the most important parameter in order to attract the attention of the investors. From the above illustration it's pretty clear that SHREE Cements lead the market which proves that they have much better corporate governance policy compare to the companies in the industry. At the same time in the following data mentioned in Table 3 we have tried to show the status of different companies in terms of PBDIT, MARKET CAP. And TOTAL LIABILITIES which can briefly explain the condition of different of different companies in the industry. The data was analyzed in the format given in Table 1 and Table 2 where in Table 1 we have considered the industry profile part and in Table 2 scoring parameter section which includes net sales(in cr.), net profit (in Rs.), earning per share, total assets, and rest of the co-related terms. And this information is being used to analyze the annual report as a whole for its content. Like corporate governance report, auditors' report, directors'

Table 3

Company Name	*PBDIT*	*Total Liabilities*	*Market Cap. (Rs. Cr.)*
ACC	3,018.17	4,459.12	11,312.53
Ambuja Cements	2,311.15	4,991.67	11,079.04
Andhra Cements	1,826.17	FOR 2007 NA	5,745.65
Barak Vally Cements	1,092.95	82.33	2,976.67
Binani Cement	897.69	992.22	2,421.32
Birla Corp	762.48	904.86	1,738.38
Burnpur Cement	634.18	34.98	1,427.96
Chetinad Cements	609.88	494.6	1,231.79
Dalmia Cement	438.84	1,768.08	1,159.30
Guj Sidhee Cements	362.4	198.52	886.33
India Cements	352.51	4,267.29	719.99
JK Cement	352.31	1,347.87	685.98
JK Lakshmi Cements	347.96	1,131.47	607.67
KCP	224.22	213.44	326.89
Madras Cements	158.7	1,343.70	323.33
Mangalam Cement	116.28	216.58	313.15
Mysore Cement	115.79	364.59	300.22
OCL India	87.93	792.52	242.37
Panyam Cements	78.52	-35.46	239.75
Prism Cement	352.49	411.22	180.62
Rain Commodities	1.13	104.15	173.58
Saurastra Cements	50.49	417.07	109.57
Shree Cements	632.88	1,383.37	101.61
Shree Digvijay	60.97	117.2	53.18
UltraTechCement	4.43	3,342.41	49.66

report and rest of the required details. During our study from the collected data we find that corporate governance is good in very few selected companies in the industry. In a study of small cap cement companies we found that there are transparency and disclosures are very low. This could be due to also the proprietary nature of their companies and also the cost of companies' regulations.

CONCLUSION

It is seen that, companies, which had very good corporate governance and had more and more exposure with the investors, survived even during the recession period. But those firms which didn't believed in that lost their investors and hence, the market cap eventually started to fall down, as a result, for transformations to take place they didn't had the capital, as they no more enjoyed the trust of their investors. Some of the firms closed down between 1999 and 2005, few merged with their parent companies or horizontal acquisitions and mergers took place. What forced these firms to merge with the peers was mainly the inability to survive the competition. But in the middle of this, the non-performance was mainly accredited to non-involvement of investors, as the investors who invested were not supplied with the sufficient information and the firms were not able to attract new investors as they do not have good reputation or the investors are not familiar with firms goals, working, capacity, plans, and other important facts that help them evaluate the firms performance. This points out towards the poor corporate governance of the firms. A very significant issue was found that some of the firms who were continuously showing recession for 3 to 4 financial terms , also closed, as they were presenting a bad image of their operations and hence, again they lost investors confidence. So their business suffered badly and hence was forced to close down. But the only good thing that was, even in the days of recession their loyal investors were with them and hence, the firms which would have closed down in a year or two, still were able to extend their operations to fight back their existence. Many of the firms have been delisted from NSE and BSE, which again points out the the linkages between corporate governance and capital markets.

REFERENCES

Gartman, Grant A., and Jack D. Isaacs (1998), *Corporate Governance State by State: A Guide to Selected Statutes*, Investor Responsibility Research Center.

Gompers, Paul A., Joy L. Ishii, and Andrew Metrick (2003), *Corporate Governance and Equity Prices, Quarterly Journal of Economics*, 118, 107-155.

Franklin Allen, Elena Carletti and Robert Marquez, August 4, (2007), *Stakeholder Capitalism, Corporate Governance and Firm Value*, the 2007 NBER/RFS Workshop.

Anderson, Kristen L., and Teri L. Yohn (2002), *The Effect of 10-K Restatements on Firm Value, Information Asymmetries, and Investors' Reliance on Earnings*, Working paper, Georgetown University.

Bebchuk, Lucian A., Alma Cohen, and Allen Ferrell (2004), *What Matters in Corporate Governance?* Working paper, Harvard Law School and NBER.

Cremers, Martijn, and Vinay B. Nair, (2005), *Governance Mechanisms and Equity Prices, Journal of Finance*, 60, 2859-2894.

Gordon, Elizabeth A., Elaine Henry, and Darius Palia (2004), Related Party Transactions: Associations with Corporate Governance and Firm Value, Working paper, Rutgers University.

Zhang, Ivy Xiying (2005), *Economic Consequences of the Sarbanes-Oxley Act of 2002*, AEIBrookings Joint Center for Regulatory Studies, 05-07.

Jayanth R. Varma, (2002), *Governance, Supervision and Market Discipline: Lessons from Enron* (October-December), Volume 14 Number 4, 559-632), The *Journal of the Indian School of Political Economy.*

Coffee, John C. Jr. (1999), *"The Future as History: The Prospects for Global Convergence in Corporate Governance and its Implications," Northwestern Law Review*, 93, 641-707.

Defond, Mark L., and Mingyi Hung (2003), *Investor Protection and Corporate Governance: Evidence from Worldwide CEO Turnover, mimeo*, University of Southern California-Leventhal School of Accounting.

Gibbons, Michael, (2002), Is Corporate Governance Ineffective in Emerging Markets? *The Journal of Financial and Quantitative Analysis*, Special Issue on International Corporate Governance.

Websites

www.google.com

www.moneycontrol.com.

www.businessbeacon.com

www.valueresearchonline.com

www.businessweek.com

14

DETERMINANTS OF POST ISSUE PROMOTER GROUPS HOLDING IN IPOs: AN EMPIRICAL INVESTIGATION

Seshadev Sahoo & Prabina Rajib

INTRODUCTION

The signaling model advocated that promoter group has more correct and rational information about the IPO firm including future cash flows and profitability. The promoter never tied up more quantity of shares in a company unless, he is absolutely confident about the wealth creation ability of the firm. Promoter groups were found investing in diversified, profitable firm by divesting their stake in non-profitable venture. To put it differently, promoters group are willing to hold a majority stake if they have private information regarding high magnitude of expected cash flows. Agency theory further strengthen the above argument by stating that more the holding by promoter, more is the incentive for the owner manager group and hence generate more cash flows. Investors in the IPOs anticipate this and motivate to assign high value to high ownership firms than low ownership firms.

Going public in many cases is a step towards the eventual separation of ownership and day-to-day control. The promoters including promoter group (pre IPO shareholders) decide to divest or sale a part of the equity in favor of the new investors. It is the magnitude of the equities retained by the promoter group in the post issue scenario provides sufficient signal to the new investors. Leyland and Pyle (1977), in their seminal article, proposed a valuation model stating that current value of the firm is positively related to the percentage of the equity retained by the promoter. They argued that the promoter knows more about the expected cash flows and profitability of the project than the potential investors. Further it is costly and risky in holding more stake in the doubtful projects. Therefore the promoter will retain shares in the IPO, only if they have private information that expected cash flows are likely to be high. Thus, they opined that greater equity ownership by the pre-IPO shareholders send a credible signal to the investment bankers, market participants and potential investors of their confidence about the company's prospects, and leads to higher valuation.

The purpose of this study is to find out the determinants for post issue ownership concentration in the context of Indian IPOs. We also document the validity of the commonly believed hypothesis that large size firms with more maturity inclined to retain more and hence divest less through IPOs. Besides, the objective in this study is to understand the role of proxies i.e. offer size, age of the firm, offer price, offer for sale, underwriting contract and appraisal of issue for defining the degree of promoters holding of equity in the post IPO scenario.

The paper is organized as follows: Section 2 provides the past studies followed by hypothesis development. Section 3 gives an overview of the Indian IPO market. Data source, Definition, Sample selection procedure and Analytical methodology are discussed in Section 4. We document the empirical findings and interpretation in Section 5 and Section 6 concludes the paper.

EXTANT LITERATURE

Early studies found focused on behavioral and signaling factors i.e. ownership retention impact on IPO valuation. Accordingly most academic IPO studies have used signaling model to explain the pricing of IPO, and the key variable has always been a signaling variable, i.e. ownership retained by insiders as evidenced by Leland and Pyle (1977). Studies by among others i.e. Ritter (1984), Kim et al (1995), Klein (1996) and Van Der Goot (1997) find that IPOs where, a larger fraction of the equity retained by pre-issue shareholders command higher after market valuations.

Hughes (1986) argued that risk-averse promoters are found all set to divest their stake in firms associated with risky cash flows in favor of the diverse portfolio of business. Retained ownership is also costly to the promoter as it forces them to bear unnecessary risk. Prior studies evidenced the use of the following as proxies for determining the degree of ownership retention by promoter groups in IPOs: (1) Leverage has an inverse relation with the proportion of post issue retention of control. Press and Weintrop (1990), Li and McConomy (1999) have documented that firms with higher leverage have a higher default risk and decreased investment opportunities. As a result, the managers of firms with high degree of leverage are expected to retain less. (2) Firms in the industries facing volatile economic conditions considered more risky than the firms in more stable industry sectors. The managers never inclined to retain more in the firms where the industry sector is unstable (Davidson and Neu, 1993). (3) Another possible motivation is to use retained ownership to affect the secondary market liquidity. Institutional investors prefer to invest in high priced issues because they are more liquid and have lower transaction costs as evidenced by Gompers and Metrick (2000). Other research by Del Gluercio (1996), Badrinath, Gay and Kale (1989) and Lipman (2000) suggests that higher retained ownership associated with the IPOs can be viewed as a prudent investment of higher quality.

Downes & Heinkel (1982), Ritter (1984) and Feltham, Hughes and Simunic (1991), among others, provide evidence on the value of ownership retention. In general, consistent with the theoretical predictions, these studies document a positive relation between IPO valuation and ownership retention. Allen and Faulhaber (1989) used a bi-variate signaling model, which is an extension of Leland and Pyle (1977). In addition to the post issue ownership retention rate being a signal of firm quality, the issuer deliberately undervalues his IPO as a second signal to convey the high quality of the company to the investors. By doing this the issuer is conveying the message that it is financially sound and will be able to recoup losses incurred by undervaluing the issue.

The possible underpricing and ownership structure nexus offers for explanation related to privatization process. The main argument is that the companies controlled by a majority share holding have smaller IPO premiums; because the market correctly understands the value of control rights and this information will reflect in the market price. The underpricing becomes even smaller if the control of a company is not expected to change hands and there is no market for corporate control. By analyzing a sample of 467 listed companies, Jian Chen & Roger Strange (2004) document that underpricing was negatively related to the proportion of shares held by largest share holder. To put it differently, the out side investors rightly perceive the attitude of the promoting group to en-cash private benefits at the cost of others.

The review of literature motivates us to find several gaps in the research that are worth addressing. First, most of the work on this area is based on the sample of late nineties. However, our study based on the sample of most recent issues, that is IPOs are issued during the period 2002-2006. Second, past research has made little effort for finding out the key determinants (or proxies) for the promoters holding of equity in the post issue scenario. We model the influence of the signaling factors which motivate the promoter group to take a position on the retention of equity, so that the rationality in the valuation could be achieved. Third, we made the sample by drawing firms across industries rather than concentrating upon a single industry. Fourth, our study is based upon the initial public offerings floated at Indian new issue market.

Contribution of empirical study to the existing literature

We extend the existing empirical studies on the determinants of post issue promoter holding. We model and provide empirical evidence regarding the determinants of the promoter groups holding in the post issue scenario of the new issues. We provide empirical evidence that promoter group retain more equity stake in the matured firms having high offer value and issue price. Our study also document empirical evidence that the post issue promoter groups holding is more in the public sector IPOs than the issues from private sector. Further, in the case of underwritten issues it is found that the magnitude of promoters holding is more than the issues which are not underwritten by underwriter.

IPO MARKET DEVELOPMENTS IN INDIA

The stock exchange as an institution and its organized functioning evolved in India since nineteenth century. The Bombay stock exchange is the oldest stock exchange in Asia was established in 1875. At the time of independence (1947) India had seven stock exchanges and 1,119 listed companies (Misra, 1997). With 9000 listed companies, India has the largest number of both small and mid-cap public companies in the world, listed on a total of 23 exchanges (Ernst & Young Global IPO trends report-2007). However, India's two primary exchanges are the Bombay Stock Exchange and National Stock Exchange. The National Stock Exchange (NSE), Mumbai is India's first fully automated and completely demutualized exchange.

In order, to effectively control the activities of primary market and to safeguard investors' interest, the Capital Issues (Control) Act (1947) came in. The new issue market started functioning under the aegis of controller of capital issues (CCI) till May 29, 1992, when it was repealed and replaced by Securities Exchange Board of India (SEBI). Henceforth SEBI became the sole regulator of the primary market and introduced many regulations and guidelines in governing the capital market in India. The new SEBI guidelines are more in line with the rules of developed markets. Besides the evidence of perverse underpricing (Shah 1995), increasing number of new issues, evolving guidelines, and a long time lag between issue date and listing date make India an important place to study IPO issues.

Indian primary market has witnessed a large number of listings in the mid-1990s. From 1993 to 1996 alone, more than 1,500 companies went public in India, from all sectors of the economy and from different ownership groups e.g., private stand-alone companies, business groups, and government-owned companies (Ghosh, 2005). However, the subsequent period was marked by a slump in the primary market, when only a handful of companies actually got listed. The dormant IPO market resumed its upward momentum in early 2002-2003 due to the active divestment of equity by public sector enterprises. In the year 2006, India's IPO market has been found fairly broad-based, although energy companies dominated with more than 50% share of funds raised (Ernst & Young Global IPO trends report-2007). With the issue proceeds of $8.3 billion through 95 IPOs in 2007, India became seventh-largest IPO market in terms of the proceeds, according to Ernst and Young Data (Business Line, December 27, 2007). All of these factors contributed to the emerging nature of the market that characterized the Indian IPO market over the past decade.

In India fixed price mechanism was used to price IPOs until 1999. These IPOs were subject to wide scale underpricing as reported in the studies i.e Madhusoodanan and Thiripalraju (1997), Shah (1995), Majumdar (1999). In 1999, the Securities and Exchange Board of India (SEBI) introduced book building process (as price discovery mechanism) in similar pattern to the USA, for IPO allocations. With the introduction of the book building process and the scrapping of the concept of par value for shares, the pricing process has become more open. It is now possible to follow the fixed price route or the book building route for the initial public offerings issued in India. The book building process is now carried out as completely automated (on-line) using the systems of the stock exchanges, and this process is known as e-IPO. This has been made possible by the compulsory dematerialization of stocks in case of secondary market transactions.

The IPO market in India has recently invited the attention of the media for scams in the allotment of shares. The charges are that few individuals managed to create multiple Demat accounts under fictitious names to gain the advantage of the provision of pro-rata allotments for retail individual investors. In this way, these unscrupulous investors managed to get a large number of subscriptions at the cost of other retail investors. The role of the banks as well as Depository Participants (DPs) has therefore come under scanner. The market regulator- Securities and Exchange Board of India (SEBI) has already passed an order asking the DPs for payment of a disgorgement amount of Rs. 1160 million approximately USD 28.3 million) Hindu Business Line, November 22, 2006. The recent scam in the allotment of shares in IPOs compels the market regulator to revamp the allocation structure starting from opening the Demat accounts to the pricing of issues.

Studying the IPOs in the Indian markets is important for another reason i.e. introducing a rating mechanism for Initial Public Offerings (IPOs) prior to their listing. With effect from May, 2007 it was made mandatory for all IPOs in India to be rated by a rating agency. While rating of debt instruments is fairly common, equity ratings is a unique concept. Ostensibly the whole objective of the market regulator is to provide some third party due diligence certificate to the potential investors in the IPO market. This rating (although SEBI claims would not be about the valuation of the issue,) is likely to serve as a signal to a retail investor about the credibility of the firm.

Global integration of Indian new issue market is taking place at an increasing pace. Keeping the objective of global importance the market regulator SEBI introduced Qualified Institutional Placements (QIPs) in May, 2006, similar to Rule 144A placements in USA. Through QIPs the Indian companies can en-cash the twin benefits of gaining access to the available capital without having an international listing, and for foreign investors to invest in Indian companies. A QIP also enables access to the global institutional market through institutional placements of equity shares, without a formal non-Indian listing.

Rising volume of new issues coupled with large number of market participants motivate the market regulator to keep regular surveillance on unscrupulous participants, so that small investors' interest could be protected. SEBI specifies that the critical data regarding the market participants needs to be disclosed. Investor Education and Protection Fund (IEPF) was created by the government of India in October, 2001 to promote awareness among investors and to protect the investors from unscrupulous market participants. In January 2003, SEBI launched a nation-wide Securities Market Awareness Campaign that aims at educating investors about the risks associated with the market as well as the rights and obligations of investors. The BSE and NSE have taken the initiative in conducting investor and market interface programme i.e. seminars and workshops and also come out with advertisement both in print and electronic media to communicate to the investors.

Dormant IPO market get a boost from public sector undertaking, divestment programme being initiated by the Government of India after 2003. The issue of Maruti Udyog Ltd. through which the Government sold part of its stake in the company, revived retail investors interest in the primary market for equity. For the first time the book building method was employed for determining the price of the IPO. The year 2003-04 and 2004-05 experienced a dramatic upsurge in the number and volume of capital raised in the IPO market, which is then continued in the year 2005-06. However it could be observed from the following chart that the small size issues are gaining more ground as the issue amount per issue declines in the year 2005-06. Thanks to the regulatory body SEBI for taking corrective measures in time i.e. path breaking initiatives for making the Indian IPO market more efficient and vibrant.

The underlying chart shows the structure of the Indian IPO market for the period 1997-98 to 2006-07. Volume of issues along with offer value and average value per issue are reflected for the whole period of study.

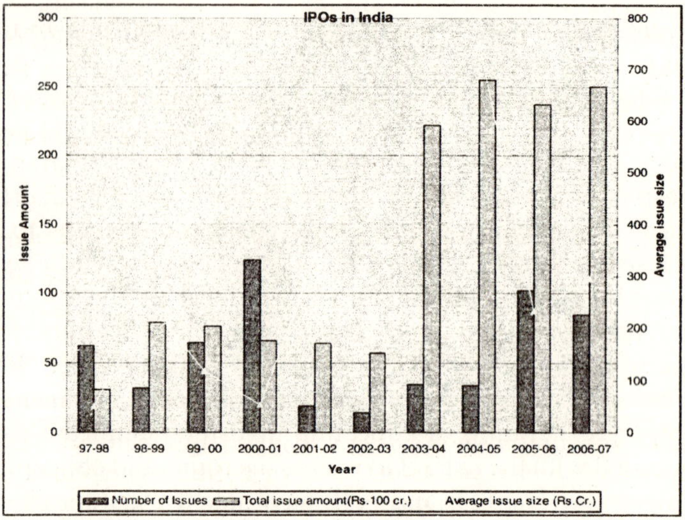

The above chart can be better understood in categorizing them for two different time periods: 1997-2001 and 2002-2006. The Indian IPO market exhibits boom for the new issues in the period 2000-2001(dot-com bubble), before it started crashing in the subsequent period. In both of the periods it is found that as the number of issues is increasing the average issue size starts falling, which can be attributed by taking the advantage of the crowd the small companies enter into the market, resulting in the investors feel the heat of risk.

Table 1

Times Subscribed	*2006-07 % of Issue*	*2005-06 % of Issue*	*2004-05 % of Issue*	*2003-04 % of Issue*	*2002-03 % of Issue*
1.5 & less	26	02	18	20	28
1.5-3 times	16	12	06	14	50
3-10 times	25	28	20	35	14
Above 10	33	58	56	31	07
Total	100	100	100	100	100

Source: Prime data base Annual Report 2006-07.

Response to the IPO in terms of frequency of over subscription is accumulating on year to year as seen from the Table 1. The data shows 56% of the IPO get subscribed by more than 10 times in the year 2004-05, which can be interpreted that the investors are gaining their confidence in the IPO market.

DATA, SAMPLE DESCRIPTION & METHODOLOGY

Defining Source

Data for the study was collected from the Prime Database annual reports from the 2002 to 2006 & the capital market data base, Capitaline.com. Further, data was also collected from various websites including: www.nseindia.com, www.bse india.com and www.sebi.gov.in and was cross-referred with CMIE (Center for Monitoring Indian Economy) prowess database.

Sample Selection Methodology

The sample used in this study comprises of 92 initial public offerings out of 102 public issues (for both equity & debt) during 2002 to 2006 available in Prime Database. Only IPOs for equity shares have been considered. As this study focuses on initial public offerings unlisted companies only, we exclude the follow on public offerings (FPOs) as well as debt issues. The following table explains the sample size and its selection methodology in the following way:

Table 2
Description of the Sample of IPO During 2002-06
Sample Selection Criterion

Universe of number of IPO offered during the period	129
Exclusion number of IPO missing offer price	07
Remaining	122
Exclusion number of IPO missing financial information	13
Remaining	109
Exclusion number of IPO missing list price	17
Remaining Total number of IPO eligible for study	92
Percentage of eligible companies in the sample for study	71.32

Measurement of Post Issue Promoter Holding (PIPH)

Post issue promoters holding (PIPH): The relationship between post issue promoters holding and underprice has been the focus of study conducted by Brennan and Franks (1997), Allen & Faulhaber (1989), Stoughton and Zechner (1998), Hill (2006). Quality companies use ownership concentration as a signal to potential investors about the quality of the firm. PIPH is defined as the percentage of shares being owned and retained by the promoter and promoter group i.e. group of insiders (promoter, manager CEO, venture capitalists and employee) in the post issue scenario. It is an important signaling variable indicating the prospects of the company to the investors.

Descriptive statistics

Predictive variables along with predictors are described in Table 3. Post issue promoter groups holding (PIPH) found an average percentage of 59.14% and the median value of 55.7%. The notable factor about the PIPH is the low degree of standard deviation, signifying a sizable segment in the sample IPOs have post issue promoter holding more than 57%. The promoters are reinstating optimum confidence regarding the business plan of the firm going public.

Among the predictive variables the role of the offer size (OS) is also analysed to define its contribution in predicting the under price. We document the offer size is not uniformly distributed throughout the sample. There is a perfect mix of both large capital and small capital issues are offered in the market during the period 2002 to 2006. Further, it is evidenced through the existence of high range. The mean OS stands at Rs.482.18 Cr. while the median value at Rs. 132.81 Cr.

Table 3
Descriptive Statistics of the Selected Sample

Variables	*Mean*	*Median*	*Minimum*	*Maximum*	*Standard Deviation*
OS (Rs.Cr.)	461.41	113.3	7.5	5428.49	1153.18
Ag (Years)	14.93	13.0	1.00	57	9.85
PIPH (%)	59.14	55.7	29.94	89.5	14.65
SS(No.)	2.84	2.00	1	6	1.43
IP (Rupees)	132.51	45	10	1100	221.21
UP (%)	48.44	29.62	25	323.50	67.58

Table 3 presents the description of all of the variables used in the model for defining the relationship post issue promoter groups holding and predictive variables i.e. OS: offer size, Ag: age of the firm, UP: magnitude of under price, PIPH: post issue promoter holding, IP: Issue Price, SS: Syndicate Size.

Average age for the Indian IPOs found to be 14.93 years and median age stands at 13 years. Low degree of standard deviation confirms that the age of the IPO firms distributed symmetrically around the median. The average percentage of under valuation is found 48.44%. The median under valuation is 29.62%; standard deviation is 67.58% implying high degree of deviations from the average, which can be shown in the spread between high value and low value.

Empirical Methodology

Multiple Regression Model: The popular method used in the valuation research is the multiple regression models. The ordinary least square (OLS) method used in the baseline approach is considered in this research for the estimation of the possible proxies for the PIPH. In this connection, we use the enter estimator technique (under sequential search method) for identifying the degree of contribution of each signalling variables to predict the magnitude of the ownership retention.

As our study is confining to a few related signalling factors, we focus on the magnitude of PIPH as dependent measure. The whole set of independent variables included in the following model (OS, Ag, IP, OFS, AP, UW) are drawn out through the literature review, to test some of the proxies of information asymmetry model along with the ownership concentration variable. However each individual (independent) variable is selected on the basis of their merit. Therefore our basic model is:

$$(PIPH)i = \alpha 0 + \beta 1(OS) + \beta 2(Ag) + \beta 3(IP) + \beta 4(OFS) + \beta 5(AP) + \beta 6(UW) + €i$$

a0: intercept, β1: degree of regression coefficient between (PIPH)i and (OS)i , β2: degree of regression coefficient between (PIPH)i and (Ag)i, β3: degree of regression coefficient between

(PIPH)i and (IP)i β4: degree of regression coefficient between (PIPH)i and (OFS)i, β5: degree of regression coefficient between (PIPH)i and (AP)i, β6: degree of regression coefficient between (PIPH)i and (UW)i, while €i: error term.

EMPIRICAL FINDINGS AND INTERPRETATION

Multiple regression method was undertaken to find out the effect of offer size (OS), age of the firm (age), issue price (IP) and Offer for sale (OFS), Appraisal of the issue (AP) and underwriting of the issue(UW) on the post issue promoter holding. The empirical result shows, the post issue promoter holding (PIPH) is adequately influenced by the magnitude of the age, offer size, issue price, appraisal of the issue, underwritten and offer for sale. We also document that the issue specific variables i.e. offer size, issue price and age bears positive regression coefficients, while offer for sale, underwriting provision and appraisal characteristics reflects an inverse relationship with PIPH. Collectively these variables explain 41.5% of the variation in the ownership concentration. Amongst all of the six variables, the issue price and offer size contributes maximum followed by the age of the issue firm. The following is the summary of the model:

The OLS model in Eq. (2) results in:

$$(PIPH)i = 58.948 + 0.149(Ag) + 6.154(OS) + 8.737(IP) \% 2.360 (OFS)\%9.261(UW)\% 1.234(AP)$$

Table 4
Model Summary

Model	*R*	*R-Square*	*Adj-R Square*	*Standard Error of Estimate*
1	.644	.415	.317	12.1058

Predictors (constant): AP,UW,OS,OFS,IP,AGDependent Variable: PIPHF value = 6.561, Statistically significant at 5% level.

Issue price found the most influential variable amongst all of the predictors use to define PIPH. We document a positive (statistically significant) impact of offer price on the post issue retention by promoter group. More is the magnitude of the issue price the likely chance is that the promoter groups hold more stakes in the post issue scenario. The following empirical result shows that the IPOs having a mean offer price of rupees 16.9 favour the promoter to hold an average of 55.41 percentage of equity, while the high priced issue (mean issue price of rupees 333) motivate the promoter to hold an average of 60.89 percentages of ownership.

Table 5

Mean IP(in Rupees)	*Mean PIPH (%)*	*Number of Companies*
16.9	55.41	26
51.3	60.64	36
333	60.89	30

Among the predictive variables the role of the offer size (OS) is also analysed to define its contribution in predicting the insider retention. We find a direct but statistically significant positive relationship between offer size and ownership retention by promoter group. Promoters and owners of large size issues found better positioned of retaining high percentage of equity in the post issue scenario. The following table also evidenced that the mega issues better poised with managing the issues with large syndicate than their counter part of small issues.

Table 6

Mean OS (in Crores of rupees)	*Mean PIPH (%)*	*Number of Companies*
21.72	55.47	24
96.41	56.58	36
1018.15	63.44	32

Age of the issuing firm documents a direct but positive relationship with post issue promoter groups holding. It is commonly expected that a private firm operating for a long period could be a reliable investment destination than a firm having short history. Further aged firm has long operational and financial history to support the promised business story in the IPO prospectus. Empirically we found, that the promoter groups retain more ownership than the firms having a short history of operation. The investment bankers found managing the issues of aged firms with the help of large syndicate size than its counterpart of start-ups. However, the result is found statistically insignificant. Underlying table evidenced the direct association of the maturity of the firm with the post issue promoter holding.

Table 7

Mean Age in years	*Mean PIPH (%)*	*Number of Companies*
5.71	53.86	28
15.38	58.84	42
42.25	63.97	30

Other Findings (Cross section comparison)

This study explores the various determinants of the post issue promoter holding. We also seek an explanation for finding out the impact of ownership concentration on underprice of the new issues for the sample of 92 companies over a period from 2002 to 2006 in India. Our study documents the following on the basis of empirical findings (details are given in Table-8):

Table 8
Cross Section Comparison of PIPH

Sector wise Distribution of IPOs			*Underwritten IPOs*			*Appraised IPOs*		
Category	*Mean PIPH*	*No. of IPOs*	*Category*	*Mean PIPH*	*No. of IPOs*	*Category*	*Mean PIPH*	*No. of IPOs*
Private sector IPOs	56.78	76	IPOs Under-written	56.64	56	IPOs Appraised	54.1	58
Public sector IPOs	65.99	16	IPOs not Underwritten	63.79	36	IPOs not Appraised	60.5	34
Mean	59.14	92		59.14	92		59.14	92

Public Vs Private Sector Companies: We document the large scale post issue promoter holding in the IPOs coming from public sector than its counter part of private sector IPOs. The promoter group in the public sector IPOs found holding an average of 65.99% of ownership stakes, while in the private sector the average retention stands at 56.78%.

Underwritten Issues: Empirical results posit less degree of post issue promoter holding than the issues which are not underwritten. On an average in the underwritten issues the promoter group holds 56.64% of equity in post issue scenario. In the case of issues which were not underwritten by any underwriter the post issue promoter holding incremented to 63.79% of the equity.

Appraised Issues: We found a large scale variation of post issue promoter holding for the IPOs among both of the category of appraised and non appraised issues. Initial public offerings appraised by financial institutions document an average of 54.1% of equity being retained by promoter in the post issue scenario, while in case of non appraised issues the post issue promoter holding incremented to 60.5%.

CONCLUSION

Our study makes a unique contribution to the literature by exploring various determinants of the post issue promoter holding. We document issue price, offer size and age of the issue firm has direct correlation with the promoter group's interest in holding the equity stake in the post issue scenario. Amongst all of the predictors, it is the offer size and issue price bears most influential impact on promoter group's retention, consistent with the prior literature. We also found that the promoter groups of the public sector firms hold more stake than the issues coming from private sectors in the post issue scenario. The promoter groups found retaining more stakes in the issues being appraised by any financial institutions than the non appraised issues. It is the preference for the promoter group to go for less percentage of retention for the issues not underwritten by the reputed underwriters.

REFERENCE

Allen F. & G. R. Faulhabar (1989), "Signaling by Underpricing in the IPO Market", *Journal of Finanacial Economics*, 23: pp. 303-23.

Badrinath, S.G., Gerald D. G and J. R. Kale (1989), "Patterns of Institutional Investment, Prudence, and Managerial Safety-Net Hypothesis", *Journal of Risk and Insurance*, 56, 605-629.

Brennan, M., Franks J. (1997), "Underpricing, Ownership and Control of Initial Public Offereings of Equity Securities in UK", *Journal of Financial Economics*, Vol. 45, pp. 391-413.

Chen J., and R. Strange (2004), "The Effect of Ownership Structure on the Underpricing of Initial Public Offerings: Evidence of Chinese Stock Markets", The Management Research Papers, King's College London, *University of London*, April.

Davidson, R. A., and Neu, D. (1993), "A Note on the Association between Audit Firm Size and Audit Quality", *Contemporary Accounting Research*, Vol. 9, No. 2, pp. 479- 488.

Downes, D. H., and R. Heinkel (1982), "Signaling and the Valuation of Unseasoned New Issues", *Journal of Finance*, 37, pp. 1-10.

Feltham, G., Hughes, J. and D. Simunic (1991), "Empirical Assessment of the Impact of Auditor Quality on the Valuation of New Issues", *Journal of Accounting and Economics*, 14, pp. 375-399.

Ghosh, S. (2005), "Underpricing of Initial Public Offerings: The Indian Experience" *Emerging Markets Finance and Trade*, Vol. 41, No. 6, pp. 45–57.

Hill, P. (2006), "Ownership Structure and IPO underpricing", *Journal of Business Finance and Accounting*, Vol. 32, Issue 1-2, pp. 102-126.

Hughes, P.J. (1986), "Signaling by Direct Disclosure under Asymmetric Information", *Journal of Accounting and Economics*, 8, 119-142.

Kim, J., Krinsky, I. and J. Lee (1995), "The After Market Performance of Initial Public Offerings in Korea", *Pacific-basin Finance Journal*, 3, 429-448.

Klein. A. (1996), "Can Investors use the Prospectus to Price Initial Public Offerings?" *The Journal of Financial Statement Analysis*, 2, 23-40.

Leland, H., and D. Pyale (1977): "Information Asymmetries, Financial Structure and Financial Intermediation", *Journal of Finance*, 32,371-387.

Li, Y., B.McConomy (1999), "An Empirical Examination of Factors Affecting the Timing of Environmental Accounting Standard Adoption and the Impact on Corporate Valuation", *Journal of Accounting, Auditing and Finance*, Vol. 14, pp. 279-313.

Lipman, Fredrick D. (2000), "The Complete Going Public Hand Book", *Prima Publishing*, Roseville, CA.

Majumdar, Utkarsh (1999)-Price Performance of Initial Public Offerings in India, *Finance India*, 1999, Volume 17, Issue 3, Page 899

Madhusoodanan, T. P. and M. Thiripalraju (1997), 'Underpricing in Initial Public Offerings: The Indian Evidence,' *Vikalpa*, Vol. 22, No. 4, pp. 17-30.

Misra M. B. (1997), "Fifty Years of Indian Capital Market: 1947-97", Reserve Bank or India Occasional Papers; 18(2&3), pp. 351-375.

Press, E., and J. Weintrop (1990), "Accounting-based Constraints in Public and Private Debt Agreements: Their Association with Leverage and Impact on Accounting Choice," *Journal of Accounting and Economics* 12, pp. 65-95.

Ritter, J. (1984), "The Hot Issue Market of 1980", *Journal of Business*, 32, 215-240.

Shah, A. (1995), "The Indian IPO Market: Empirical Facts—Technical Report." *Centre for Monitoring Indian Economy*, Mumbai, May 1995.

Stoughton N, and J. Zechner (1998), "IPO Mechanisms, Monitoring and Ownership Structure", *Journal of Financial Economics*; Vol. 49, pp. 45-77.

15

ARTIFICIAL NEURAL NETWORKS: THE NEW AGE TECHNICAL ANALYST

Munmun Mohanty

INTRODUCTION

Much of economic and financial theory is based on the notion that individuals act rationally and consider all available information in the decision-making process. This idea had its foundation in the very old and accepted model of neo-classical man. The neo-classical economic perspective is the concept of rational self-interest. Individuals attempt this via what is often referred to as the rational, utility maximizing behaviour who settles only for the best. The widely accepted theory on the working of the stock market called Efficient Market Hypothesis (EMH) is based on this economic man model.

DEVELOPMENT OF RANDOM WALK AND EMH

The foundation of research into random walk or efficient markets is generally agreed to begin in 1900 when a doctoral dissertation published by Louis Bachelier (Reprinted in cootner, 1962) began to seriously explore the theory of speculation. His statement of the fundamental principle of equity pricing, "The mathematical expectation of the speculator is zero", laid the foundation for what we know today as the random walk theory. Put simply, the mean of past prices is the best estimation of future prices. Extensions of his work were not undertaken for more than fifty years, but seemed rather to restart as new streams of research.

An important parallel to the early work in financial fields was unfolding in science, mathematics and statistics. Holbrook Working wrote in 1934 what would become an important study of random differences in time series analysis. John Von Neumann (who later went on to make contributions to game theory, quantum mechanics and high-speed computer information system) did a study on mean squared successive differences. He wrote an application on the distribution of the ratio of mean squared successive differences to the variances. These studies could have been applied to financial theory quite accurately but did not partly because they were developed in different fields of study. Years later Working's early material and a later piece in 1960, became fuel for economists to better understand the dynamics of market pricing.

Kendall (1953) made a significant contribution to the growing foundation of applying probability to finance with his extensive work on economic time series and stock prices. Kendall's research found no logical or predictable pattern in stock prices. Based on these findings, he theorized that prices evolved randomly. This disturbed financial theorists and led them to conclude that these random price movements, in fact, indicated an efficient market and not an unpredictable one, as Kendall has postulated. This supposition, referred to as the Random Walk Theory, was first seriously presented by Samuelson (1965), who proposed that randomness is realized through operative participation of many investors seeking wealth. Unable to control their appetite for profits, investors pounce on even the most negligible informational advantage at their disposal, and in doing so, they amalgamate their information into market prices and quickly eliminate the profit opportunities that led to their aggression. Financial theorists espoused the idea that the stock prices should follow a random walk made a case for the idea that markets are in fact efficient.

In 1965, Fama published a foundation piece of research that extended prior work on market randomness. This framework has received wide acceptance and subsequently textbook standard. The framework provides three categories of empirical tests: Tests of weak form, semi strong from and strong form efficiency. Fama defines efficient markets in terms of a fair game where prices fully reflect all available information. The expected value of excess returns in such a perfectly efficient market is zero. He defined three different degrees of market efficiency depending the information set.

Weak from EMH

In the weak from EMH the information subset of interest is restricted to historical prices. If the markets are efficient in weak form, investors should not be able to consistently earn abnormal gains by analyzing the historical prices. The reason behind such logic is that current prices of stocks already fully reflect all the information that is contained in the historical sequence of prices. This form of EMH is popularly known as the Random Walk Theory.

Semi Strong form EMH

The semi strong form of EMH says that current prices of stocks not only reflect all informational content of historical prices, but also reflect all publicly available knowledge about the corporations being studied. Furthermore, the semi strong form says that efforts by analysts and investors to acquire and analyse public information will not yield consistently superior returns to the analyst. Examples of public information are corporate reports, corporate announcements, information relating to corporate dividend policy, forth coming stock splits etc.

Strong form EMH

The strong form EMH maintains that not only is publicly available information useless to the investor or analyst, but all information is useless. Specifically no information that is available, public or inside can be used to earn consistently superior investment return. Being an extreme hypothesis, it is not expected to hold good in any security market.

This theory focuses on three assumptions, all focusing on investor behaviour. These are:

- Investors are fully rational and respond rationally to all changes within the market. This may go so far as saying that investors subconsciously use tools like Bayesian probability to analyze probabilities and make decision.
- Irrational investors trade randomly, and as such, all random investments cancel themselves out, leaving no effect on the market.
- Even if investors' irrational decisions do not cancel out through probabilistic methods, other rational investors will take advantage of these irrational decisions to make a profit, which bring the market back to efficient state.

KEEPING EMH IN PERSPECTIVE

Over the past 35 years, there has been considerable investigating testing of the statistical validity of EMH. The EMH has been robustly examined from both theoretical and empirical positions. In 1990s Markowitz, Miller and Sharpe shared the Nobel prize for their work in equity valuation theory. Markowitz was recognized for developing modern portfolio theory, Miller for his theory of corporate finance and Sharpe for developing Capital Asset Pricing Model (CAPM).

However, some authors have presented respectable and convincing evidence that are inconsistent with the determination of market rates according to the EMH and CAPM. The crux of their argument is as follows:

- From experience we know that investors may temporarily pull financial prices away from their long term trend level. Over-reactions may occur, so that excessive optimism (euphoria) may drive prices unduly high or excessive pessimism may drive prices unduly low.According to the efficient market hypothesis (EMH), only changes in fundamental factors, such as profits or dividends, ought to affect share prices. But the efficient-market hypothesis is sorely tested by such events as the stock market crash in 1987, when the Dow Jones index plummeted 22.6 per cent— the largest-ever one-day fall in the United States. This event demonstrated that share prices can fall dramatically even though, to this day, it is impossible to fix a definite cause.

- This largely theoretic academic viewpoint of efficiency also predicts that little or no trading should take place, since prices are already at or near equilibrium, *having priced in all public knowledge,* bringing the market to a halt. Disequilibrium or market inefficiency provides a constructive force that leads to a healthy trading environment. They argue that security markets in fact work because they are informationally inefficient and it is a necessary requirement along with costly information.
- On a simple behavoural lavel it is clear that people do not use Bayesian probability to learn from their mistakes (Shleifer, 2000) and are rarely fully rational.
- The theory also assumes that every investor has access to all the required information to value a stock. This problem of "perfect information" is its interpretation– while financial statements and economic statistics are widely available, one cannot assume that such information is interpreted correctly by all investors (Dyckman & Morse, 1986).
- In terms of large groups, one of the biggest problems with EMH is that the assumptions imply investors act independently of each other i.e. a naïve investor making mistakes will be taken advantage of by a rational investor. However it is often the case that investors act in unison said to follow *Herd mentality* (Shleifer, 2000), as can be seen during periods of irrationally increasing prices, like the late 1990's dot-com stock boom.

- The last and most convincing proof against market efficiency is the presence of well documented *market anomalies* (Dimson, 1988) like the January effect, the weekend effect, the low P / E effect etc.

TECHNICAL ANALYSIS

The above mentioned discussion though, does not summarily discard the EMH as an explanation of stock prices, definitely encourages analysts to undertake the painful activity of stock price prediction. Stock price prediction may take any of the two routes of *Fundamental analysis and Technical analysis* though, not as substitutes of each other. The fundamental analysis posits that companies that do well in their line of work, be it having high profits, a good managerial structure, a successful focus on research and innovation, or any other similar factors, will do well in the stock market. So to predict whether a company will do well in future, the fundamental analyst looks at a host of factors starting from the economy to industry to company's operation and its profitability. Whereas the assumption inherent in technical analysis is that all such required information is available in a share's past prices. Bodie (1998) defines technical analysis as "an attempt to exploit recurring and predictable patterns in stock prices". Charles Dow the father of technical analysis is recognized for the establishment of the Dow theory, a technique that attempts to recognize trends in the market price of stocks. Dow is also credited with developing in 1897, the industrial average, a general index containing 12 blue chip stocks, and the rail average, a 20 stock rail industry index. Dow originally looked at these tow indicators, which we now call the Dow Jones Industrial Average (DJIA) and the Dow Jones Transportation Average (DJTA) in an attempt to determine the trend of the market.

The way technical analysis helps predict whether a stock will increase or decrease in value is by signaling trend reversals. According to technical analyst, many securities exhibit different types of growth over time, and the key to making a profit in the stock market is to predict when a stock's tendency to increase in value will rise, or a falling stock price will stop and begin to rise. By viewing a stock's past performance, one may begin to understand how people investing in that stock act and which prices they are comfortable with. Indeed, some researchers (Warneryd, 2001; Iihara, Kato & Tokunaga, 2001) have compared the theory behind technical analysis to herd behaviour in the stock market.

The use of technical analysis within investment decisions has been controversial. Technicians often referred to as chartists; remain oblivious to the fundamental reasons for a change in stock price, looking only to identify a trend which is completely divergent to the idea of an efficient market. Technicians are substantial computer users because of their indifference to fundamentals and exclusive interest in share price and volume (Cringley, 1994). However, the critics of EMH feel that technical analysis is an extremely useful tool to predict trend reversals and stock price fluctuation (Brock, Lakonishok & LeBaron, 1992).

However, the problem in technical analysis arises due to the large volume of data regarding past prices which are often available on a real time basis. The data is quite extensive as well, including daily high and low prices, adjusted closing prices to account for dividends and share splits, and numerous other variables. Indeed, the problem of technician is that there is so much of data and forms of analysis that he does not know what to do with it. For example, *Technical Analysis from A to Z* (Achelis, 2001,) a reference guide for technical analysts, lists 135 different tools for doing such analysis. But many of the details regarding these tools are subjective. It is upto the investors to choose values for the variables within each tool, and it is the investor's decision to follow a buy or sell signal from a technical indicator. With so many options, technical analysis sometimes looses its simplicity and predicting ability.

ARTIFICIAL INTELLIGENCE TO THE RESCUE

While computers have found widespread application in the financial industry, they are commonly used only for tabulation, accounting and various linear quantitative optimizations. Given the significant noise in financial time series data and the chaos of daily market fluctuation, it has been traditionally thought that the usefulness of computers to an investor was limited to simple book-keeping.

Many investors operate on haunches and feelings, and not on numerical calculations which could easily be automated. Clearly, designing a computer to emulate the elements of Byzantine human intuition is beyond our present level of understanding. It has been thought that without such intuitive cognition, a computer could never trade on a par with humans. Yet despite the inherent stumbling blocks, the few years have seen artificial Intelligence (AI) slowly creep into the financial sector. While industry skepticism of AI remains high, smatterings of innovative AI applications have emerged. There are two general classes of AI techniques that have found application in finance. The first class is comprised of expert system architectures that use knowledge-based or rule based reasoning to make decisions about a market. Typically, a sufficiently large knowledge-base of financial know-how is developed and is used to assist a real human trader in making decisions. The second major area is the application of connectionist networks and a surrounding body of non-linear techniques to predict new market data from historical databases. In some sense, these systems have no inherent knowledge of their own. Instead, they develop behaviours that predict the market based on a trial-and-error methodology. The Artificial Neural Networks belong to this second category.

ARTIFICIAL NEURAL NETWORKS (ANN)

An Artificial Neural Network (ANN) is an information processing paradigm that is inspired by the way biological nervous systems, such as the brain, process information. These biologically inspired neural networks are systems loosely modeled after the human brain. They attempt to replicate the multiple layers of simple processing elements called neurons (Figure 1).

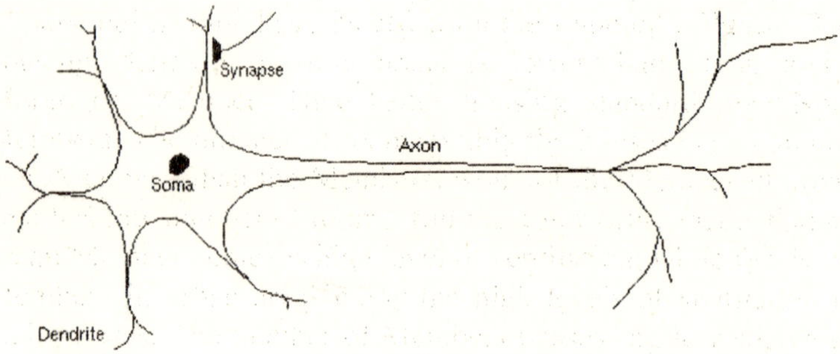

Figure 1: A Biological Neuron

Each of the estimated 100 billion neurons in the human brain represents a primary working unit of the brain. Each neuron carries messages through an electromechanical process and is linked to some of its neighbours with varying co-efficients of connectivity that represents the power of these connections. Each neuron performs three basic functions: receiving input, processing and sending output signals (Figure 2).

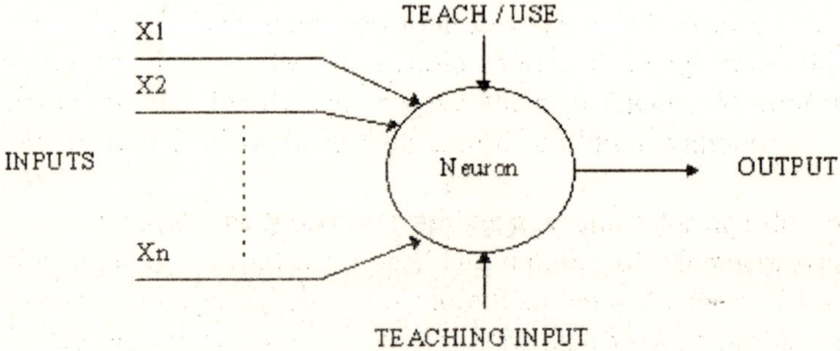

Figure 2: An Artificial Neuron

An artificial neuron is a device with many inputs and one output. The neuron has two modes of operation; the training mode and the using mode. In the training mode, the neuron can be trained to fire (or not), for particular input patterns. In the using mode, when a taught input pattern is detected at the input, its associated output becomes the current output. If the input pattern does not belong in the taught list of input patterns, the firing rule is used to determine whether to fire or not. ANNs, like people, learn by example. An ANN is configured for a specific application, such as pattern recognition or data classification, through a learning process. Learning in biological systems involves adjustments to the synaptic connections that exist between the neurons.

Unlike traditional time series analysis where rules and instructions are central and some mathematical equation describes the dynamics; neural networks do not perform according to preset rules. When displayed to data the network gains experience, learns from regularities in the past and sets its own rules. The learning is accomplished by amending the strengths of neural connections to cause the universal network to yield suitable results. More simply, layers of these artificial neuron-like devices are adjusted until they synergize to look for patterns and to produce results based on the recognition of patterns. (Figure 3).

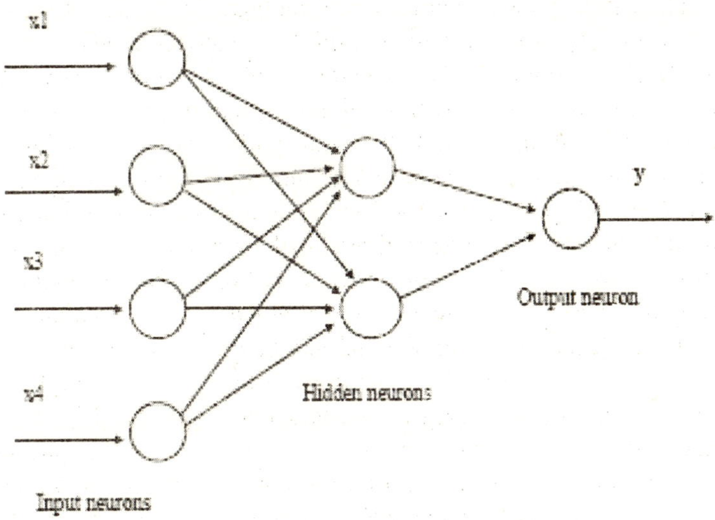

Figure 3: A simple Neural Network

ANNs are not programmed with descriptions or patterns to be recognized: they are trained to recognize these patterns as a result of the iterative process performed (Turban, McLean and Weatherbe, 1999). ANN discerns relationships among inputs by observation and progressive refining. It thus learns through adaptation. In addition, it is the nature of ANN to arrive at educated guesses or to infer from previous inputs and experience. ANN are a series of processing elements, with each one having only one output, but many inputs. The output of one processing element becomes an input to another processing element (Trippi, *et al*, 1992).

Advantages of ANN

Neural networks have several advantages. Most important is the ability to learn from data and thus potential to generalize i.e. produce an acceptable output for previously unseen input data. This even holds when input series contain low quality or missing data. Another valuable quality is non-linear nature of neural network. Potentially a vast amount of problems may be solved. Furthermore, no expert system (typically a programmer coding rules in a computer programme) is needed which makes the network extremely flexible to changes in the environment. One only has to retain the network.

Table 1
Summary of Benefits and Drawbacks

Benefits	*Drawbacks*
ANNs are able to learn any complex non-linear mapping, and approximate any continuous function	ANNs lack theoretical background concerning explanatory capabilities
Like non-parametric methods, ANNs do not make *a priori* assumptions about the distribution of the data or input-output relationship	ANN architecture topology and parameter selection lacks theoretical background. Still trial and error.
ANNs are very flexible with respect to incomplete, missing and noisy data (fault tolerant)	ANN learning process can be very time-concuming
ANN models can be easily updated and are therefore well suited for dynamic environments.	ANNs can over-fit the training data, and thus generalizability.
ANNs overcome limitations of other statistical methods while generalizing them	There are no explicit rules to select ANN paradigm/learningalgorithm.

Regarding downsides, the *black box property* first springs to mind. Relating one single outcome of a network to a specific internal decision (known as credit assignment problem) is very difficult. Noisy data also reinforce the negative implication of establishing incorrect causalities, *overtraining (overfitting)*, which will harm generalizations. Finally, a certain degree of knowledge in current subject is required as it is not trivial to assess the relevance of chosen input series. A short summary of benefits and drawbacks are presented in the table:

WHY ANNS MAY BE BETTER TECHNICAL ANALYSTS

In 1990, most computer financial applications centered on expert systems. Hawley et al postulate that ANN are the only systems suitable for financial decision making and may well prove to be one of the most significant endeavours of finance in the next decade. They believe that there is no better suited area than financial decision making for the application of ANN. Neural networks, with their remarkable ability to derive meaning from complicated or imprecise data, can be used to extract patterns and detect trends that are too complex to be noticed by either humans or other computer techniques. A trained neural network can be thought of as an "expert" in the category of information it has been given to analyse. Other advantages include:

(1) Adaptive learning: An ability to learn how to do tasks based on the data given for training or initial experience.

(2) Self-Organisation: An ANN can create its own organisation or representation of the information it receives during learning time.

(3) Real Time Operation: ANN computations may be carried out in parallel, and special hardware devices are being designed and manufactured which take advantage of this capability.

(4) Fault Tolerance via Redundant Information Coding: Partial destruction of a network leads to the corresponding degradation of performance. However,

some network capabilities may be retained even with major network damage.

Turban et al (1999) refer to neutral computing as distinct approach to intelligent systems because it uses a structure that mimics certain of the processing capabilities of the brain. The results of the neural system are based on analogous processing, speedy recovery of vast amounts of information and the capability to recognize patterns in the data. The ability to recognize patterns in the data is what differentiates these systems from standard computing systems.

In addition, artificial neural networks are often able to detect subtle patterns and trends that may be too intricate for humans to identify. Individuals cannot digest and incorporate more that two or three variables simultaneously; ANN can simultaneously recognize correlations among hundreds of variables (Bylinsky, 1993). ANN are also gifted with the ability to "extract hidden trends and relationships from huge volumes of data" (Dineley, 2001).

Advantages of ANN include giving the investors a competitive advantage because of the ANN's agile nature. Individuals are often at a disadvantage while making decisions because of biases, which occur when emotions become a part of the decision making process. The human may see a pattern, but discount it because it is not what is desired. ANN do a more thorough and consistent job, with no emotional involvement in the decision making process. ANN learn by example and by their mistakes. They have no ego that prevents them from admitting their errors.

ANN IN FINANCIAL MARKETS

ANNs have made big inroads into the financial world. Banking, credit card companies and lending institutions deal with decisions that are not clear cut. There are instances of firms using several neural architectures to deal with these decisions. Neural networks are also being used in all of the financial markets: stock, bonds, international, currency and commodities. Some users are crackling that these systems make them see green. For example, it is known that Fidelity

Investments have many funds that use neural networks to manage over $ 3 billion (Ridley, 1993). Indeed, neural networks are reported to be highly successful in the Japanese financial market. Daiichi Kangyo Bank has reported that for Government bond transactions, neural networks have boosted their hit rate from 60 % to 75 %. Daiwa research institute has reported a neural net system which has scored 20 % better than the Nikkei average. Daiwa securities' stock prediction system has boosted the companies hit rate from 70 % to 80 %. Nikko Securities claims that a simulation of theirs rated corporate bonds correctly 24 out of 25 times. It reputedly ran over 40 times faster than traditional quantitative simulations.

Trippi *et. al* (1992) reviewed the financial applications of ANN in a variety of investment management scenarios. They specifically focused on a simple ANN-based intraday trading system for S 7 P 500 futures contracts. They found ANN technology well suited for the pattern recognition, association and classification deemed necessary for this type of analysis.

Swales and Yoon (1992) studied the use of ANN as opposed to multiple discriminant analysis (MDA) in differentiating between stocks that perform well and stocks that perform poorly. They note that this superiority might well be attributed to the ability of ANN to accommodate fuzzy inputs; hence they are better able to compute qualitative rather than quantitative data.

Williams (2001) discusses some of the practical applications of ANN stock selection currently being used by a small group of mutual fund and pension fund managers. He postulates that the ANN are employed by this specialized group because of the ability of ANN to analyse more variables than a human possibly can and their ability to learn from their mistakes.

CONCLUSION

All the above discussion may seem that the ANN is the magic box where historical data about stocks can be used to predict the future stock prices and may encourage investors to rush and buy an ANN package and start training. But the next question that comes to mind is that with so many bright analysts, money managers and scholars rigorously and continually researching, are only the inexpert and overconfident under the assumption that they are smarter than the market? The answer to that question is that because of these rational, well-informed traders who are continuously sharing knowledge among themselves, the markets are forced to be efficient in the long run, but in the short run this does not hold up. It is the behavior of investors that is the cause of the short lived inefficiencies. The period of inefficiency could be minutes, hours or days. Many cite the informational capacities of the internet to be a boon to the efficiency.

What does all these knowledge mean? It means that we should mean market efficiency because investing is a long-term activity. Further the time and risk incurred to attempt to beat the market may not pay off because the cost of capitalizing on the short tem market inefficiency may well be gobbled up by transaction costs and tax ramifications.

ANNs are by no means an empirical panacea and cannot foretell the future. The true lesson is that all the areas where ANN make sense share commonality, in that decisions are best made without bias and the nuances of human behaviour that appear to be the origin of these inefficiencies. With the plethora of noise about, the investing publis needs guidance more than ever. They need the discipline because the investors' greatest enemy is his own emotions. Hence the ANN have a scope of dealing with this scenarion in a subjective manner. So it said about the ANNs that they are unique and powerful techniques that can provide better forecasting capabilities than any other methods. However, the inherent limitations should be understood and used to prevent inappropriate applications.

REFERENCES

Achelis, S. B. (2001), *Technical Analysis from A to Z,* United States: McGraw-Hill.

Bodie, Z. & Kane, A. (1998), *Essentials of Investments,* Boston, Massachusetts: Irwin McGraw-Hill, pp. 232-253

Brock, W., Lakoniskok, L. & Lebaron, B. (1992), "Simple Technical Trading Rules and the Stochastic Properties of Stock Returns", *The Journal of Finance,* Vol. 47, pp. 1731-1764.

Bylinsky, G. (1993), "Computers that Learn by Doing", *Fortune,* Vol. 128, No. 5, Sept.6, pp. 96-10.

Cootner, P. H. (1962), "Stock Prices: Random vs Systematic Changes", *Industrial Management Review,* Vol. 3, No. 2, pp. 24-45.

Cringley, R. (1994), "Fast Money", *Forbes,* Vol. 153, No. 8, pp. 74 - 80

Dimson, E. (Ed.). (1988), *Stock Market Anomalies,* Cambridge: Cambridge University Press.

Dineley, D. (2001), "Knowledge Management with Human Smarts", *Infoworld,* Vol. 23, Iss. 6, Feb. 5, pp. 50-51

Dyckman, T. R. & Morse, D. (1986), *Efficient Capital Markets and Accounting: A Critical Analysis,* Untited States, Prentice Hall.

Fama, E. F. (1965), "The Behaviour of Stock Market Prices", *Journal of Finance,* Vol. 38, pp. 34-105.

Hawley, D., Johnson, J., and Raina, D. (1990), "Artificial Neural Systems: A Simple Specifications Test for Financial Decision-Making", *Financial Analysts Journal,* pp. 63-72.

Iihara, Y., Kato, H. K. & Tokunaga, T. (2001), "Inverstos' Herding on the Tokyo Stock Exchange", *International Review of Finance,* Vol. 2, pp. 71-98.

Shleifer, A. (2000), *Inefficient Markets: An Introduction to Behavioral Finance,* Oxford: Oxford University Press.

Swales, G. and Yoon, Y. (1992), "Applying Artificial Neural Networks to Investment Analysis", *Financial Analyst Journal,* Vol. 48, No. 5, pp. 78-82

Trippi, R., and DeSieno, D. (1992), "Trading Equity Index Futures with a Neural Network", *Nournal of Portfolio Management,* Vol. 19, No.1, pp. 27-34

Turban, E., McLean, E. and Weatherbe, J. (1999), *Information Technology for Management* (2nd ed.), New York: John Wiley and Sons Inc.

Warneryd, K. E. (2001), *Stock Market Psychology,* United Kingdom: Edward Elgar

Williams, F (2001), "Artificial Intelligence has Small but Loyal Following", *Pensions & Investments,* Vol. 29, No. 10, pp. 4124-4128.

16

NEURAL NETWORK AND FORECASTING PROBLEMS IN BUSINESS ENVIRONMENT

Dushmanta Mallick & Anil Kumar Mishra

INTRODUCTION

The objective of prediction of stock market prices is financial gain of market. Any company that gives good profit continuously in the market that would make the owner of the system very wealthy. So investors and researcher looking for the superior system which gives high return.

The efficient market hypothesis states that no system continuously gets profit in the market. If this system becomes public, everyone will try to get profit and negating its potential gain. Thus there has been an ongoing debate about the EMH, and some researchers attempted to use neural networks to propose their claims.

Neural networks are very useful to predict stock market prices because neural networks are able to learn nonlinear mappings between inputs and outputs. In stock market prediction, neural networks have been trained to perform a variety of financial tasks. There are experimental and commercial systems used for tracking commodity markets and futures, foreign exchange trading, financial planning, company stability, and bankruptcy prediction. Banks use neural networks to scan credit and loan applications to estimate probabilities of bankruptcy, while money managers can use neural networks to plan and construct profitable portfolios in real-time. The application of neural networks in the financial area is so vast, this paper will focus on stock market prediction. Finally, neural networks are used primarily as an application tool in the financial analysis, several research improvements have been made during their implementation.

Overview of Artifitial Neural Network

The calculator is first invented by Abacus which is in the form of wooden frame consisting of sliding beads in the wires helped in counting Arabic numerals by the Fisherman, Merchants and Clarks. In the year 1623 Wilherm Schickand developed an arithmetic calculator called calculating clock simplified the day to day calculation. During the year 1643 the French philosopher Blaise Pascale develop an arithmetic calculating device called Pascaline which is considered as the first calculating device used in Tax calculation in France till 1799. In the year 1822 the difference engine due to Charles Babage helps to simplify the operation on numbers up to 31 decimals degits in the Arithmetical Calculation. The modified machine due to George Scheistz which is a piano like structure can be able to create logarithmic table which was demonstrated at the exposition universelle in Paris in 1855. Due to the constant effort of scientist such as Martin Wiberg (1875), Dorr E. Felt (1884), William.S (1891), Howard Aiken (1938), Atanasaff Berry (1942) and J. Prisper Ecket and John Mauchly (1946) many changes have been made in calculating device. During the period of world war II, though John V. Atansoff, a professor of physics and Clifford E. Berry, a graduate student at Iowa State College, started constructing an electronic computer but unable to complete it. However, due to the constant attention in this regards Atansoff Berry completed the same in 1939 and used in the work. The machine Electronic Numerical Integrator and Calculator(ENIAC) invented by J. Presper Eckert and William Maavchley which is big in size containing 18,000 vacuum tubes could able to perform Arithmetical calculation at the rate 5000 addition per second helps in solving mathematical problem. Impressed upon the work of Charles Babage and George Scheistz, John Van Neuman invented first digital computer which is named as first generation of computer gives immense help to the mathematician, scientist and technologies for the various research work.

A machine designed at Bell Laboratory during 1947 using transistor put a remarkable change in the evolution of calculating device and it is called as second generation of computer. Due to constant research and effort in this direction in the year 1956, a new computer called Leprechaun built in Bell laboratory using integrated circuits could able to improve machine for better form. The microprocessor was a large scale integrated circuit which contains thousands of transistors and the transistors on the chip were capable of performing logical and mathematical calculation called central processing unit in the system. The reduced size, reduce cost and increased speed of the microprocessor led to the creation of the first personal computer. The first Apple computer due to Steve Jops and Steve Wozniak (1976) and subsequently by IBM (1981) made revolunary changes in the invention of personal computers which has a great impact on the society. Subsequently the uses of Silicon chips enable the scientist to indent the machines and in 1971, Intel developed micro computer using microprocessor. Now a day's researcher trying to develop intelligent machines to solve the complex nature problems. Artificial neural systems are examples of such machines that have great potential to improve the quality of our life. Traditionally the term neural network has been used to refer to a network of biological neurons. The modern usage of the term refers to artificial neurons or nodes. Thus the term Neural Network has two distinct usages. Biological neural networks are made up of real biological neurons that are connected or functionally related in the peripheral nervous system or the central nervous system. In the field of neuroscience they are often identified as groups of neurons that perform a specific physiological function in laboratory analysis.

In general biological neural network is composed of a group or groups of chemically connected or functionally associated neurons. A single neuron may be connected to many other neurons and connections in a network may be extensive. Neural network is defined as a simplified models of the biological neuron system is a massively parallel distributed processing system made up of highly inter connected neural computing elements that have the ability to learn and there by acquire knowledge and it is able for use in different problems. Various learning rules are adopted for acquiring knowledge for better efficiency. Neural network is classified due to its learning mechanism and other features. Artificial neural networks are made up of interconnecting artificial neurons. Artificial neural networks may either be used to gain an understanding of biological neural networks or for solving artificial intelligence problem without necessarily creating a model of a real biological system.

The concept of neural networks was worked upon in the late 1800.It was an effort made by the researchers to understand the functioning of human mind. The pioneering work Mc Culloch and Pitts in 1943 put a foundation stone for the beginning of the golden era in the field of neural network and he considered as the father of Artificial Neural Network. These models are based on several assumptions on the functioning of neurons as there was not much known about the functioning of neurons. Their networks were based on simple neurons, which were considered to be binary devices with fixed thresholds. The results of their models were simple logic function OR and AND such as "X or Y" and "X and Y".In late 1940's Donald Hebb made first hypothesis for neural plasticity (learning low neuronal connections are enforced in mammalian brains).This is also a technique of weight selection in artificial neural network which helps in training the neural network. In early 50s Friedrich Hayek was the first to come out with the idea of spontaneous signals arising due to decentralized network of neurons. The suggestion due to Von Neuman in his papers for design a brain like processing unit subsequently helps Neumann to designed a new technology for the construction of electronic discrete variable automatic computer which is developed out of electronic numerical integrator and the machine so designed was the first general purpose electronic computer which was built at Moore school of Electrical Engineering of University of Pennsylvania with some correction due to Aspray and Buck.

Human brain serves as an information processor in the human body. Many researchers use the structure, function and the association of the human brain as a model for building intelligent machine systems, still there is not much information available on the functioning of human brain. It is believed that the brain cells help us think related things and memorize. The struggle to understand the brain has been made easier due to the pioneering work of Romon Cajal who introduced the idea of neurons as structural constituents of the brain. A brain consists of 10^{10} basic units called neurons. A neuron is a small cell that receives electro chemical signals from its various sources and in terms responds by transmitting electrical impulses to other neurons. A neuron is composed of a nucleus of a cell body known as soma. The signals generated in soma are transmitted to other neurons through an extension on the cell body called axon or nerve fibres.Another kind of extensions around the cell body like bushy tree is called dendrites which are responsible from receiving the incoming signals generated by other neurons by Nokes [20].The incoming signals are processed by soma and then the soma converts the processed signals into an output. The axons from two different neurons meets in a gap called synaptic gap containing synaptic fluid which regulates the signals generates different neurons to improve the signals given in Figure 1.

After studying 25 years about the system of nervous system neuro-physiologist Walter MC-Culloch and Yang mathematical prodigy Walter Pitts wrote a paper on how neurons mights work and hence they built a primitive artifitial neural network using simple electrical circuits. The theory developed by them is called as MC Culloch-Pitts theory of formal Neural Network which is a major area in the information technology in the 21st centutry.According to MC Culloch-Pitts model, An Artificial neural network is an information processing system that has certain performance characteristics in common with biological neural networks. Artificial neural networks have been developed as generalization of mathematical models of human cognition of neural biology based on the following assumptions: (i) Information processing occurs at neurons. (ii) Signals are passed between neurons over connection links. (iii) Each connection link has associated weights which, in a typical neural net, multiply the signal transmitted. (iv) Each neuron applies an activation function (usually nonlinear) to its net input (sum weighted input signals) to determine its output signals.

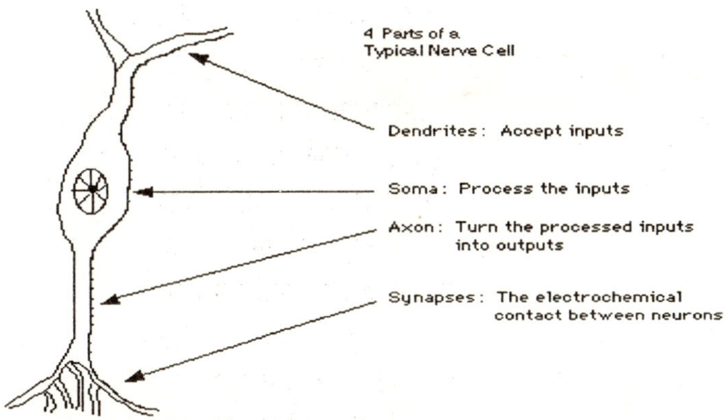

Figure 1 : Part of Typical Nerve Cell

A neural network consists of a large number of simple processing elements called neurons. Each neuron is connected to other neurons by means of directed communication links and each links with an associated weight. The weights represent information being used by the network to solve problems. Each neuron has an internal state called its activation or activity level which is a function of the inputs it has received. Typically a neuron sends its activation as a signal to several other neurons and a neuron only send single signal at a time.

Let us consider $x_1, x_2, \ldots x_n$ are n input signals and the corresponding weight $w_1, w_2, \ldots . w_n$.As the biological neurons receives all inputs through dendrites sum them and produce an output if the sum is greater than a threshold value in the similar fashion if the weighted sum is greater than a threshold value then it give an output to the next neuron.

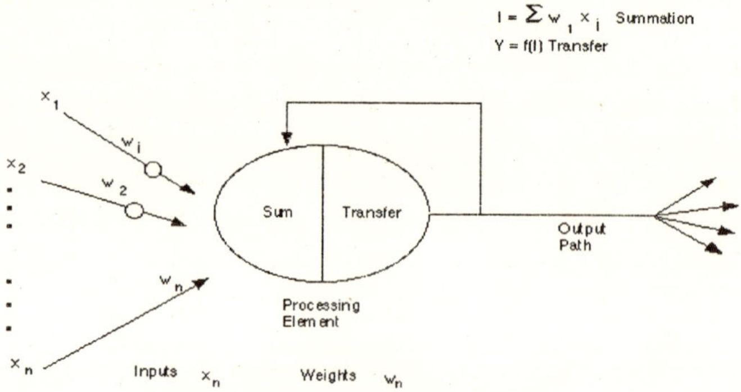

Figure 2 : Part of Typical Nerve Cell

Let I be the total input received by the soma of the artificial neuron given by

$$I = w_1x_1+w_2x_2+....+ w_nx_n=\Sigma w_ix_i$$

If 'Y' be the final output of the neuron then

$$Y= \phi\ (\Sigma w_ix_i-\theta)$$

where θ is the activation function and q being the threshold value.

The output 'Y' can be given as discrete which is given by

$$Y = F(x) = \begin{cases} 1, 1 > \theta \\ 0. 1 \leq \theta \end{cases}$$

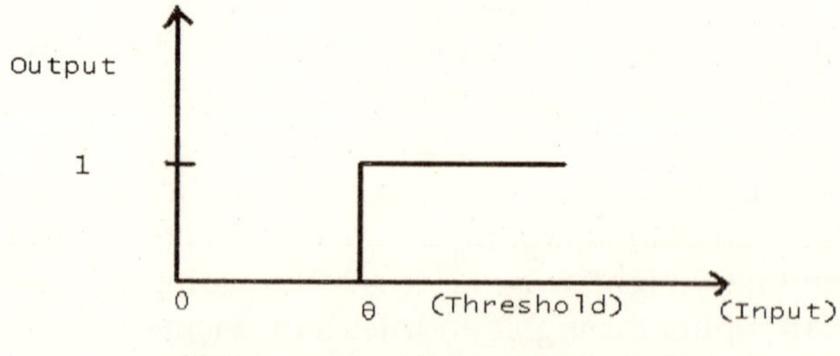

Figure 3 : Part of Typical Nerve Cell

The continuous activation function is said to be sigmoid function has a greater role in neural network which is given by

$$\Phi(I) = \frac{1}{e^{xI}}$$

where 'a' is the slope parameter of the sigmoid function.

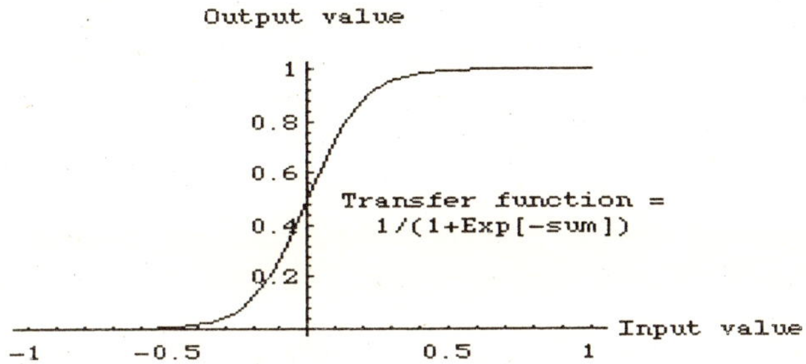

Figure 4 : Part of Typical Nerve Cell

which adjust the abruptness of the function between the two asymptotic values.

The other activation function such as linear type given by f(x) = kx, k being the real constant and ramp function by

$$f(x) = \begin{cases} 0, \; x \le 0 \\ \frac{z}{k}, 0 < x \le k \\ 1, \; k < x \end{cases}$$

is used in the different problems of neural network.

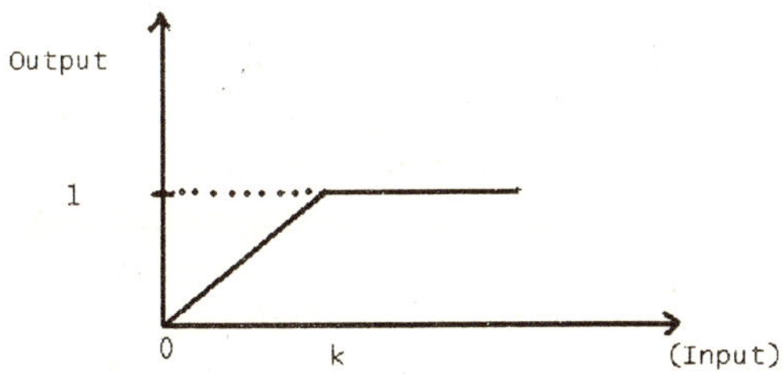

Figure 5 : Part of Typical Nerve Cell

ANALYTICAL METHODS

People traded stocks and commodities primarily on intuition before the age of computers. So people searched for tools and methods that would increase their gains while minimizing their risk. Statistics, technical analysis, fundamental analysis, and linear regression are all used to attempt to predict the market's direction. None of these techniques has given the consistently correct prediction tool that is desired, and many researchers argue about the usefulness of many of the approaches. However, these methods are presented as they are commonly used in practice and represent a base-level standard for which neural networks should outperform. Also, many of these techniques are used to preprocess raw data inputs, and their results are fed into neural networks as input.

Application of Neural Networks to Market Prediction

The ability of neural networks to discover nonlinear relationships in input data makes them ideal for modeling nonlinear dynamic systems such as the stock market. Various neural network Configurations have been developed to model the stock market. Commonly, these systems are created in order to determine the validity of the efficient market hypothesis or to compare them with statistical methods such as regression. Often these networks use raw data and derived data from technical and fundamental analysis.

The networks are examined in three main areas:

(1) Network environment and training data

(2) Network organization

(3) Network performance

Multiple Regression Analysis: Multiple regression analysis is a method to define the relationship between a dependent variable and one or more independent variables. In the case of a product that is sold to a final consumer, MRA calls for determining the quantitative relationship with the following variables for determining retail sales forecasting:

$$Y = f(X_1, X_2, X_3, X_4, X_5, \ldots)$$

where,

Y = Market demand for the product

X_1 = Consumers' disposable income

X_2 = Population size

X_3 = Product price

X_4 = Substitutes price

X_5 = Complementary products price

The manager must specify a family of equations in the form of regression curves and select the member of the family that best fits the data. The quality of fit is measured in terms of an error term. Normally the least square method is used to fit the equation.

CONCLUSION

In general, we can say that neural network approaches differ from traditional statistical techniques in several ways, and the differences can be exploited by the application developer. They are powerful alternative tools and a complement to statistical techniques when data are multivariate with a high degree of interdependence between factors, when the data are noisy or incomplete, or when many hypotheses are to be pursued and high computational rates are required. With their unique features, both methods together can lead to a powerful decision-making tool. Studies and investigations are being made to enhance the applications of ANNs and to achieve the benefits of this new technology.

REFERENCES

Aspray.W and Bucks. A. (1986), Papers of John Von Neumann on Computing and Computer Theory, Charles Babbage Institute Reprint Series for the History of Computing, Vol. 12, Cambridge MA, MIT Press.

Aldenderfer, M.S. and Blashfield, R.K. (1987), Cluster Analysis, Sage Publications, London.

Burke, L. (1991), Introduction to Artificial Neural Systems for Pattern Recognition, *Computers and Operations Research,* Vol. 18 No. 2, pp. 211-20.

Churchill, G.A. (1991), Marketing Research: Methodological Foundations, The Dryden Press, New York, NY.

De Groot, C. and Wurtz, D. (1991), Analysis of Univariate Time Series with Connectionist Nets: A Case Study of Two Classical Examples, Neuro Computing, No. 3, pp. 177-92.

Dibb, S. and Simkin, L. (1991), Targeting, Segments and Positioning, *International Journal of Retail & Distribution Management*, Vol. 19 No. 3, pp. 4-10.

Dillion. W.R and Mulani. N (1989), "LADI: A Latent Discriminant Model for Analyzing Marketing Research Data, *Journal of Marketing Research,* Vol. XXVI. pp. 15-29.

Eisenbeis, R. A. (1977), Pitfalls in the Application of Discriminant Analysis, *Journal of Finance*, No. 32, pp. 875-900.

Hand, D. ·J. (1981), Discrimination and Classification.Wiley, New York, NY.

HNC (1990), Neuro Software.HNC Inc. San Diego. C. A.

Hruschka.H (1993), Determining Market Response Functions by Neural Network Modelling: A Comparison with Econometric Techniques, *European Journal of Operations Research,* No. 66. pp. 27-35.

Huang, W.Y. and Lippman R. P. (1987), Comparisons between Neural Net and Conventional Classifiers, IEEE 1st International Conference on Neural Networks IV, pp. 485-93.

Hebb (1949), The Organization of Beviour.A Neuro Psychological Theory, Newyork, John Wiley.

Jurik, M. (1993), Consumers Guide to Neural Network Software, Futures: The Magazine of Commodities and Options, pp. 36-41.

Kohonen; T. (1988), Self-organisation and Associative Memory, Springer, New York, NY.

Kotler, P. (1991), Marketing Management, Prentice-Hall, Englewood Cliffs, NJ.

Lippman, R.P. (1987), An Introduction to Computing with Neural Nets, IEEE ASSP Magazine, April, pp. 4-22.

Mc Culloch.W.S and Pitts.W (1943), A logical Calculus of the Ideas Imminent in Nervous Activity, *Bulletin of Mathematical Biophysics,* Vol. 5, pp. 115-153.

Neumann Von.J (1986), Papers of John Von Neumann on Computing and Computer Theory. W. Aspray and A.Bruks, Eds, Cambridge, M.A: MIT Press.

Nokes.L.D.M, D. Jennings, A. Flint (1995), Introduction to Medical Electronics Applications. Edward Arnold, Hodder Headline PLC, London.

Nelson, M.M. and Illingworth, W.T. (1991), A Practical Guide to Neural Nets, Addison-Wesley, New York, NY.

Proctor, R.A. (1992), Marketing Decision Support Systems: A Role of Neural Networking, *Marketing Intelligence & Planning,* Vol. 10 No. 1, pp. 21-6.

Romon Cajal.S (1911), Histologic du systems nerveux de'I hommect des verte bres.Pairs: maloine.

Stone, B. (1988), Successful Direct Marketing Methods, 4th ed., Lincolnwood, IL.

Subramanian, V., Hung, M.S. and Hu, M.Y. (1993), An Experimental Evaluation of Neural Networks for Classification, *Computers and Operations Research,* Vol. 20, No. 7, pp. 769-82.

Tam, K.Y. and Kiang, M. Y. (1992), Managerial Applications of Neural Networks: The Case of Bank Failure Predictions, *Management Science,* Vol. 38 No. 7, pp. 926-47.

Thall, N. (1992), Neural Forecasts: A Retail Sales Booster, *Discount Merchandiser,* Vol. 32 No. 10, pp. 41-2.

Von Neumann.J (1958), The Computer and the Brain. New Haven, CT: Yale University Press.

V.Venugopal and W.Bates (1994), Neural Networks and Statistical Techniques on Marketing Research: A Conceptual Comparison, Marketing Intelligence and Planning, Vol. 12, No. 7, pp. 30-38.

Weiss, S.M. and Kulikowski, C.A. (1991), Computer Systems That Learn, Morgan Kaufmann, CA.

White, H. (1989), Neural Network Learning and Statistics, AI Expert, Vol. 4, No. 12, pp. 48-82.

SECTION–III

MICROFINANCE

17

MICROFINANCE INDUSTRY: YESTERDAY, TODAY AND TOMORROW

N. K. Mohanty

Poverty is the central focus of microfinance industry, as the vast majority of the poor suffer financial apartheid. It is exclusively associated with deprivation of income and consumption, leading to social inequality, marginalization, loss of self-worth and personal dignity. This financial exclusion destroys their dignity and self-respect, erodes hope and create a sense of helplessness. The microfinance movement has tried to change that through the provision of a range of financial services like thrift and savings, credit, insurance, payment and transfer services.

The concept of micro finance rests essentially on the premise that: self-employment or enterprise formation is a viable alternative means of reducing poverty; secondly, lack of access to capital assets/credit acts as a constraint on existing and potential micro enterprises and thirdly, the poor are capable of saving despite their low level of income .Empirical evidences suggest that micro finance services have helped the poor, among others, to improve their income, smoothen their consumption, build their assets gradually, enhance their ability to face shocks, manage their risks better and enjoy improved quality of life. The outstanding difference of micro loans from others in the money lending, debt and credit business is that it is relatively quick and easy to obtain financial support; there is no red tape and procrastination and they are geographically located close to their clients. The services offered are from three types of sources : formal institutions, semiformal institutions such as NGOs and cooperatives, and informal sources such as moneylenders and shopkeepers etc. In India, the characteristic feature of the micro finance program is the thrust given to the formation of Self-help groups (SHGs) of the poor, with the intermediation of NGOs and subsequently linking it with formal credit institutions. These SHGs are formed and usually promoted by NGOs as voluntary associations of the poor with a commonality of interests to achieve social and economic goals, through activities of thrift and savings mobilization, credit facilities for emergent consumption and production requirements and mutual help. The process of building up SHGs involve three phases – that is identification and formation of the groups at the initial phase with a time dimension of around five months; next as stabilization process; and final being consolidation stage where the group members collectively assumes roles and responsibilities. Many NGOs, of late, have assumed the role of financial intermediation either directly or through working with smaller NGOs or by promoting federation of the SHGs and other outfits like Multi-purpose Cooperative Societies. Broadly, Micro finance Institutions are classified as (a) not for profit MFIs (b)Mutual Benefit MFIs like Credit Cooperatives and (c) for profit MFIs, which are called Non-Bank Financial Institutions (NBFIs) registered under Companies Act, 1956.

Micro finance is a movement that first emerged in India 40 years ago and has ramped up significantly in the last decade. Viewed from a historical perspective, the origin of the industry started in informal sector of the economy and is traced back to the beginning of the co-operative movement in Germany where the problem started in the field of credit when the peasants were perpetually dependent on the merchant-userer and could not arise out of poverty and squalor. The enactment of

Co-operative Credit societies Act in 1904 could be considered as the beginning of micro finance in India., which was established primarily to combat the problems of usury and indebtedness of the farmers to moneylenders and to bring together people of small means for promoting thrift and mutual help. After independence, the Government of India initiated measures to review the arrangements for institutional credit delivery system. Here again the main focus was, largely, sector-oriented rather than people-centered and therefore providing access to institutional credit for the asset less rural poor was visibly absent.

As explained above, SHGs form the pivot around which the existing MF models in India revolve. They work on the principles of peer pressure as the new collateral and this acts as a boon to the asset less people who seldom have any collateral. Through the provision of loans, rather than grants, the micro-credit providers become, largely, sustainable by recycling resources over and over again. Thus this style of intermediation at the grass roots level makes sincere attempt to deliver the "holy trinity" of outreach, impact and sustainability. The repayment rates in the SHG-based–credit system are found to be much better than other credit system which is around 90 to 95 % factors which, to-day, contribute to the success of micro-finance programs in the country are: (i) organizing the poor into homogeneous and cohesive groups (ii)inculcating the habit of thrift amongst the members of the groups (iii)reducing transaction costs to the borrowers and lenders (iv) providing timely credit (v) freedom to the group to charge interest rates as per their perceptions (vi) efficiency in recovery of loans through peer pressure and (vii) stress on empowerment of women, who have remained marginalized for years.Viewed against the extent of financial exclusion in the sector, it projects a concerted effort to promote micro finance innovations as complementary to the mainstream credit delivery mechanism.

There exist a wide range of Micro finance models in India and among them, four types of credit delivery model are popular and each one succeed well in its respective sphere.

Micro finance Institutions(NGO-MFIs, Mutual benefit MFIs, and for profit-MFIs) in the country have adopted various traditional and innovative approaches for increasing credit flows to the unorganized sector. They are: (i) SHG-NGO-Bank model (ii) SHG-Federation-Bank model (iii) SHG-cluster-Federation-Bank model and (iv)SHG-Bank–Federation-NGO model. The first model acts as a pseudo bank by taking over the functions of the bank like providing credit facilities and performing the savings functions of the SHGs. Under second model, the federation provides credit facilities and assists in savings function of the SHGs, thus functioning as an MFI and acting as an intermediary between the bank and the SHG. The third model implements cluster concept while the final one attempts at establishing linkages between the SHGs and the bank with NGOs or federation, playing the role of a facilitator. Almost two thirds of SHGs formed in India are of this model with minor contextual operation .The reasons behind the existence of above models in the country are: geographical size of the country; existence of a wide range of social and cultural groups; the emergence of different economic classes and a strong NGO movement.

Products development forms a critical part of the competitive strategy of micro finance which, in its vision, concentrates on flexibility, client-friendly approach, designed as per contextual needs of the beneficiaries and its variation and promotional strategies are the key determinants of market share. Marketing is the analytical tool that helps increase the number of clients, identify market share and target market, identify the needs of the clients, define appropriate products to the clients, position the products and finally promote them. In other words, the products of micro finance transactions need to be based on market analysis so as to meet the needs and preferences of the target clients while keeping the Micro finance outfit profitable or breaking-even. In our country as in case of a few other developing countries around the world it is, unfortunately, supply-driven instead of being demand-driven in the sense that micro finance delivery system simply copies the products, procedures, manuals, etc. of another MFI without market studies and recognizing the heterogeneity of the poor to identify the needs of the people and exploit market niches. In the Indian context to be specific, similar to loan and savings products, insurance as a product has not well thought of so far. .But there are needs to implement insurance products such as life, health, damage, disability etc. so that it matches with the needs of the clients and at the end of the day, it is proved that insurance products for the poor are business-oriented and worth as service providers.

Today micro finance as an industry, which continues to be used as vehicles of credit to the rural and low-income household, has achieved substantive geographic spread across the country due to the reason that SHG financing modalities significantly reduce both the covariant risk and transaction costs. More importantly, the institutions are operating in many of the poorest districts across the country especially in the south, and the east. It also demonstrates the extent of outreach and deepening of providing the services to segmented markets of clients belonging to scheduled castes and tribes where formal finance have found it difficult to venture. Two apex level financial institutions, which are promoting, supporting and financing micro finance programs in the country are NABARD and Small Industrial Development Bank of India (SIDBI). NABARD's involvement in promoting micro finance, through the concept of SHGs, which started back in early eighties, have gone through many innovations, improvement in terms of relationship banking and culminating in Linkage banking program which establishes synergy between the banks as the financial supporters and the NGOs as the mobilizer of the helpless poor to build up their capacity for availing loans from the banks and eventually to graduate to a level from where they can access larger amounts without intervention of NGOs. As of now, nearly 30 lacs self help groups, covering around 400 lacs of poor families have been linked with the formal banking system. NABARD has plan to promote and credit-link an additional one million SHGs during the eleventh plan. In order to link Micro finance Institutions with Banks, several steps are in progress. In the private and joint sectors, achievements in extending savings and credit facilities by SEWA, an NGO in Ahmedabad, FWWB, Ahmedabad, an affiliate of Women's World banking, New York, MYRADA, an NGO based in South India are impressive. An important aspect of the credit-plus role performed by above NGOs in the micro-credit delivery system has been capacity building and the development of human resource capital of the poor by meeting their training needs, providing inputs for sustained production and marketing of their finished products for remunerative prices.

Tomorrow the sector will witness a sea change. It will be a sector–vibrant, all inclusive, coordinated, focused and long-term sustainable sector in the country. Financial inclusion has become a major concern and the issue has, of late, been close to the heart of the policy makers. The sector is rapidly witnessing a steady migration of NGO-MFIs in the last few years from the society and trust form of registration to the company form of incorporation, most of them becoming NBFCs, but a few of them preferring to retain their not-for-profit status. Likewise a number of NGOs have started experimenting with various initiatives like replication of Grameen, networking with NGOs and financing through SHG federations and co-operatives to take financial services to the poor clientele. It is thought and perhaps rightly so that SHG-bank linkage program being a major plank of the strategy to deliver sustainable financial services to the poor, the supply-side efforts alone will not achieve desired results. Demand-side efforts, which will improve human and physical resource endowments, enhance productivity, mitigate risk and strengthen market linkages and create absorption capacity for financial services which have been evaluated to formulate micro finance regulation bill for an orderly development of the sector. Since different structures and organizations are operating under diverse legal framework it is increasingly being felt that a suitable regulatory framework with universally accepted yard stick in place will help the operators to follow a common set of guidelines. The Micro Financial Sector Development and Regulation bill seeks to do three things: to allow micro finance institutions to offer the valuable financial services of providing an outlet for savings of their poor clients;. Second, to introduce a measure of consumer protection by providing for the redressal of grievances through an Ombudsman. and thirdly, to promote the "orderly growth of the sector" by setting performance and accounting standards, creating a reporting system and database , supporting research, promoting consumer education, disseminating information relating to fair practices and laying a code of conduct. It is for all of us to wait and see how the industry grows and grows well from strength to strength, linking yesterday with today and planning for tomorrow.

18

MICROFINANCE–A STRATEGY FOR JOB CREATION AND SELF-SUFFICIENCY

Sunanda Asuti

IN RETROSPECT AS A BACKWARD NATION

Indian economy is yet described as an underdeveloped country because of two characteristics-low National Income(as well as per capita income) and limited size of the market; although it is true that it no longer suffers from stagnation.

Even after 61 years of independence and more than five decades of planned economic development, sixty percent to seventy percent of its population seeks employment from agriculture. PCI is low, in addition rate of capital accumulation also low. Widespread unemployment is a normal feature. Ranking our economy on the basis of PCI our position is slightly above Nigeria, Tanzania, Zambia, Ethiopia, Bangladesh and Nepal. Rest of the 3rd world has PCI higher than India. Not only that we are poor, but the economic distance between most Developed countries and India has also increased over the years. *WDI figures show a per capita income figure of $470 in 2002, $530 in 2003, and $620 in 2004 and $820 in 2006. This is one-fifth of US' PCI!*

Moreover distribution of income clearly reflects inequality in household expenditure. WDR 2005 recorded that in 1999-2000, lowest 20% of households earned 8.9% of aggregate household expenditure, whereas share of top 20% was 41.6%.Middle 60% accounted for 50% of aggregate expenditure. For modern business firms lowest 40% of households are irrelevant due to their meager purchasing power.

Going by calorie consumption, 36% of population in 1993-94 was below poverty line. Although it is true that after liberalization there has occurred significant decline in incidence of poverty to 27.5% by 2004-05; nevertheless this is an alarming situation even after six decades of independence.

75% of the poor are in rural areas with most of them comprising daily wage earners, self-employed households and landless laborers. Near about 1/4th of our population neither has capacity to contribute to capital accumulation nor to generation of large demand for industrial goods.

Widespread unemployment is the most striking symptom of inadequate development of our economy.

Table 1
Current Daily Status Unemployment Rate Per Thousand

Year	*Rural Males*	*Rural Females*	*Urban Males*	*Urban Females*
1993-94	56	56	67	105
1999-2000	72	70	73	94
2004-05	80	87	75	116

The above data shows that during 1993-94 to 2004-05 unemployment situations has worsened in all 4 segments which also prove the fact that *growth was jobless* in post liberalization period In contrast to the West, where unemployment is cyclical, in India it is chronic and results from structural defects in the economy. Open, disguised, seasonal industrial and educated are major types of unemployment in our economy.

TOWARDS SOCIAL AND ECONOMIC JUSTICE

Among all efforts towards social and economic justice, the most commendable was in the form of bold decision of Nationalization of banks by the then PM Smt. Indira Gandhi. With nationalization, banks became dynamic catalytic agent for promoting economic growth. A number of specific programmes emerged to help the poorer sections of society with gainful employment and asset creation. Mention must be made of priority sector lending, Lead bank scheme, opening branches in rural areas, adoption of villages for specific schemes for agricultural and non-agricultural credit, and *last but not the least SHGs-Bank Link up in Rural Credit.*

As per the NABARD data, as on March 31, 2006 22.5 lakh SHGs were linked to 545 banks in India covering 3.33 crore families in their effort to come out of poverty. As a pilot project, initially 13 states were selected which accounted for 70% of rural poor population. Today the programme has assumed the status of 'Micro-finance movement. The success of this programme can be judged from the fact that target of covering 1/3rd of rural poor by 2007 was realized much ahead by March, 2004. More than 1/4th of SHGs are three years old and therefore many can hope to be converted into micro-enterprises however this change is not smooth due to many obstacles.

WHAT IS MICRO-FINANCE?

Definition

Micro-finance is the provision of broad range of financial services such as deposits, loans, payments, money transfers and insurance to the low income households and their micro enterprises to break out of poverty.

Purpose

Providing the beneficiary access to financial assistance including credit to the poor so that he/she is enabled to start or expand micro enterprises and expand them over a period.

How does it help the needy?

Micro credit enables the poor people to be thrifty and helps them in availing credit and other financial services for improving income and living standards.

How does the Formation of SHG Take Place?

The poor are encouraged to voluntarily come together to save small amounts regularly and extend micro loans among themselves. The focus is on those poor and underprivileged groups who need finds in small amount but frequently but unfortunately have no sustainable access to formal banking system.

Who are the Target Groups?

Women; small and marginal farmers; agricultural and non-agricultural laborers; artisans and craftsmen; migrant workers and all those who are engaged in small businesses like vending, hawking etc.

Who are the Helping Agencies?

Since India has adopted multi-agency approach, all major credit institutions as commercial banks, co-operative banks, RRBs along with NGOs are associated with the micro-credit programme.

Models of Micro-finance

There are three models of Micro-finance.

Model I—Here bank takes lead in forming and nurturing SHG; opens savings account and provides bank loan.

Model II—In this case SHGs are formed by NGOs and formal agencies but SHGs are directly financed by banks.

Model III—SHGs are financed by banks through NGOs and other agencies

Statistical observations

Following table shows performance of Micro-finance facilities as on March 31, 2006.

(i) As per NABARD website information, 74% was share of Model II, 20% of Model I and just 6% of Model III. Obviously lion's share of loans sanctioned came through Model I.

Particulars	*Cumulative*
No. of SHGs linked to banks	22,38,565
% of women groups	90
No. of participating banks	545
No. of districts covered	583
No. of partners covered	4896
Bank loan Rs. in billion	113.98
No. of poor households assisted (in million)	32.98
Avg. loan/SHG Rs.	50,917

(ii) There is a positive growth of SHGs linked to banks from2, 63, 825 to22, 88, 565 i.e. by 67%during 2001 to 2006.

(iii) The southern region accounted for 71% of SHGs in 2001 however by 2006 it's share went down to 54%; the share of North-eastern region which was conspicuously low at 0.0001 went up to 0.027and that of Northern region from 0.0034 to 0.059.

(iv) The amount of loans disbursed through banks has increased from Rs.571 million to Rs. 113975million i.e. about 20,000times.

(v) Approximately 3.33 crore families are helped to come out of poverty by 2006.

(vi) SBI credit linked the highest number of SHGs followed by Indian bank and Canara bank in 2006.

(vii) All 158 RRBs participated in the programme.

(viii) The number of co-operative banks participating increased to 340 because of amendments made in co-operative society's acts by various states. SHG-Bank linkage have accounted for nearly 16% from co-operative banks.

HISTORY OF MICRO-FINANCE... BANGLADESH EXPERIENCE

Micro-finance movement as a tool for alleviating poverty got maximum success and yielded maximum benefit in Bangladesh in the form of Grameen Bank Movement started by Mr. Muhammad Yunus in 1976.It's tremendous success for

Bangladeshis as well as Nobel Peace Prize to its promoter brought a hype or fashion among the global financial sector. The impact was so much so that year 2005 was declared by UN as 'Year of Micro credit'.

Described by its founder, Muhammad Yunus, as a "socially conscious capitalist enterprise," the much-lauded Grameen Bank in Bangladesh seems to be one of the Third World's brightest success stories. By viewing poor people as potential entrepreneurs, the bank has helped village people, especially women, to better their lives in small but significant ways. Bornstein, a Canadian journalist based in New York City, concludes, "The lesson of Grameen is not extrapolation from abroad but the importance of seeking new solutions to and institutions for complex social problems."

As a young Economics professor at Chittagong University in Bangladesh in 1976, Muhammad Yunus lent $27 out of his own pocket to a group of poor craftsmen in the nearby town of Jobra. To boost the impact of that small sum, Yunus volunteered to serve as guarantor on a larger loan from a traditional bank, kindling the idea for a village-based enterprise called the Grameen Project. It never occurred to him that his gesture would inspire a whole category of lending and propel him to the top of a powerful financial institution.

Today, Yunus runs Bangladesh's Grameen Bank, a leading advocate for the world's poor that has lent more than $5.1 billion to 5.3 million people. The bank is built on Yunus' conviction that poor people can be both reliable borrowers and avid entrepreneurs. It even includes a project called Struggling Members Program that serves 55,000 beggars. Under Yunus, Grameen has spread the idea of micro credit throughout Bangladesh, Southern Asia, and the rest of the developing world

Yunus' innovation has broad appeal. In 1997 only about 7.6 million families had been served by micro credit world wide; according to the 2005 State of the Micro credit Summit Campaign Report. As of Dec. 31, 2004, some 3,200 micro credit institutions reported reaching more than 92 million clients, according to the report.

When Yunus started Grameen, he wanted to turn traditional banking on its head. One of his first moves was to focus on women because they are most likely to think of the family's needs. This was a radical step in a traditional Muslim society, and it took Yunus six years to reach his initial goal of a 50-50 gender distribution among borrowers. Today, 96% of Grameen's borrowers are women.

The innovation of Grameen in particular and of microfinance in general—is to collateralize the asset of future access to loans. In this sense, microfinance in low-income countries works a lot like credit cards in high-income countries; borrowers repay because they want to preserve future access to loans. Default by one group member leads to loss of access for all members. *This joint liability reduces risk in three ways:*

- *First,* joint liability gives members an incentive to exclude known bad risks. For outsiders, knowledge of individual character is costly, but, for villagers, it is often a sunk cost. Thus, joint liability can cut the cost to screen potential borrowers.
- *Second,* joint liability gives members an incentive to make sure that their fellows do not squander their loans; this can cut the cost to monitor borrowers.
- *Third,* joint liability gives members an incentive to coax comrades out of arrears or even to repay their debts for them. Members may also mentor each other. This can cut the cost to enforce repayment.

MICRO FINANCE NEITHER HYPE NOR A HOPE BUT REALITY

For India micro finance is neither hype nor a hope, but it is the reality –tool for alleviating poverty. In India, trusts and societies constitute the vast majority of Micro Finance Institutions. MFIs as corporate entities are allowed to access the capital markets for generation of funds; RBI has given them option to solely not depend on bank lending, grants and donations. A MFI may lend to individual beneficiary, to partner –NGO or to SHGs or allocate funds among different categories of borrowers.

A SHG is an informal group of rural poor consisting of not more than 20 members who have volunteered to organize themselves into a group with a motive to eradicate poverty of the members. They agree to save regularly and convert their savings into a common fund. They agree to use all common funds so secured. The SHG movement in Andhra Pradesh and Karnataka has become successful models of 'Empowerment of Women'. The SHGs take up diverse income generating activities like dairying, manufacturing of readymade garments, candle-making, petty businesses, production of organic manure, mat-weaving, and making pickle, papads, condiments etc.

Advantages of SHG-Bank Linkage are 4-fold

(1) Satisfactory recovery performance (100%) compared to ordinary rural lending (50%-60%).

(2) Intermediation through SHG significantly reduces transaction costs both by bank and MFIs thereby increasing margins.

(3) Bank branches have the opportunity of getting future quality clients both for deposits and loans.

(4) SHGs successfully provide both credit and saving services to the poor.

This success of SHG-Bank linkage led RBI to issue instructions to banks to treat it as a business opportunity or corporate plan. As a result both PSBs and Pvt. Sector banks as ICICI, Citi Bank, ABN-Amro have taken it on priority basis.

As per ICICI Report, 2003 there is a huge gap between demand and supply of credit in India. The gap can be known from the figures—Annual Demand equals Rs. 135 to 400 billion, Annual supply equals Rs. 9000 to Rs. 13,000 million. This attracted the attention of players as commercial banks, development banks, SIDBI, NABARD, RRBs, SHGs, MFIs, and NGOs, to play significant part.Commercial banks, development banks and private banks are actively trying to enter into rural microfinance sector.

AREAS TO CONCENTRATE

Rural Agro Business

Generation of income is possible through establishment and running of agro-based units or agro-processing units. In developed countries, up to 14 per cent of the total work force is engaged in agro-processing sector directly or indirectly. However, in India, only about 3 per cent of the work force finds employment in this sector revealing its underdeveloped state and vast untapped potential for employment. In the report entitled *Prosperity 2000 – Strategy to generate 100 Million Jobs in India through Accelerated Development of Commercial Agriculture and Agro-based Industries* by Dr. G. Rangaswami, Former Vice-Chancellor, and Tamil Nadu Agricultural University following key observations were made.

India—with its conducive and varied climate, the largest irrigated area of any country in the world and still substantial untapped irrigation potential, its vast population and huge reservoir of technical and scientific manpower, and four decades of experience in raising food production to meet the needs of an expanding population—is today poised for a breakthrough in agriculture that can double food production and total exports, virtually eradicate rural unemployment and poverty, and energize the entire economy for rapid growth. In order to achieve full employment and raise its entire population above the poverty line by the year 2000, India needs to create additional employment for 100 million persons and raise the incomes of millions of under-employed persons.

The study team suggested the programme with the anticipation of doubling agricultural production in ten years, achieving complete nutritional self-sufficiency for the country, and generating Rs. 400,000 million in exports of sugar, fruits, vegetables, fish, silk and cotton textiles. This program will generate a minimum growth rate of more than 4% in the agricultural sector, generate at least 100 million new jobs, add an additional Rs. 750,000 million to rural incomes, and raise virtually 100% of rural families above the poverty line. The multiplier effect of skyrocketing rural demand will stimulate sufficient increases in the income and employment for the urban poor to raise nearly all urban families above the poverty line, eliminate the country's foreign exchange crisis and transform India into a world market leader in several categories of agriculture-based exports.

Micro-finance in Housing

There has been pro-rich orientation in respect of housing loans by both commercial banks and housing finance corporations. More than 90% of individual housing finance exposures of commercial banks and housing finance corporations go to the salaried class and balance to business or professional class, the share of the poor whether urban or rural remains meagre.

Housing problem in urban India is more acute than that in rural India. As per NSSO data, 2007, there exists tremendous gap between number of dwelling units targeted and constructed in respect of both of two special schemes-housing for economically weaker sections and housing for low income group. For the former it is 80% and for the later 90.62%.Result:The really deserving sections of society do not have access to the system. The challenge for Indian housing finance system is how to make it more inclusive and equitable. By 2030, 60% of urban population is expected to be urban; unfortunately the worst part of urbanization is formation of slums.60% of urban population lives in slums but occupies only 5% of urban land. Remaining 95% of urban land goes to the privileged rest i.e. 40%.The result is—*Slum formation takes place almost at the same pace as the urbanization.*

To solve this problem India would require to construct 5, 00,000 housing units every year for next 20 years. It is obvious that market will not meet this huge demand. Even regulatory regimes like ULCRA are not so effective because of poor governance.

It is interesting to know how other countries have solved this problem. China through tax incentives to developers and equity grants to slum dwellers could develop more than 20 million housing units during 2002-08; Chile implement capital subsidy programme to eliminate slums from cities; South

Africa, Singapore, Cuba and Sweden were best success stories in 'social housing'; Thailand keeps aside a sum of *US $ 1650 per family for infrastructure subsidy and housing loan interest subsidy*. These and other countries therefore practice partnership form of development. Indonesia, Myanmar, Sri Lanka are able to avert slum formation by accurate planning and investment in low cost housing.

The problem can be solved by government taking the role as a facilitator, providing fiscal concessions to builders and developers. Besides NGOs, SHGs, community organizations should come forward to set up MFIs.

Empowerment of Women

Empowerment is the process of enabling women to acquire and possess resources to make decisions on their own or resist decisions that are made by others. Among various interventions recommended the most accepted or popularized was SHGs. The concept of SHG revolves around women. The finding in Andhra by Nirmala and others revealed that SHGs not only help in raising income levels but lead to improvement in access to credit facilities and reduction in workload. Moreover they become more self-confident and this assures better status and decision making power. They are able to tackle in a better way issues related to injustice and family violence. Their leadership qualities improve and they become more aware about health and education. Research done by Purushottam revealed that many benefits were reaped through micro credit interventions to women entrepreneurs in the form of shifting from wage earning to self-employment, repayment of old debts, sending girl child to school and so on.

Despite this success in women empowerment, gender discrimination continues which is very much shown in wage differential between male and female laborers. Thus women's empowerment is successful functionally but not structurally.

This analysis leads us to realize the fact that credit is not the only factor to bring transformation of power.

Micro Enterprises

Micro enterprises are businesses in which people invest small amount of capital to earn some return. Investment may range between two thousand rupees to ten thousand rupees. Activities undertaken are as follows-milking, trading in seasonal agricultural products, tailoring, grocery, vegetables or fruits, petty shops and handicrafts.

A study undertaken for some selected districts in Tamil Nadu by Joseph and Lissy revealed following facts:

(a) 99% of micro enterprises were making profits.

(b) 70% of them with profits upto Rs. 25,000 p.a.

(c) Weaving and petty business were most profitable whereas traditional activities as agriculture and milking were least profitable.

(d) Investment in handicrafts was not profitable at all (60% facing losses).

(e) 60% of respondents felt that financial viability was strong while 28% found it difficult to continue.

Off course economic impact of micro enterprises is two-fold: increase in savings and improvement in developmental consumption. 48% of respondents had savings between Rs. 2500 to Rs. 5000 thanks to SHG membership and their weekly and monthly schemes. Among different options of savings most prominent were contribution to SHGs and LIC premia .55% of respondents experienced rise in investment in children's education while more than 58% viewed that there was no improvement in housing, livestock and household equipments.

Suggestions emerging from this research are:

(a) Training in marketing and accounting skills organized by MFIs will be of great help.

(b) SHGs should make effort to withstand competition from market.

(c) MFIs can give consultancy services to their clients to select right micro enterprises.

(d) Aid in preparing 'interim profitability statements' by banks would make micro entrepreneurs aware about profitability and take corrective steps to control expenses.

(e) Self help promoting institutions should provide support in distribution so that products reach centre of demand i.e. urban areas.

Financial Inclusion

Even today banks have not been able to bring vast segments of population into their fold especially the economically weak and underprivileged sections of society which is true globally also. Financial exclusion may lead to social exclusion. The best solution to this issue would be financial inclusion.

Financial inclusion is delivery of banking services at affordable cost to LIGs. It is done either voluntarily or through state regulation. Regulators step when desired attention is not paid by banks.

The most serious ill effects of financial exclusion are increased unemployment and borrowing at exorbitant rates of interest.

Following efforts were made in Indian economy during 80s towards financial inclusion:

(i) Expansion of bank branch network

(ii) Setting up of RRBs

(iii) Focus on rural credit

(iv) Priority sector lending

(v) Interest rate ceiling and

(vi) Formation of co-operatives

Although four decades of banking, have led to our success of financial access to masses, it is doubtful how far this achievement is good enough implying tremendous scope for financial coverage.

Banks are competing with each other to achieve high targets and see that more saving accounts are open; moreover they have come out with Kisan credit cards, Artisan credit cards etc. Does this help solve basic problem of 'poor? Unfortunately not! Finance is everything for poor man to save from day to day hardships .The poor requires not only capital but real services.

Suggested Measures

Public sector banks are the best mode of change towards financial inclusion as they have desired linkages and can support organizations. In addition social responsibility of Indian private banks and foreign banks need to be increased.

Attention needs to be diverted from major urban areas to secondary towns and semi-urban areas. To achieve this government can make use of incentives as tax concessions, tax exemptions and tax holidays to these banks and other financial institutions.

PSBs should be persuaded to go for physical expansion in under-banked areas by sensitizing them about business opportunities.

RBI can make use of some prudent norms.

(i) A bank office/ co-operative credit society for every Gram Panchayat would go a long way in achieving desired goal.

(ii) Banks should continue their policy of resource mobilization through measures as pigmy collection, so that rural people develop relationship with banks.

(iii) Need for fresh look into financial services.

(iv) Financial Inclusion Fund on the same lines as RIDF (Rural Infrastructure Development Fund) of NABARD needs to be created. This fund could be utilized for assisting financial institutions in the building of physical and social infrastructure.

Micro Pensions

Pension scheme is yet another financial service not reaching deserving low-income groups. Although structural reforms are undertaken by many countries in their pension schemes, the number of beneficiaries is as low as11% of wage earners and that too those who contribute to private pension plan or social security plan. The poor are not in a position to contribute to regular salary deductions.

Pension schemes are not available to those in informal sector, micro entrepreneurs etc. If micro pensions are started, they will go a long way in making people avert 'poverty trap' in their later years of their life when they are economically unproductive.

The schemes can be implemented most professionally—Pensions would be collected by professional fund manager as voluntary savings accumulated over long period, then they would be invested in capital market .Withdrawal could be as per pre agreement lump sum or annuities.

So far the successful effort towards micro pensions has been taken by UTIAMC in collaboration with SEWA Bank of Gujarat and SHEPHERD of Trichirapalli for their members.

Micro pensions would serve as insurance against old age. NGOs and MFIs can provide the service to develop such funds. Mutual Funds can collect periodical contributions by facilitating pension products. The beneficiaries would be individuals in unorganized sector, economically weaker rural/semi urban /urban families.

Though the UTIAMC scheme is showing good performance, overall there is unawareness about micro pensions among people.

Uthira D and Hansa L.Manohar in their paper have suggested following models:

(a) Partnership models (involving NGOs, Banks and Industrial Houses)

(b) Grameen model (with involvement of MFIs)

(c) Agency model (through service provider)

(d) Micro-agent model (networking agency)

Grameen Bank of Bangladesh has launched Grameen Pension Savings(GPS). Here a borrower contributes minimum taka 50(=.86US$) per month for 10 years at least , after 10 years he/she is assured of almost double of accumulated amount. The scheme is become extremely attractive .People are contributing even taka 500 per month. Bank is able to collect over taka100 million as deposits.

Bank or MFI can derive the advantage in the form of opportunity to utilize the collection of pension amount for its own business.

Though conceptually very ideal micro pension scheme is practically very challenging to implement as it requires dealing with masses who are illiterate, with low financial literacy, with irregular patterns of income. If community based pension models are utilized, and initiative is taken NGOs/MFIs/SHGs/ Banks then micro pension will help not only alleviate poverty but bring assured, sustainable economic development.

GLOBAL AND INDIAN SUCCESS STORIES

Bolivia—Credit-Con Education Rural (CRACER)

Bangladesh—Bangladesh Rural Advancement Committee (BRAC)

Kenya—KWFT, K-rep (NGO), KSTES, SMEP, ECOLOF are MFIs

With countrywide outreach

Honduras—Save the Children

India—SHARE (Society for Helping Awakening Rural Poor through Education——Andhra Pradesh); SEWA (Self Employed Women's Association—Gujarat); ADITHI —Bihar; ASA –Tamil Nadu; SHEPHERD; Oriental Bank in Deheradun (Uttaranchal)

CONCLUSION

Micro credit helps the poor beneficiaries to move out of poverty trap but fails to work for economic deprivation of very poor and destitute. Families with children under 18 years should be given preference in Micro- finance. Micro finance should not stop at economic support. Co-chair UN Council Micro Credit Summit Noeleen Heyzer rightly pointed out "——It is about women achieving economic and political empowerment within their homes, their villages, their countries". Microfinance has a positive impact far beyond the individual client. The vast majority of loans go to women as they make use of these funds and earning generated for reinvestment in their businesses and their families. When families cross poverty line and micro businesses expand, entire communities benefit. Jobs are created, knowledge is shared, civic participation increases and women are recognized as valuable members of their families and communities.

REFERENCES

Can India grow without Bharat? By Acharya Shankar.

India Business Year book-2007.

OECD Economic Survey-2007.

Financial Institutions and Markets By Bhole L.M.

Economic Environment of Business By S. K. Puri.

Micro finance and poverty Eradication–Indian and Global Experiences Edited by Dr. Daniel Lazar and Professor P. Palanichamy. Pondicherry University.

Indian Financial System By M. Y. Khan.

References also include articles on relevant subjects in different National and local Newspapers, as well as Blogs on Topic Micro finance on Websites and Papers presented at National Seminar on Micro finance, Self-employment and poverty Alleviation on March 17.2006 by Department of Economics, University of Mumbai.

19

ROLE OF MICROFINANCE INSTITUTIONS IN FINANCIAL INCLUSION

Hareram Mohanty & Pradeepta Kumar Samanta

INTRODUCTION

Financial Inclusion has become a buzzword throughout the world including India which has adopted financial inclusion rather late compared to many other countries like UK, Canada and USA. Financial Inclusion (FI) is all the more important for India as it has 203 million households of which 147 million are rural and out of the rural households more than 70% have no access to formal credit. Hence it is needless to emphasize the degree of Financial Exclusion in India. Nearly 41% of adults of the country do not have bank accounts let alone availment of bank credit. FI has been though late, given due importance by the Government and almost all financial agencies have been exhorted to take up FI in a big way. In fact 100% FI is the target to be achieved in the shortest period. Attempt has been made by the authors to carve a place for the MFIs scattered throughout the country in different names and forms to contribute towards FI which essentially includes provision of financial services, adequate formal credit, micro-insurance etc.

Different definitions for financial inclusion have evolved and it is worth while to study the definitions evolved in Indian context.

Mr. P Chidambaram, former Finance Minister defined financial inclusion as "The process of ensuring access to timely and adequate credit and financial services by vulnerable groups at an affordable cost". Ms. Usha Thorat, Deputy Governor, RBI delineated financial inclusion as "Financial inclusion imparts formal identity, provides access to the payments system and to savings safety net like deposit insurance. Hence financial inclusion is considered critical for achieving inclusive growth." Mr. Y V Reddy the then Governor of RBI defined financial inclusion as "Ensuring bank accounts to all families that want it". Mr. C Rangarajan Committee defines financial inclusion as "The process of ensuring access to financial services and timely and adequate credit where needed by vulnerable groups such as weaker sections and low income groups at an affordable cost."

Before studying financial inclusion process in India it is relevant that the Rangarajan Committee Report is available for analysis and understanding the programme of financial inclusion as envisaged in India.

RECOMMENDATIONS OF RANGARAJAN COMMITTEE

A few major recommendations are:

(i) Launching of a National Rural Financial Inclusion Plan (NRFIP)

(ii) Constitution of two funds with NABARD

  (a) The Financial Inclusion Promotion and Development Fund (FIFP)

  (b) Financial Inclusion Technology Fund (FITF)

(iii) Deepening the outreach of micro-finance programme through financing of SHGs/JLGs (Self Help Groups; Joint Liability Groups)

(iv) Use of PACs as Business Facilitators and Correspondents.

(v) Micro Finance–Non Banking Finance Companies (MF-NBFCs) could be permitted to provide thrift, credit, micro-insurance, remittances and other financial services up to a specified amount to the poor in rural, semi-urban and urban areas.

(vi) Opening of specialized micro finance branches/cells in potential urban centers for exclusively catering to micro finance and SHG-bank linkages requirements of the urban poor.

It is obvious from the various policy measures and developmental activities that concerted efforts are being made by all concerned to achieve total financial inclusion in India. However the aggregate effort made are not adequate. The implementing institutions are mainly banks and their achievements have been discussed in the following paragraphs. Banks have been advised to adopt the opening of no frills accounts as means for achieving Financial Inclusion.

Table 1
No-Frills Accounts opened by Banks

Category	*March 31, 2006*	*March 31, 2007*	*March 31, 2008*
Public Sector Banks	332,878	5865,419	13,925,674
Private Sector Banks	156,338	856,495	18,879,073
Foreign Banks	231	2,753	33,115
Total	489,497	6,724,667	15,837,862

Source: RBI

Assuming that the financially excluded category of prospective accounts were 893 lac and of which 158.37 lac no-frills accounts have been opened by all types of banks taken together, the gap is still huge. As per NSSO data 459 lac farmer households do not have access to credit. This is more than 51 per cent of the farmer households. It is further disheartening that only 27 per cent of the total households avail credit from formal sources. Hence the need for financial inclusion, primary step for which is opening of bank accounts for all the excluded households. No doubt it is a tall order for all banks taken together.

At this point emphasis may be made on the 5th recommendation of Rangarajan Committee which states that Micro finance is general and MF-NBFC in particular may be emphasized for bridging the gap and achieving total financial inclusion expeditiously.

WHAT ARE MFIs

MFI has been defined as an organization or association of individuals legally constituted as society, trust, cooperative society, mutual benefit society, mutually aided society, cooperative bank etc. for the purpose of carrying on the business of extending microfinance services.

Micro-finance institutions in legal framework are not unique. They operate in different forms and two basic forms are:

(i) NGO-MFI

(ii) MFI-NBFC

It is interesting to note that there are more than 1000 NGO-MFIs in India and MFI-NBFCs might exceed 20. Though less in number, MFI-NBFCs account for more than 80 per cent of the microfinance loans.

MFIs may be:

- Association/society under Societies Registration Act 1860
- Trust under Indian Trust Act 1920
- Company under Indian Companies Act 1956. It may be a Sec 25 Company, Company for mutual Benefits and Non-Banking Finance Company

To define MFIs, it is necessary to have a legal base and that would be provided by the proposed Microfinance sector (Development and Regulation) Bill 2007 introduced in March 2007. The proposed bill defines microfinance services as providing financial assistance to an individual or an eligible client either directly or through a group mechanism for:

(i) An amount not exceeding Rs. 50,000 per individual for small and tiny enterprises, agriculture and allied activities.

(ii) An amount not exceeding Rs. One lakh fifty thousands for housing purpose.

MFIs & FI

MF-NBFCs have been visualized by the Rangarajan Committee as a very powerful medium for achieving total financial inclusion. As reported, MFIs have grown rapidly during 2003-2008 and their number of borrowers increased from 11 lac to 140 lac.

These non-banking financial companies are required to take up

- Mobilization of low cost deposits
- Providing microcredit
- Providing micro-insurance
- Providing miscellaneous financial services up to a specified limit

The financial services generally include

- Savings
- Credit
- Insurance
- Payments and Remittances

To make it more specific the micro credit should mean and include;

(i) Purpose: Agriculture, allied and non-farm activities
Amount: Maximum Rs. 50,000

(ii) Purpose: Housing Loan
Amount: Rs. 1,50,000 maximum

(iii) Purpose: Risk mitigation services
Tool: Micro Insurance

MFIs AS BUSINESS CORRESPONDENTS

It is expected that MFIs as business correspondents should take up inter-alia the following activities:

(a) Opening of deposit accounts

(b) Collection and payment of small value deposits up to Rs. 10,000

(c) Disbursement of loans up to Rs. 10,000 after due documentation

(d) Recovery of loans

(e) Selling insurance and other financial products of small value

(f) Providing small remittance facility say up to Rs. 10,000

RESTRUCTURING OF MFIs

To achieve the financial inclusion target in a holistic manner it is required that many MFIs be restructured.

Purpose:

(i) Reaching out to the poor

(ii) Understanding of their needs especially financial needs

(iii) Acceptability among the poor and it is a very sensitive point

(iv) Ensure legitimacy, accountability and transparency

Restructuring should enable MFIs to

(a) Take and use savings available at low cost

(b) Avail adequate debt and equity fund

(c) Abiding by regulatory norms and expand beyond a geographical area

(d) Act as correspondents of banks for providing limited financial and insurance services.

AN ORDERLY GROWTH REQUIRED

It is enough to mention that growth of MFIs in India has not been orderly and has not given any distinct picture both structurally and statistically. Hence it is opportune time that a systematic coordination and development be ensured through the enactment of the micro finance sector (Development and Regulation) Bill, 2007 which in any count, is delegated and need to be passed to meet the urgent requirement of financial inclusion.

As to the involvement of Banks, public and private sector, Regional Rural and Cooperative all taken together the reach would be rather limited due to structural and attitudinal reasons. Microfinance is the solution and it has been proved in aplenty but in pockets scattered all over the country. It is now imperative that the examples set in various locations – districts, states be emulated by the rest of the country and the required push be provided by the enactment and the regulatory as well as extension agencies so that the total financial inclusion could be achieved throughout the country. Before the supremacy of MFIs in implementing financial inclusion is appreciated, it is necessary to identify the pros and cons of the financial institutions like Regional Rural Banks, Commercial Banks, *vis-à-vis* MFIs.

RRBS VS MFIs

It is worthwhile to make a comparative study between MFIs and RRBs as RRBs as financial institutions are expected to cater to the financial requirements of rural households. RRBs were originated with the expectation that these banks would provide the advantages of commercial banking and cooperative banking to their rural clients. However over three decades of their existence and growth the achievements have not been quite encouraging. Now the MFIs should learn lessons from both RRBs and Cooperative Banks and adopt the best approach suited for the rural ethos and sentiment of poor households in every nook and corner of India. It is important that the new agencies devoted to financial inclusion implementation should have the right attitude and skills available to handle the millions of rural poor in India.

COMMERCIAL BANKS VS MFIs

There can not be level playing field between Commercial Banks and MFIs for reasons of sizes and operations. However, the role of MFI towards FI cannot be outweighed in view of the colossal presence of Commercial Banks' branches numbering more than 33,500 in rural and semi-urban centers of India. The reason is, though semi-urban and rural branches try to cater to the households in their areas of operation, the large number of households shown under Financial Exclusion, elsewhere in this paper points out at the wide gap. The MFIs in existing form and in restructured form post MFI Act, would well take care of the financially excluded households without posing any competition whatsoever to the Commercial Banks.

SIDBI and MFI

Role of SIDBI in developing MFIs for catering to the financial need of the poor needs no emphasis. MFIs have been constantly delivering credit to the poor though their sustainability due to lack of legal status for mobilizing resources is not strong. SIDBI has been trying to strengthen the MFIs by augmenting their capacity through need-based capacity building support, technical assistance and operational support. Liquidity management in case of many MFIs has been a difficult task and SIDBI is providing equity capital to eligible institutions. SIDBI is assessing the MFIs as to their experience in managing microcredit programs, their growth potential, track record, professional expertise and enabling them to take up efficient credit dispensation through on-lending.

ACHIEVEMENTS OF FINANCIAL INCLUSION BY VARIOUS AGENCIES

It is heartening that India's attempt to achieve financial inclusion has been greatly supplemented by the self-help groups (SHGs). Indirectly millions of poor people mostly women below poverty line being members of SHG have achieved access to the financial system through bank linkages. The essential part of the linkage being supply of adequate credit it is satisfying that more than 223 lakh SHGs (March 2006) have been credit linked. Taking an average of membership as 15 the individual getting to credit through SHGs would exceed 330 lakhs. This is no less achievement and with the thrust being given to financial inclusion through SHGs and MFIs, the number of poor below poverty line to get access to credit will be greatly enhanced. The current figure of accounts through SHGs and MFIs of 40 lakh and 14 lakh appear to be realistic though accelerated growth is desirable. The savings created through SHGs at Rs. 3500 crore appear commendable and indicated how empowerment of rural poor has come up.

CASE OF ORISSA

The authors have studied the level of Financial Inclusion in the State of Orissa as it is a very backward state and as many as 47.2% of the state's population are living below poverty line. The state has extreme regional imbalance and financial exclusion had been a bottleneck in the state's overall growth. The Table 2 shows the progress regarding Financial Inclusion as of November 30, 2008.

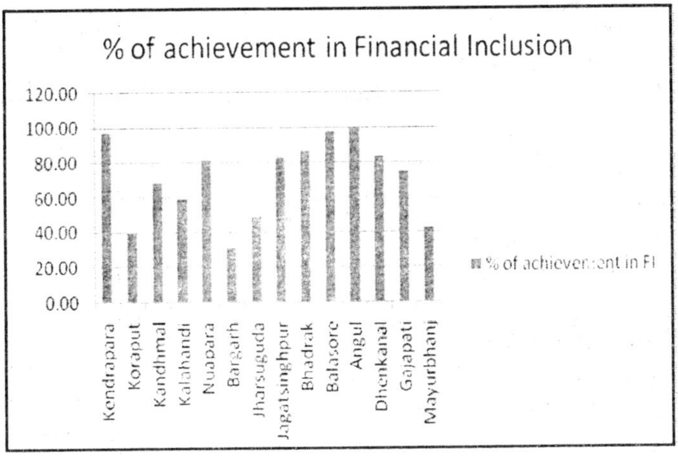

Figure 1 : % of Achievement in Financial Inclusion

Out of 30 districts of the state it is heartening that 6 districts namely Cuttack, Ganjam, Puri, Rayagada, Nayagarh, and Keonjhar have achieved 100%. The table shows case of 14 districts as data could not had for rest 10 districts. It may be seen from the diagram that all 14 districts are yet to complete opening of bank accounts for even the financially excluded households (Figure 1).

The subsequent steps such as providing regular financial services and especially financial assistance to all these households would not be easy for Banks to accomplish. Hence

Table 2
Progress Report / Information Regarding Financial Inclusion (As Of 30.11.2008)

(Amt. in lacs)

Name of the District	No. of Household Identified for Financial Inclusion	No. of Household Covered Under Financial Inclusion so far (as of 30.09.2008)	No. of Household Excluded/ remained for Financial Inclusion	No Frill A/c Opened		GCC Issued		% of Achieve-ment	Remarks (Data as on)
				Account	Amount	Account	Amount		
Kendrapara	156080	152576	3504	43267	1.72			97.75	30.11.2008
Koraput	61580	24516	37064	24516	2.66			39.81	30.11.2008
Kandhmal	69933	47896	22037	47896	10.81			68.49	30.11.2008
Kalahandi	323135	191602	131533	47966	47.98			59.29	31.10.2008
Nuapara	125390	102510	22880	21310	43.65			81.75	30.11.2008
Bargarh	232942	72657	160285	18312	14.13			31.19	30.11.2008
Jharsuguda	82923	40655	42268	8730				49.03	30.11.2008
Jagatsinghpur	116458	96551	19907	30623	506.00			82.91	30.11.2008
Bhadrak	60264	52620	7644	83488	22.40			87.32	30.11.2008
Balasore	322852	316395	6457	161325	17.50			98.00	30.11.2008
Angul	198841	198388	453	43802	119.71			99.77	30.09.2008
Dhenkanal	85015	71326	13689	65005	38.26	316	61.58	83.90	30.11.2008
Gajapati	111405	83553	27852	83553	25.82			75.00	30.11.2008
Mayurbhanj	202655	85980	116675	86860	18.30	7115	1215.20	42.43	30.11.2008

Cuttack,Ganjam, Puri, Rayagada, Nayagarh, Keonjhar has achieved 100% Financial Inclusion

Source: SLBC, Orissa

MFIs are the institutions to serve the poor households in every nook and corner of the state. From various sources it has been compiled that 9 reasonably large MFIs are operating in Orissa and their lending to the SHGs are shown in the table below.

Table 3
MFIs in Orissa as on March 31, 2008

Amount (in lacs)

Name of the MFI	*On Lending to SHGs*
Adhikar	320.00
Asmitha Microfin	5562.90
BISWA	57.85
BSFL	297.50
Gram Utthan	126.34
KAS Foundation	50.00
Mahashakti Foundation	14.00
RGVN	84.94
Swayamshree Micro Finance Services (SMCS)	182.00
	6698.03

Source: SLBC Report, Orissa

Other than the large nine MFIs mentioned in the table (Table 3) there are many NGOs which have taken up micro financing activities in the state. As a result of the MFI enactment, the NGOs might become legally constituted MFIs and take up all the activities under Financial Inclusion.

CONCLUSION

The advantages of MFIs *vis-à-vis* Commercial Banks, Regional Rural Banks and Cooperative Banks, lead us to infer that the purpose of financial inclusions as contained in the definitions discussed, may be well achieved through the MFIs, be it NGO-MFI, NBFC-MFI or self-help groups as they are. The passage of MFI Bill will go a long way in strengthening the MFIs, providing them a strong legal status, defining the operational authority etc. Poor rural households despite financial inclusion through opening of no-frills accounts or ordinary bank accounts may have to look up to the MFIs operating in the vicinity for financial assistance and allied support as well as micro insurance. It is never meant that MFIs can exclusively discharge these responsibilities nor banks can be fully loaded with those. The best arrangement would be total achievement of FI through Banks and MFIs complementing each other.

REFERENCES

Chakrabarty, K C. (2006), "Financial Inclusion: Reaching the Unreached", The Analyst, The Icfai University Press, Hyderabad.

Leladhar, V. (2006), "Taking Banking Services to the Common Man-Financial Inclusion", Reserve Bank of India Bulletin.

Mahendra Dev, S. (2006), "Financial Inclusion: Issues and Challenges", *Economic and Political Weekly.*

Thorat, U. (2006), "Financial Inclusion and Millennium Development Goals", *Reserve Bank of India Bulletin.*

Thorat, U. (2006), "Treating Bank Customers Fairly–Regulatory Initiatives", *Reserve bank of India Bulletin.*

Thorat, U. (2008), "Financial Inclusion and Information Technology", *Reserve Bank of India Bulletin.*

http://www.iibf.org.in

http://www.monycontrol.com

http://www.thehindubusinessline.com

http://theeconomictimes.com

20

MICROFINANCE: AN INNOVATION FOR DEFEATING RURAL POVERTY

Bibhudatta Nayak

THE NICHE DIVERSIFICATION OF POVERTY IN INDIA

India is a land of richness lived by poor–the development planners have kept this fact in view while drawing the planning process for the country. Despite the emphasis on sectoral developments through the initial four Five Year Plans, there was no much dent on rural poverty in the country. The study on *Poverty in India* by Prof. Dandekar and Rath in 1971 made the conviction strong that poverty and misery were widespread in India and there was an urgent need to address this issue in the planning process. Area and target group specific poverty alleviation programmes were thus introduced in the Fifth Five Year Plan for directly defeating poverty. By the end of Seventh Five Year plan, it was realized that the trickledown approach did not yield the desired effect (Ahluwalia 1986, Bardhan 1986) in tackling poverty in India-. These programmes fell short to break the jinx of poverty mainly as these were marred with:

- supply driven approach–flowing from top to down;
- met only short run objectives through providing wage employment which kept poverty in abeyance but not eradicated it;

- no social inputs to augment family welfare and social security and also address issues like inefficient house keeping, migration, wasteful practices like alcoholism, gambling, etc.;
- lack of social and economic justice to women who constituted about half of the population in India; and
- structural constraints are so pervasive that the rich and middle classes managed to derive far more benefits than those for whom the poverty alleviation programmes were meant.

There was need for reorienting poverty alleviation programmes to build 'group power' for preventing perpetuation of exploitative practices and for channelizing purchasing power in favour of low income households (Parthasarathy 1985). The poverty persisted because of government and market failure in the 'top-down' approach of managing poverty. This was the phenomenon in most of the developing economies of the world. There were instances in the seventies and the eighties in other developing countries like Kenya, Korea, Bangladesh and Nepal where various credit programmes for agriculture and rural development when modeled on participatory approach showed better impacts and results. Based on these experiences, group mode was thought of in the process for breaking the vicious circle of poverty on the following *socio-politico-economic* background of rural poor in India:

- Debt trap and resource constraints are major causes of poverty. The poor always wanted to get rid of the exploitation by the usurious informal lenders.
- Public policies often aimed at dismantling the informal credit systems but did not offer alternate sources of credit to the poor. Rather extra precautionary attitude of formal lending agencies deprived the rural poor of institutional credit.
- Rural poor, during a certain period of year, earn more than consumption. If the surplus during the glut were saved then it would help in the dearth season.

- People with homogeneous socio economic conditions at a particular locality can fight a problem common to all with a handholding support system.

MICROFINANCE AS A TOOL FOR POVERTY ERADICATION

The key to break the vicious circle of poverty was to garner savings potential of the poor and keep the poor away from borrowing from the informal lending agencies. Institutional sources could be the credit alternative, provided the poor get a reach to it. Thus a system was thought up to unite the poor into a socially homogenous group for self-help through linkage with various developmental and financial agencies under microfinance. The old practices of Rotating Savings and Credit Associations (ROSCA) and Regular Savings and Credit Associations (RESCA) were used as instruments for garnering savings of the poor and redistributing as credit among members. The research project on microfinance by Mohammad Yunus in 1979 in Bangladesh and subsequently establishment of Grameen Bank (GB) in 1983 laid the foundation of modern microfinance movement. The third international symposium on the *mobilisation of personal savings in developing countries* (1984) organised by the United Nations also highlighted the strength of internal savings to provide the basis for credit programmes for poor. In India, the accidental initiation of Self help Affinity Groups (SAGs) in the early 1980s (Fernandez 2006) graduated to SHG Bank Linkage Programme pioneered by National Bank for Agriculture and Rural Development (NABARD).

The first official interest in microfinance in India took shape during 1986-87 when NABARD supported an action research project on 'Savings and Credit Management of Self Help Groups' of Mysore Resettlement and Development Agency (MYRADA). Findings of a study in 1988-89 to examine the functioning of SHGs and possibilities of collaboration between the banks and SHGs in the mobilization of rural savings and improving the delivery of credit to the poor encouraged NABARD to take a pilot project in 1991-92 to promote 500

SHGs. Microfinance through SHG Bank linkage programme was formally launched in India in 1992-93. SHG has become synonym to Microfinance.

During the last a few years, the microfinance movement has taken a distinct shape in India with the support of many governmental and nongovernmental agencies. People on a large scale, specially the women from socially and economically backward classes, have adopted it with a great deal of sanguinity and commitment. Microfinance in India has passed through three distinct Phases. First was the Research and Development Stage, that continued until 1992-93. During this stage various studies and impact assessments were conducted to assess the problems and prospects of microfinance and different models of micro finance were developed. The second stage was the Promotional Stage that lasted up to 1999-2000. Development agencies, NGOs and government organizations introduced a host of programmes for capacity building and empowerment process for popularizing microfinance movements. Model units were established and success stories were documented and disseminated for a demonstration effect. The Growth Stage has started since 2000-01. This stage witnessed rapid growth in formation of SHGs, credit linkage and disbursement of credit flow and also graduating the SHGs to micro entreprises. Microfinance has grown rapidly and covered a large section of poor across the globe and became world's largest socio-economic movement in a span of a decade or so. By the end of March 2008, a cumulative of Rs.22,133 crore of bank credit was disbursed to 34.78 lakh SHGs in India. Around 5.8 crore poor households were benefited under microfinance in the country (NABARD 2008) making the programme the largest in the world. Microfinance in India enabled 41.60 lakh SHGs to save Rs.3513 crore outstanding with the banking sector as on 31 March 2007 (NABARD 2007). More importantly, microfinance proved the maxim that 'the poor are bankable and they can save'.

Microfinance means transactions in small amounts of both credit and saving, involving mainly small-scale and medium-scale businesses and entreprises. The poor, especially the women in rural area, are the prime reason for microfinance intervention in the developing world, including India. The poor, who cannot start a small business because of want of investments or capital, benefits the most from microfinance system. The question of whether microfinance really benefits the poor and to what extent, depends on how poverty is defined and what kind of support services microfinance offers to the poor to overcome poverty. What microfinance can do for alleviating poverty also depends on the willingness and ability of the poor to utilize what microfinance offers to them. In general, microfinance provides a window of opportunity for the poor to access easy and low cost borrowings on the one hand and provides saving facilities and induces the poor for regular savings on the other. Microfinance organizations with their credit support can only alleviate liquidity constraints of the resource-poor households. Success in such a business depends on the skill and entrepreneurship of the poor as well as local economic conditions. Many poor participants do lack such skills and benefit very little from microfinance. Keeping this in view, the microfinance promoting agencies like development banks and government and non government agencies also provide the poor with entrepreneurship and skill building training, arrange for travel and visit programmes, exposure visits, etc. Microfinance thus proffers organizational help, training, safety nets, empowerment and credit plus support services.

Microfinance in India has made great strides in delivering financial services (savings and credit) to the poor in rural areas. Strategies such as collateral-free, group-based lending and mobilization of savings increased the financial outreach of the poor. Microfinance programmes support production and consumption needs of the poor. Easy loan repayment terms level out consumption and help the unemployed to become self-employed. In certain cases the SHGs were also engaged to assist in building community roads, schools, or health facilities, and lease in common resources like panchayat ponds, land, village commons, etc. for commercial utilization. The successful SHGs were also supported with assistance from donor agencies and government poverty alleviation programmes like Revolving Fund Assistance (RFA), subsidy linked credit programmes, entrepreneurship development programmes, etc. For government and donor agencies the issue is clear. If microfinance programmes did not benefit the poor in a sustainable way, then efforts to channel resources into microfinance would be misplaced.

INSTANCES OF MICROFINANCE OVERCOMING POVERTY

The SHGs have been graduated with the increasing linkages, higher savings by members and more funds at disposal. Over the years in India rural credit, poverty alleviation and microfinance have strongly entwined to empower the rural poor, both socially as well as economically. Microfinance, though was initially designed as a tool to widen credit linkage to the inaccessible ones in rural areas, of late has been acknowledged as a development paradigm for alleviating poverty through mobilization of savings and creating investment opportunities. These programmes have provided ample scope to the borrowers to uplift their income through entrepreneurial activities and employment opportunities and consequently beat poverty. Low cost and easy credit under microfinance enabled the members to stay away from the usurious money lenders. The empowerment process through microfinance system also improved the social conditions by way of reducing alcohol consumption, family quarrels, infrastructure development, etc. While the financial review of microfinance programs in India is less promising than one would expect, their socioeconomic benefits are substantial. Findings differ from study to study because of the underlying impact assessment methodologies, but impact assessments indicate that these programs help the poor, although all participants may not benefit equally.

Khandker (1998) estimated that in the world about 5 per cent of borrowers under microfinance programme lift themselves out of poverty each year. This 5 per cent of the microfinance borrowers represents only about one per cent of the population, which means that the aggregate poverty impact of microfinance program is quite negligible. But the potential of microfinance in reducing poverty cannot be denied. We can say microfinance created scope and opportunity for the poor to overcome poverty, which was not with him/her. One has to fight the battle with exploring the skill, initiatives, entrepreneurship and market linkages available with him/her individually or in a group.

The Evaluation Study on SHG Bank Linkage Programme in Kalahandi District of Orissa (NABARD 2005) revealed that out of 997 sample members of 80 SHGs, 71 per cent of SHG members were BPL, the average annual savings of members was Rs.336, credit was accessible to poor women at a modal interest of 2 per cent per month, and the most important is, after formation of SHGs not a single member borrowed from any moneylender rather they have repaid all the old debts of money lenders. Members could access credit facilities for consumption, repayment of old debt and also commercial ventures. Microfinance could create entrepreneurship opportunities, reduced migration from rural areas and gainfully employed the rural poor in the non-agriculture seasons. The study revealed that the borrowers earned an average annual additional income of Rs.5,248 from the ventures through microfinance. It was further revealed that 25 per cent of the members were earning an annual incremental income of more than Rs.8000 while 17 per cent were not able to add to their regular income as a major chunk of their borrowings were utilized in consumption, health and other nonproductive expenditures. We can say the supplementary income had definitely helped 83 per cent of borrowers to enhance their income and made the path easy to cross the poverty line.

The study conducted in Koraput district of Orissa (Meher 2003) highlighted that that the income of all the five sample SHGs increased between 50 and 226 per cent after formation of SHG and availing microfinance facilities. In absolute terms the average household income of the SHG members have gone up by somewhere between Rs.3075 and Rs.13776. While SHG members with an annual income below Rs.10000 declined by from 67 in the pre SHG period to 36 in the Post SHG period, it in the income group between Rs.10000-20000 increased from 9 to 30 and in the income group of above Rs.20000 gone up from one to 7. Microfinance, the study highlights, reduced the extent of poverty among the SHG members.

The study of Comparative Cost Models for SHGs in Dakshin Kanada, Mysore and Hasan districts of Karnataka (NABARD 2006) also revealed evidences of attack on rural poverty through microfinance by way of increase in savings and income of the SHG members. It was estimated in the study that microfinance enabled the SHG members to save on an average Rs.780 per annum and the average annual net income per member was Rs.6482. The economic success of microfinance over time gradually increased the amount as well as frequency of regular savings of members.

A study in Chittoor, Nizamabad and Warangal districts of Andhra Pradesh(NABARD 2007a) came out with the substantiation that microfinance supported the rural women to take up micro-enterprises that could augment their income and savings. The average annual incremental income of the sample SHG members was around Rs.14,115. Members of older SHGs could earn up to an average annual incremental income of Rs.22,389. This indicated a convincing propensity of microfinance for poverty alleviation though self help.

Microfinance through SHG movement not only fetched additional income to the rural poor women but also empowered them with dignity, identification, recognition and respect. The male members and other members of the family changed their attitudes towards the women folk with the SHG movement taking off in rural areas. (Nayaka2006). SHGs grow financially and socially strong over time. Locational advantages like places with transport and communication facilities, market potential, etc. add to the vigour of effectiveness of microfinance. Handholding support from Self Help Promoting Institutions and forward and backward linkage supports help the SHGs to productively utilize the small fund they borrow under microfinance. The contentment of income through a venture from microfinance inspires the rural poor for further progress. This also creates the demonstration effect and invites others to participate and grow through microfinance.

ISSUES

Since microfinance transactions with the poor are very small, the accrued benefits from microfinance may also be small. In such a case, the important policy question is whether microfinance is indeed a real help to the poor; and whether such benefits are sustainable. Studies revealed that very few SHGs do sustain for a long period with the continuation of viable economic activity. The situation of capital constraint with the resource poor is broken by way of either savings or credit or both in the microfinance system. But this may not create a situation where the resource poor would take adequate interest to take up a viable economic activity. In many cases the enthusiasm among the members do not last for a long period and the members' intention diverts more towards getting RFAs or subsidy linked credits than undertaking self propelling viable economic activities. In such a situation making regular income log a long period is a question.

Microfinance by default has been women centric. In developing countries like India, financial and entrepreneurial decisions are mostly taken by the male members of the family. Women, especially in a rural base, are to some extent constrained to take up an entreprise beyond a certain limit because of a host of reasons and to cross this limit they have to depend on the support of the male members of the family. There are instances where the women SHG members borrow from the group or provider and hand over the entire borrowings to their male members who in turn spend waste the money in alcohol, gambling and so like vices. In many cases the male members of the families who are otherwise not eligible to avail credit from banks because of defaulting earlier borrowings or such reasons persuade the ladies to join SHGs so that bank credit can be availed by them. In such cases chances of not utilizing the borrowings in any economic venture and non-repayment of the borrowings are very high. This not only distorts the economic and social life of the poor

SHG member but also is one of the main reasons for breaking up of the SHGs. In all, motivation of the SHG members as well as their family members for resource management is utmost important for realizing the poverty alleviation potential of micro finance.

CONCLUSION

There are adequate evidences that microfinance has the force and potential to attack strongly on rural poverty. Even though poverty decreases through microfinance, albeit at a slow rate, poverty is widespread in a country like India. Microfinance is not to be blamed for this high incidence of poverty. On the other, it is significant for poverty alleviation no matter how small is its aggregate impact. Microfinance is only one among a large number of poverty reduction strategies that are pursued to reduce poverty. Microfinance borrowers or the SHGs need to be graduated to take up Income Generating Activities, Micro Entreprises and processing the local resources for Value Addition such that these can fetch good remuneration for the borrowers. Though institutional credit support is not a constraint to performing SHGs, good market linkage for the raw materials and the produce under economic venture is an essential requisite for all micro entrepreneurs. Extension supports for market oriented designs of arts and crafts, value additions to locally available raw materials and resources, sharpening the skill and artisanship of the borrowers, etc. shall definitely boost the turnover of SHGs. A concerted effort from SHG Promoting Institutions, government and development agencies can infuse a sustainable force in microfinance to almost eradicate poverty from rural India.

REFERENCES

Ahluwalia, M. S. (1986), "Rural Poverty, Agricultural Production and Prices : A Re-examination" in John W. Mellor and Gunvant M Desai (eds) *Agricultural Change and Rural Poverty*, Oxford University Press, New Delhi, p. 69-72.

Bardhan, Pranab K (1986), "Poverty and Trickle down in Rural India: A Quantitative Analysis" in John W Mellor and Gunvant M Desai (eds) *Agricultural Change and Rural Poverty*, Oxford University Press, New Delhi, p. 77-78.

Dandekar, V. M. & Rath, Nilkanth (1971), "Poverty in India", *Economic & Political Weekly*, Mumbai.

Fernandez, Aloysius P. (2006), "Sustainability of Self-Help Affinity Groups or SAGs as understood by MYRADA" in *Towards a Sustainable Microfinance Outreach in India; Experiences and Perspectives*, NABARD, GTZ and SDC.

Khandker, S. R. (1998), *Fighting Poverty with Microcredit: Experience in Bangladesh*, Oxford University Press.

Meher, Shiblal (2003), *Self-Help Groups and Poverty in Orissa*, Nabakrushna Choudhury Centre for Development Studies, Bhubaneswar, Orissa, India.

NABARD (2005), *Evaluation of SHG-Bank Linkage Programme in KBK Region of Orissa*, National Bank for Agriculture and Rural Development, Orissa Regional Office, Bhubaneswar, Orissa, India.

NABARD (2006), Comparative Cost Models for SHG in Karnataka – MFI vs. NABARD Model, National Bank for Agriculture and Rural Development, Karnataka Regional Office, Bangaluru, Karnataka, India.

NABARD (2007), Status of Micro Finance in India 2006-07, National Bank for Agriculture and Rural Development, Mumbai, India.

NABARD (2007a), Microfinance for MicroEntreprises : An Impact Evaluation of Self Help Groups, National Bank for Agriculture and Rural Development, Andhra Pradesh Regional Office, Huderabad, Andhra Pradesh, India.

NABARD (2008), Annual Report 2007-2008, National Bank for Agriculture and Rural Development, Mumbai, India.

Nayak, Bibhudatta (2006), "Socio Economic Change in KBK Region through SHG-Bank Linkage Programme", in: Prasad R R & Rajnikanth G (Eds), Rural Development and Social Change, National Institute of Rural Development, Hyderabad, India,: 372-392.

Parthasarathy, G (1985), "Reorientation of Rural Development Programmes : A note on Some Basic Issues", *Economic & Political Weekly*, November 30, pp. 2125-28.

21

MICROFINANCE–TOWARDS FINANCIAL INCLUSION OF THE POOR

G. A. Narasimham

THE CONCEPT

Micro finance is positioned as a development strategy for anti-poverty programs micro finance is considered as financing the poor. Microfinance consists of making small loans, usually less than $200, to individuals, usually women, to establish or expand a small, self-sustaining business. The micro credit delivery systems through informal channels like SHGs are considered as micro finance. Broadly micro finance includes-targeting the poor, organizing them into a group economic activity, inculcating thrift habit among members in the group, quick disbursement of small loans without any collateral at market determined interest rates, provision of financial and non-financial packages for the poor. The present paper focuses on the role of micro finance models in financial inclusion and what are the challenges of micro finance models to achieve the objective of financial inclusion and also empowerment strategy of SHGs to measure the performance indicators for effective functioning through networking in India.

There are about 200 million house holds that have no access to banks or formal financial services. A World Bank study assessing access to financial institutions found that amongst rural households in Andhra Pradesh and Uttar Pradesh, 59% lack access to deposit account and 78% lack access to credit. Considering that the majority of the 360 million poor households (urban and rural) lack access to formal financial services, the numbers of customers to be reached, and the variety and quantum of services to be provided are really large.

Micro finance in India has emerged as a powerful tool for financial inclusion reaching out to poor households as well as non-poor households who have yet to be reached by the formal sector. In the financial year 2007-08, Microfinance in India through its two major channels – SBLP and MFIs – served over 33 million Indians, up by 9 million over the previous financial year. 4 out of 5 microfinance clients in India are women. The outstanding micro-credit portfolio of India Microfinance was about Rs. 22,000 crore. 75% are accounted for by SBLP, 20% by large MFIs and 5% by medium and small MFIs. SBLP reports over Rs. 3,500 crore savings of SHG-members (2006-07). MFIs are prohibited from accepting savings; however, one third of their clients are served under the SHG-model and thus encouraged to save among themselves and/or open savings accounts with banks.

What is beginning to happen in microfinance can be seen from the perspective of what has happened to phones in India. With the right enabling environment, and intense competition amongst private sector players, mobile phones in India expanded by 160% during just one year 2003-04 (from 13 to 33 million). Mobile tariffs fell by 74% during the same period. While this is heady progress, there is a less heralded but even more powerful nationwide success on access. Microfinance is not yet at the centre stage of the Indian financial sector. The knowledge, capital and technology to address these challenges however now exist in India, although they are not yet fully aligned. With a more enabling environment and surge in economic growth, the next few years promise to be exciting for the delivery of financial services to poor people in India.

SEEDS OF CHANGE

Micro finance is often considered one of the most effective, flexible, and sustainable strategies in the fight against global poverty. The potential of these SHGs to develop as local financial intermediaries to reach the poor has gained recognition due to their community based participatory approach and sustainability–recovery rates have been significantly higher than those achieved by commercial banks inspite of loans going to poor, unorganized individuals without security or collateral. Once the NGOs have done the capacity building, it is much easier to the banks to lend to the poor since the cost of intervention through micro finance institutions is low. Success stories in neighboring countries, like Grameen Bank in Bangladesh, Bank Rakiat in Indonesia, Commercial & Industrial Bank in Philippines, etc., gave further boost to the concept in India in the 1980s. The Global Summit on Micro Finance held in Washington in February 1997 set a global target of covering 100 million poor families with credit by 2005 - it was expected that 25-30 million of these could be in India alone.

ACCESS TO CREDIT BY POOR

The poor in India define the micro-finance market. The Planning-Commission estimate of 2007-08 says 25% of the population or 250 million people live below the poverty line - there would be 140-150 million women alone living below the poverty line. Assuming that only 25% of the country's poor women are ready to adopt micro-finance as a method of poverty alleviation, it is estimated that 40-45 million poor women would need credit. Financial services could enable the poor to leverage their initiative, accelerating the process of building incomes, assets and economic security. However, conventional finance institutions seldom lend down-market to serve the needs of low-income families and women-headed households. They are very often denied access to credit for any purpose, making the discussion of the level of interest rate and other terms of finance irrelevant. Therefore the fundamental problem is not so much of unaffordable terms of loan as the lack of access to credit itself.

MICRO FINANCE AND FINANCIAL INCLUSION

In India the formal financial institutions has not been able to reach the poor households, and particularly women, in the unorganized sector. The first and the foremost significance is that the rapid spread of micro finance has provided competition to rural money lenders. Structural rigidities and overheads lead to high cost of making small loans. Organizational philosophy has not been oriented towards recognizing the poor as credit worthy. The problem has been compounded by low level of influence of the poor, either about their credit worthiness or their demand for savings services. Micro-finance programmes have often been implemented by large banks at government behest. Low levels of recovery have been further eroded due to loan waiver programmes leading to institutional disenchantment with lending to small borrowers. All this gave rise to the concept of 'micro-credit' for the poorest segment along with a new set of credit delivery techniques. Funding is no longer a problem, primarily because banks now see micro finance as a profitable opportunity to deploy their funds cost effectively by meeting their priority sector targets. Recently banks are expanding their network of operations for financial inclusion of all sections of the society The demand for credit from people earning less than 1$ a day has often been estimated at Rs.50,000 crores but more recent studies say that the actual number could be double. The scope of micro finance is much larger than what we understand today. Whoever is underserved or unserved by banks can really become a micro finance client.

TOWARDS INSTITUTIONALIZATION

With the support of NGOs an informal sector comprising small Self Help Groups (SHGs) started mobilizing savings of their members and lending these resources among the members on a micro scale. Several former NGO-MFIs are seeking to transform themselves into NBFCs. There is a changing trend towards formalization of NGOs which are buying out existing ones that have ceased operations. The MFIs are also acting as agents for insurance companies and offering micro insurance.

A growing number of MFIs are also offering health insurance, community insurance in collaboration with charitable institutions and hospitals.

SHG-BANK LINKAGES

The SHGs form the basic constituent unit of the micro finance development in India. The SHGs are informal association of 10-20 members mostly women who contribute small amounts to the savings pool. After saving for some time the lending activity begins among the members and maintaining their own accounts preferably the SHGs are linked to a bank with savings bank account and it offers loans upto four times their savings. While a census of NGOs in micro-finance is yet to be carried out, there are perhaps 250-300 NGOs, each with 50-100 Self Help Groups (SHG). Few of them, not more than 20-30 NGOs have started forming SHG Federations.

There are also agencies which provide bulk funds to the system through NGOs. Thus organizations engaged in micro finance activities in India may be categorised as Wholesalers, NGOs supporting SHG Federations and NGOs directly retailing credit borrowers or groups of borrower. The Wholesalers will include agencies like NABARD, Rashtriya Mahila Kosh-New Delhi and the Friends of Women's World Banking in Ahmedabad. Few of the NGOs supporting SHG Federations include MYRADA in Bangalore, SEWA in Ahmedabad, PRADAN in Tamilnadu and Bihar, ADITHI in Patna, SPARC in Mumbai, ASSEFA in Madras etc. While few of the NGOs directly retailing credit to Borrowers are SHARE in Hyderabad, ASA in Trichy, RDO Loyalam Bank in Manipur. The MFIs on the other hand tap loans from private banks, SIDBI, and foreign investors The average loan size for an SHG is less than Rs.4,000 and for MFI it is about Rs.5,000. Currently there are 800 MFI and 22 lakh government backed SHGs that are working as principal sources of micro credit.

The various models followed for lending include the SHGs have direct access to loans from financing banks based on their independent credit standing and saving accounts of the group are maintained and operated at the financing branch. The credit decisions are based on appraisal of individual SHGs.

SHGS–NGO MODEL

NGOs play a major role in taking initiative to promote SHGs and hold them till they stabilize. They ensure regular interaction among the members of the group in maintaining the accounts and monitor the progress of the business. After doing capacity building they dissociate with the groups giving them independence to work and manage on their own. In some models the NGOs does not dissociate with the SHGs instead they see that the group remains vibrant and also help other groups or clusters. It also continuously oversee the functioning of the group and ensure sustainability of the groups so that they do not wither away after some time loosing interest. Many of the NGOs are now looking at the sustainability of the SHGs in the country so that the groups benefit in the long run. Some of the NGOs are following business facilitator model and some are following business correspondence model for rendering financial services to various SHGs.

BANK–MFI BULK LENDING MODEL

Under this model an aggregate amount is placed with NGO-MFI by the lending institution as a term loan or as a facility out of which the MFI draws funds for lending to SHGs. In this model the appraisal of functions is done to MFI rather than to SHGs. Channelising funds from financial institutions to MFIs is feasible for effective distribution of funds among different groups.

BANK–MFI PARTNERSHIP MODEL

This model has potential of expanding the outreach of banks which are having limited network of operations. The MFIs sources loans directly from the banks This released the MFIs from capital constraints and allows them to achieve rapid increase in the outreach of self help groups. In this model the credit risk is left to the bank which makes effective used of the streangths of both the partners since the MFI/NGO continues to play the intermediary role.

THE SHG EMPOWERMENT STRATEGIES

Matured SHGs need to be encouraged on a continuous basis. This requires facilitating continuous interactions among different groups and support agencies. Right from the framing of rules and regulations for operating and managing the group to preparing an agenda for doing an economic activity or a social activity and obtaining loan from the bank or various agencies,the developments should be constantly monitored to improve the strength of the group for long run sustainability. Chanalizing the funds effectively for a stated purpose by the members should be seen and make them accountable for their achievements. This should help the group to reduce the cost of financing and risks. At a latter part of the stage they should form themselves in to mutually aided cooperative societies and formally into a local area bank which can fulfill the needs of a large community.

THE ROAD AHEAD

Despite lending credit to the millions of unserved poor consumers, the MFIs have certain roadblocks in their functioning. Reserve Bank of India came with a code of conduct for MFIs and now the central government is working on a Micro Finance Bill which is approved by the cabinet and is likely to be implemented. The bill may help to pave the way for MFIs to access savings instead of being excessively leveraged. The bill also proposes to reduce the capital requirement for MFIs with an investment of Rs.2.0 crores to Rs.25 Lakhs to register as an NBFC. The question is that whether the micro finance is serving to lift the poor people from poverty or is it serving merely as a band-aid to heal their poverty. The fact is that with the growing disbursement of banks in the SHG-Bank linkage programs over 50% of loans micro finance is one of the fastest growing areas of bank finance.

CONCLUSION

Some valuable lessons can be learned from the experience of successful Microfinance institutions. First of all, the poor repay their loans and are willing to pay for higher interest rates. The solidarity group pressure and sequential lending provide strong repayment motivation and produce extremely low default rates. The poor save and hence microfinance should provide both savings and loan facilities. This implies that banking on the poor can be a profitable business. However, attaining financial viability and sustainability is the major institutional challenge. Deposit mobilization is the major means for microfinance institutions to expand outreach by leveraging on equity. In order to be sustainable, microfinance lending should be grounded on market principles because large scale lending cannot be accomplished through subsidies.

The challenge lies in finding the level of flexibility in the credit instrument that could make it match the multiple credit requirements of the low income borrowers without imposing unbearably high cost of monitoring its end-use upon the lenders. A promising solution is to provide multi-purpose loans or composite credit for income generation, housing improvement and consumption support. Consumption loan is found to be especially important during the gestation period between commencing a new economic activity and deriving positive income. Eventually it would be ideal to enhance the creditworthiness of the poor and to make them more "bankable" to financial institutions and enable them to qualify for long-term credit from the formal sector. Microfinance institutions have a lot to contribute to this by building financial discipline and creating awareness among the poor about its long term benefits.

REFERENCES

"Micro Finance and Poverty Alleviation" Piyush Tiwari and S.M. Fahad, Housing Development Finance Corporation, Mumbai.

"The Future of Microfinance in India": The Microfinance India Conference and a Look at an Expanding Market.

Small Customers, Big Market: Commercial Banks in Microfinance, Edited by Malcolm Harper and Sukhwinder Singh Arora.

Barry, N.(1995), "The Missing Links: Financial System that Works for the Majority," Women's World Banking, New York.

Chriseten, R.Peck Rhyne, Elisabeth and Vogel, Robert C. (1994), "Maximizing the Outreach of Microenterprise Finance: The Emerging Lessons of Successful Programs," September IMCC, Arlington, Virginia.

Churchill, C.F. (1996), "An Introduction to Key Issues in Microfinance: Supervision and Regulation, Financing Sources, Expansion of Microfinance Institutions," Microfinance Network, Washington, D.C. February.

Ghate, P. *et. al* (1992), Informal Finance: Some Findings from Asia, Oxford University Press, Hong Kong.

Grameen Trust (1995), Grameen Dialogue No. 24, Dhaka, October. 2006.

Otero, M. and Rhyne, E. (1994), The New World of Micro-enterprise Finance-Building Healthy Financial Institutions for the Poor, Kumarian Press, West Harford, Connecticut.

Phelps, P. (1995), "Building Linkages Between the Micro Enterprise and Shelter Sectors: An Issues Paper," GEMINI, Betuesda, Maryland.

Women's World Banking (1994), "United Nations Expert Group on Women and Finance," New York.

"Performance of Micro Finance in India"–*Business Today*, Dec, 2006.

22

MICROFINANCE IS POWERFUL–BUT IT IS NO PANACEA FOR ECONOMIC DEVELOPMENT

Svetlana Tatuskar & Gazia Sayed

HISTORY OF MICRO FINANCE IN INDIA

India has supported social banking for a long time. Policy directions to rapidly expand rural branches, mandate credit allocations for priority sectors (including agriculture), deliver large subsidy oriented credit programmes to serve marginal communities and poor households and control interest rates have been tried for over 35 years.

The new generation microfinance was slow in coming to India. Low levels of grants to microfinance institutions, an unfavorable policy environment, substantial traditional banking infrastructure and a search for context specific solutions has constrained rapid scale up. The first breakthrough emerged from policy support to enable informal self help groups of 15-20 members (mainly women) to transact with commercial banks. These groups build up and rotate savings amongst themselves, open bank accounts and take responsibility for lending and recovering money financed by banks. With the missionary zeal of the National Bank for Agriculture and Rural Development (NABARD), insights gained by NGOs, the increasing enthusiasm of bankers and politicians and emerging successes in repayment and social impacts, this national movement now encompasses 1.4 million such groups (over 20 million members).

At a time when many questioned the need for specialized microfinance institutions (MFIs) in India, the Small Industries Development Bank of India recognized the opportunity and started implementation of an ambitious national programme. Providing loan and capacity building support to MFIs and capacity building and rating support for sector development, this programme already supports 70 MFIs and has disbursed US$46 million. A Task Force on Microfinance recognized in 1999 that microfinance is much more than microcredit, stating: "Provision of thrift, credit and other financial services and products of very small amounts to the poor in rural, semi-urban and or urban areas for enabling them to raise their income levels and improve living standards". The Self Help Group promoters emphasizes that mobilizing savings is the first building block of financial services. For many years, the national budget and other policy documents have almost equated microfinance with promoting SHG links to the banks.

The central bank notification that lending to MFIs would count towards meeting the priority sector lending targets for Banks offered the first signs of policy flexibility towards MFIs. One could argue that MFIs are small and insignificant, so why bother. The larger point is about policy space for innovation and diversity of approaches to meet large unmet demand. The insurance sector was partially opened to private and foreign investments during 2000. Over 20 insurance companies are already active and experimenting with new products, delivery methodologies and strategic partnerships.

Microfinance programmes have rapidly expanded in recent years. Some examples are:

Membership of Sa-Dhan (a leading association) has expanded from 43 to 96 Community Development Finance Institutions during 2001-04. During the same period, loans outstanding of these member MFIs have gone up from US$15 million to US$101 million.

The CARE CASHE Programme took on the challenge of working with small NGO-MFIs and community owned-managed microfinance organizations. Outreach has expanded from 39,000 to around 300,000 women members over 2001-05, Many of the 26 CASHE partners and another 136 community organizations these NGO-MFIs work with, represent the next level of emerging MFIs and some of these are already dealing with.

ICICI Bank and ABN Amro

In addition to the dominant SHG methodology, the portfolios of Grameen replicators have also grown dramatically. The outreach of SHARE Microfin Limited, for instance, grew from 1,875 to 86,905 members between 2000 and 2005 and its loan portfolio has grown from US$0.47 million to US$40 million.

Since banks face substantial priority sector targets and microfinance is beginning to be recognized as a profitable opportunity (high risk adjusted returns), a variety of partnership models between banks and MFIs have been tested. All varieties of banks - domestic and international, national and regional - have become involved, and ICICI

Bank has been at the forefront of some of the following innovations:

- Lending wholesale loan funds.
- Assessing and buying out microfinance debt (securitisation).
- Testing and rolling out specific retail products such as the Kissan (Farmer) Credit Card.
- Engaging microfinance institutions as agents, which are paid for loan origination and recovery, with loans being held on the books of banks.
- Equity investments into newly emerging MFIs.
- Banks and NGOs jointly promoting MFIs.

The 2005 national budget has further strengthened this policy perspective and the Finance Minister Mr P. Chidambram announced "Government intends to promote MFIs in a big way. The way forward, I believe, is to identify MFIs, classify and rate such institutions, and empower them to intermediate between the lending banks and the beneficiaries."

What is beginning to happen in microfinance can be seen from the perspective of what has happened to phones in India. With the right enabling environment, and intense competition amongst private sector players, mobile phones in India expanded by 160% during just one year 2003-04 (from 13 to 33 million). Mobile tariffs fell by 74% during the same period. While this is heady progress, there is a less heralded but even more powerful nationwide success on access. In the late eighties, the phone infrastructure was the monopoly of public sector institutions. Phones were difficult to get and even more difficult to use for those lacking ownership. Realization that users need not own a phone to access one led to privatization of the last mile - where a phone user could interface with a private sector provider using the public sector telecom infrastructure. Even with this policy change, today there are 2.5 million entrepreneurs selling local, national and international phone services through the length and breadth of India. Many of these are now graduating to sell internet services and could potentially be banking agents - that is the evolving story.

Small-scale enterprises form an important sector in most of the economies. In recent years, financial support for this sector has become a major component of the strategy for poverty alleviation. Several Micro-finance schemes provide loans to enable potential entrepreneurs start small-scale enterprises. Unfortunately these schemes only provide subsistence living for the proprietor with no possibility of providing jobs for others in the community.

In order to move the activities of micro-finance schemes from subsistence living to small-scale enterprises it is necessary to inject technology into the various activities.

Technology has a very important role to play in the transformation of client activities. It can improve the rate of production, level of productivity and income of the clients' operation. Furthermore, use of better technology in the management of Micro-Finance Institutions (MFI) can improve efficiency, reduce cost of administration and facilitate access of their clients to information that will improve their operations.

Indeed, most micro-finance schemes have credit policies that favour only investments that yield profit over a very short term. Since technology-driven activities tend to be usually profitable only over long-term, they are not supported. In order to change this situation, it is necessary to identify and promote policies that can enhance the technological capacity of the small-scale enterprises. The promotion of rapid socio-economic development and the eradication of poverty will require the transformation of small-scale income earning activities from subsistence living to micro-enterprises that provide jobs for others. Through the additional employment created, the operations or activities will increase the impact of the microfinance schemes and accelerate the rate of poverty reduction. It will enable the poor to become not only income-earners but also employers of the poorest of them (those that may not even qualify for micro-credit).

WHAT IS MICROFINANCE?

Microfinance (MF) is the provision of credit, savings, and other financial products.

Microfinance is provided in small amounts primarily to poor customers·usually assumed not to have the ability to save as well as being incapable to pay the high interest rates necessary to cover credit transaction costs.

Microfinance comprises different types of financial projects. Some of them are provided exclusively to women; furthermore, microfinance projects directed to other groups have women as their majority customers as well, since the majority of the poor are women.

Microfinance refers to the provision of financial services to poor or low-income clients, including consumers and the self-employed. The term also refers to the practice of sustainably delivering those services.

More broadly, it refers to a movement that envisions "a world in which as many poor and near-poor households as possible have permanent access to an appropriate range of high quality financial services, including not just credit but also savings, insurance, and fund transfers"

"Microfinance is much more than simply an income generation tool. By directly Empowering poor people, particularly women, it has become one of the key driving Mechanisms towards meeting the Millennium Development Goals, specifically the Overarching target of halving extreme poverty and hunger by 2015." Mark Malloch Brown Administrator of the United Nations Development Programme (UNDP).

"Sustainable access to microfinance helps alleviate poverty by generating income, creating jobs, allowing children to go to school, enabling families to obtain health care, and empowering people to make the choices that best serve their needs. Together, we can and must build inclusive financial sectors that help people improve their lives."

Kofi Annan, Former UN Secretary-General

A good investment climate is important because it attracts investments, which in turn leads to economic development. Microfinance (MF) is one way of creating a better investment climate for small entrepreneurs. Thus, MF may be an important tool in decreasing poverty among the people of a country.While microfinance programs mainly have been funded by donors and governments, efforts are now shifting towards promoting commercial microfinance institutes. This is commonly being done by removing regulatory obstacles, supporting credit information agencies, and making sure that non-commercial entities do not weaken market development.

Microfinance Institution (MFI) is financial institution which can be non-profit organizations, regulated financial institutions or commercial banks providing microfinance to poor clients.

Micro credit is a part of microfinance. Micro credit is the supply of credit to poor entrepreneurs, which is sometimes referred to as micro loan. Micro credit can be offered, often without collateral, to individuals or groups. Group lending is a method of micro credit that permits a number of individuals to get loans through group repayment pledges. The incentive to repay is based on peer pressure; if one individual in the group fails to repay, the other group members are responsible to make that payment. Individual micro lending, on the other hand, focuses on one individual and does not demand other individuals to offer bonds.

Micro saving is part of microfinance. Micro saving is deposits made with MFIs in the microfinance sector (Basu *et al.*, 2004, p.4). It is sometimes argued that poor people are too poor to save, but the poor already save in ways that we may not consider as "normal" savings. This is done by investing in assets that can be exchanged to cash in the future (e.g. gold jewellery, domestic animals, building materials).

GROWTH OF MICROFINANCE

The growth of microfinance is visible in many aspects. There are more than 2000 NGOs involved in the NABARD SHG-Bank linkage program. Out of these, approximately 800 NGOs are involved in some form of financial intermediation. Further, there are 350 new generation co-operatives providing thrift and credit services. According to our estimate, the present total outstanding , including Sa-Dhan members and bank linkages is approximately Rs.700 crores (Rs. 150 crores of Sa-Dhan members and another Rs. 550 crores from the Banking system). The total client base is estimated at 6-8 million as opposed to the Government of India (GOI) intention to reach 25 million clients. The growth of community institutions has taken place with the role to take social and financial intermediation. A numbers of community banks have come into existence at village and block levels call ' Federation of Self Help Groups'.

The inadequacies of the formal financial system to cater to the needs of the poor and the realization of the fact that the key to success lies in the evolution and participation of community based organizations at the grassroots level led to the emergence of new generation of MFIs.

One kind of MFI is an NGO engaged in promoting Self Help Groups (SHGs) and their federations at a cluster level and linking SHGs with Banks under the Scheme. Examples are Myrada in Karnataka, which has promoted Sanghmitra, a company of its village saving and credit sanghas, PRADAN which has established a large number of SHGs and federated them under Damodar in Bihar, Sakhi Samiti in Rajasthan. Another kind is NGO-MFI directly lending to the poor borrowers, who are either organized into SHGs or into Grameen Bank type of groups after borrowing bulk funds from SIDBI, RMK and FWWB. Examples in this category are Rashtriya Gramin Vikas Nidhi (RGVN) which runs credit and savings programme in Assam and Orissa on the lines of Grameen Bank, Bangladesh. Also we have SHARE in AP, ASA in Tamil Nadu under this category.

There are MFIs which are specifically organized as cooperatives, such as over 500 Mutually Aided Cooperative Thrift and Credit Socities (MACTS) in AP, promoted among others by Cooperative Development Foundation (CDF) and the SEWA Bank in Gujarat which also runs federations of SHGs in nine districts.

Then we have MFIs, which are organized as Non-Banking Finance Companies (NBFC) such as BASIX, CFTS Mirzapur, SHARE Microfin. Ltd and Sarvodaya Nanofinance Ltd.

THE DEVELOPMENT PROCESS THROUGH MICRO FINANCE

Micro finance is expected to play a significant role in poverty alleviation and development. The need, therefore, is to share experiences and materials which will help not only in understanding successes and failures but also provide knowledge and guidelines to strengthen and expand micro finance programmes.

In India, a variety of micro-finance schemes exist and various approaches have been practised by both GOs and NGOs. In the development sector, credit has been viewed as one of the missing inputs and therefore, a growing emphasis on re-formulating and re-strengthening micro credit programmes is observed. There are examples of spectacular successes and there are also examples of not-so-successful programmes which experienced high default rates and were unable to provide financial services in the long run. Ultimately the aim is to empower the poor and mainstream them into development. Amongst different approaches of micro-finance schemes, the process and stages remain more or less the same.

The development process through a typical micro-finance intervention can be understood with the help of Chart - 1. The ultimate aim is to attain social and economic empowerment. Successful intervention is therefore, dependent on how each of these stages have been carefully dealt with and also the capabilities of the implementing organisations in achieving the final goal, e.g., if credit delivery takes place without consolidation of SHGs, it may have problems of self-sustainability and recovery. A number of schemes under banks, central and state governments offer direct credit to potential individuals without forcing them to join SHGs. Compilation and classification of the communication materials in the directorv is done based on this development process.

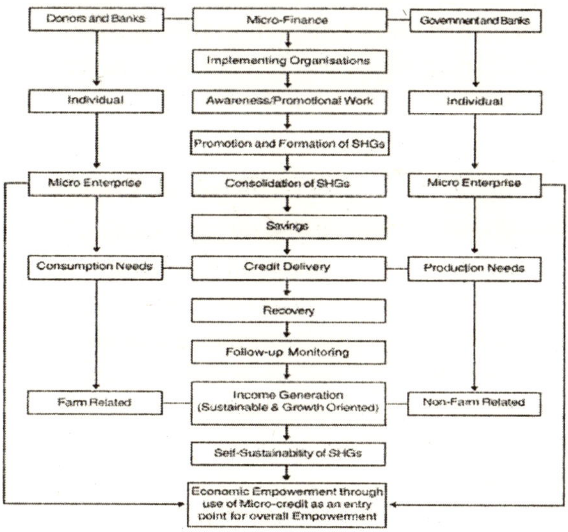

Chart 1 : Development Process through Micro-Finance

MICROFINANCE ACTIVITIES

Economic activities base upon sellers and buyer and their capacity. Sellers, before market their product, look at buyer intention and capacity. On the other hand, banking activities depend on both sellers and buyers. Lenders (financial institutions) finance both sellers and buyers for their activities. Commercial Banks invested in projects at large scale while with this, banks invested in consumer finance also. While MFIs usually don't invest in consumer finance, but give finance only for micro enterprise. MFIs encourage people to lift up their standards by doing businesses and earning from them and this is a consistent and sustainable way. In fig (2), microfinance is dedicated only to poor and explicitly for business activities. But with this, there are some indirect impacts of microfinance on the micro borrower which are alleviation of poverty, improvement in healthcare, increase in literacy and other social impacts

Many activities and characteristics are included in microfinance. Some are:

- Small and short term loans.
- Social collateral rather than financial collateral.
- Access to larger amount of loan if repayment performance is positive.
- Search and access the real poor and their business demand.
- Continuous monitoring of business.
- Loan on higher interest rates due expensive financial transactions and risk factor.
- Easy way to access finance, therefore not too much paper work, and easy and short procedures.
- Offering saving services to borrowers even for smallest amount.
- Offer training services to borrower's business development.
- Literacy training to borrowers so that they can come up with competence to daily business problems and its solutions.
- Health care, social services and other skill training services to provide borrower a sustainable base for their business development.

MICRO-FINANCE AND POVERTY ALLEVIATION

Most poor people manage to mobilize resources to develop their enterprises and their dwellings slowly over time. Financial services could enable the poor to leverage their initiative, accelerating the process of building incomes, assets and economic security. However, conventional finance institutions seldom lend down-market to serve the needs of low-income families and women-headed households. They are very often denied access to credit for any purpose, making the discussion of the level of interest rate and other terms of finance irrelevant. Therefore, the fundamental problem is not so much of unaffordable terms of loan as the lack of access to credit itself (Kim 1995).

The lack of access to credit for the poor is attributable to practical difficulties arising from the discrepancy between the mode of operation followed by financial institutions and the economic characteristics and financing needs of low-income households. A large number of small loans are needed to serve the poor, but lenders prefer dealing with large loans in small numbers to minimize administration costs. They also look for collateral with a clear title-which many low-income households do not have. In addition, bankers tend to consider low income households a bad risk imposing exceedingly high information monitoring costs on operation.

Over the last ten years, however, successful experiences in providing finance to small entrepreneur and producers demonstrate that poor people, when given access to responsive and timely financial services at market rates, repay their loans and use the proceeds to increase their income and assets. Community banks, NGOs and grassroot savings and credit groups around the world have shown that these microenterprise loans can be profitable for borrowers and for the lenders, making microfinance one of the most effective poverty reducing strategies.

To the extent that microfinance institutions become financially viable, self sustaining, and integral to the communities in which they operate, they have the potential to attract more resources and expand services to clients. Despite the success of microfinance institutions, only about 2% of world's roughly 500 million small entrepreneur is estimated to have access to financial services (Barry et al. 1996). Although there is demand for credit by poor and women at market interest rates, the volume of financial transaction of microfinance institution must reach a certain level before their financial operation becomes self sustaining. In other words, although microfinance offers a promising institutional structure to provide access to credit to the poor, the scale problem needs to be resolved so that it can reach the vast majority of potential customers who demand access to credit at market rates. The question then is how microenterprise lending geared to providing short term capital to small businesses in the informal sector can be sustained as an integral part of the financial sector and how their financial services can be further expanded using the principles, standards and modalities that have proven to be effective. To be successful, financial intermediaries that provide services and generate domestic resources must have the capacity to meet high performance standards. They must achieve excellent repayments and provide access to clients. And they must build toward operating and financial self-sufficiency and expanding client reach. In order to do so, microfinance institutions need to find ways to cut down on their administrative costs and also to broaden their resource base. Cost reductions can be achieved through simplified and decentralized loan application, approval and collection processes, for instance, through group loans which give borrowers responsibilities for much of the loan application process, allow the loan officers to handle many more clients and hence reduce costs (Otero *et al.* 1994).

Microfinance institutions can broaden their resource base by mobilizing savings, accessing capital markets, loan funds and effective institutional development support. A logical way to tap capital market is securitization through a corporation that purchases loans made by microenterprise institutions with the funds raised through the bonds issuance on the capital market. Microfinance institutions can either provide savings services directly through deposit taking or make arrangements with other financial institutions to provide savings facilities to tap small savings in a flexible manner (Barry 1995). Convenience of location, positive real rate of return, liquidity, and security of savings are essential ingredients of successful savings mobilization (Christen et al. 1994).

Once microfinance institutions are engaged in deposit taking in order to mobilize household savings, they become financial intermediaries. Consequently, prudential financial regulations become necessary to ensure the solvency and financial soundness of the institution and to protect the depositors. However, excessive regulations that do not consider the nature of microfinance institution and their operation can hamper their viability. In view of small loan size, microfinance institutions should be subjected to a minimum capital requirement which is lower than that applicable to commercial banks. On the other hand, a more stringent capital adequacy rate (the ratio between capital and risk assets) should be maintained because microfinance institutions provide uncollateralized loans.

Governments should provide an enabling legal and regulatory framework which encourages the development of a range of institutions and allows them to operate as recognized financial intermediaries subject to simple supervisory and reporting requirements. Usury laws should be repelled or relaxed and microfinance institutions should be given freedom of setting interest rates and fees in order to cover operating and finance costs from interest revenues within a reasonable amount of time. Government could also facilitate the process of transition to a sustainable level of operation by providing support to the lending institutions in their early stage of development through credit enhancement mechanisms or subsidies.

One way of expanding the successful operation of microfinance institutions in the informal sector is through strengthened linkages with their formal sector counterparts. A mutually beneficial partnership should be based on comparative strengths of each sectors. Informal sector microfinance institutions have comparative advantage in terms of small transaction costs achieved through adaptability and flexibility of operations (Ghate et al. 1992). They are better equipped to deal with credit assessment of the urban poor and hence to absorb the transaction costs associated with loan processing. On the other hand, formal sector institutions have access to broader resource-base and high leverage through deposit mobilization (Christen et al. 1994). Microfinance institutions could also serve as intermediaries between borrowers and the formal financial sector and on-lend funds backed by a public sector guarantee (Phelps 1995). Business-like NGOs can offer commercial banks ways of funding micro entrepreneurs at low cost and risk, for example, through leveraged bank-NGO-client credit lines.

MICRO FINANCE INSTITUTIONS

Indian microfinance is dominated by two operational approaches: self-help groups (SHGs), and microfinance institutions (MFIs), in addition to a few cooperative forms. The SHG model was initiated by the National Bank for Agriculture and Rural Development (NABARD) through the SHG-Bank Linkage Programme in the early 1990s. Today the SHG model, which links informal groups of women to the mainstream banking system, has the largest outreach to microfinance clients in the world. MFIs emerged in the late 1990s to harness social and commercial funds available for on-lending to clients. Today there are over 1,000 Indian MFIs.

Formal Sectors

Traditionally, the formal sector Banking Institutions in India have been serving only the needs of the commercial sector and providing loans for middle and upper income groups. Similarly, for housing the HFIs have generally not evolved a lending product to serve the needs of the Very LIG primarily because of the perceived risks of lending to this sector.

Following risks are generally perceived by the formal sector financial institutions:

- Credit Risk
- High transaction and service cost
- Absence of land tenure for financing housing
- Irregular flow of income due to seasonality
- Lack of tangible proof for assessment of income
- Unacceptable collaterals such as crops, utensils and jewellery.

As far as the formal financial institutions are concerned, there are Commercial Banks, Housing Finance Institutions (HFIs), NABARD, Rural Development Banks (RDBs), Land Development Banks and Co-operative Banks (CBs). As regards the Co-operative Structures, the Urban Co-operative Banks (UCB) or Urban Credit Co-operative Societies (UCCS) are the two primary co-operative financial institutions operating in the urban areas. There are about 1400 UCBs with over 3400 branches in India having 14 million members. Their total lending outstanding in 1990-91 has been reported at over Rs 80 billion with deposits worth Rs 101 billion.

Similarly there exist about 32000 credit Co-operative societies with over 15 million members with their total outstanding lending in 1990-91 being Rs 20 billion with deposits of Rs 12 billion. Few of the UCCS also have external borrowings from the District Central Co-operative Banks (DCCBs) at 18-19%. The loans given by the UCBs or the UCCS are for short term and unsecured except for few which are secured by personal guarantees. The most effective security being the group or the peer pressure.

The Government has taken several initiatives to strengthen the institutional rural credit system. The rural branch network of commercial banks have been expanded and certain policy prescriptions imposed in order to ensure greater flow of credit to agriculture and other preferred sectors. The commercial banks are required to ensure that 40% of total credit is provided to the priority sectors out of which 18% in the form of direct finance to agriculture and 25% to priority sector in favour of weaker sections besides maintaining a credit deposit ratio of 60% in rural and semi-urban branches. Further the IRDP introduced in 1979 ensures supply of credit and subsidies to weaker section beneficiaries. Although these measures have helped in widening the access of rural households to institutional credit, vast majority of the rural poor have still not been covered. Also, such lending done under the poverty alleviation schemes suffered high repayment defaults and left little sustainable impact on the economic condition of the beneficiaries.

Informal Financial Sources

The informal financial sources generally include funds available from family sources or local money lenders. The local money lenders charge exorbitant rates, generally ranging from 36% to 60% interest due to their monopoly in the absence of any other source of credit for non-conventional needs. Chit Funds and Bishis are other forms of credit system operated by groups of people for their mutual benefit which however, have their own limitations. The experience of these informal intermediaries shows that although the savings of group members, small in nature do not attract high returns, it is still practiced due to security reasons and for getting loans at lower rates compared to that available from money lenders. These are short term loans meant for crisis, consumption and income generation needs of the members. The interest rates on such credit are not subsidized and generally range between 12 to 36%. Most of the loans are unsecured. In few cases personal or group guarantees or other collaterals like jewellery is offered as security.

MODELS OF MICROFINANCE

Grameen Model

In Grameen model, primary unit to whom lending fund is a group of 5 members that organize and apply for loan. In first round, loan is granted for two members to invest in their business. If these two members become successful to repay amount, then four to six weeks later, next two members are granted for loan. Last one member will be eligible for loan if previous two repay loan successfully. Repayment of loan open door for next loan and then go on if all members repay loan successfully. If anyone of group member will default in her loan, whole group will be disqualified for further loan. So this rather to financial collateral, social collateral is involved.

Each group has its own president and secretary to coordinate all activities among their own group and to communicate and coordinate with other groups. Eight groups are then organized at center level, by which a bank officer deals with these all eight groups. This center of eight groups has its own center chief and center group leader (Khan, Rehman, 2007). According Sengupta, Aubuchon (2008), first time, bank granted loan $100 and bank require to repayment of 10 percent amount, at rate of per annum, weekly. This repayment ensures to user for loan security, and also encourages them for savings. Along with five percent of loan deposited in group account for emergency and social need. For example, in case of need of health care of any one member, in case of emergency, this five percent deposit will be use.

In Grameen model, unique and innovative approach of group lending is used. As Sengupta, Aubuchon (2008) described that group lending have many benefits. First, group usually organize in members who are neighbor to each other, those can understand each other well and recognize their needs. Second, if anyone of group member will not present in group meeting, leader or other member can pay its installment. We can say that there is a kind of mutual understanding between all members. Third, in south Asia generally, and in Bangladesh specially, there are social pressures among members of society with social bindings with them. If one member of group will not pay even one installment, social pressure will be levied from all eight groups on this member. Ultimately she will try to pay installments. This leads to the reduction of risk.

Progressive Lending-Banco Sol Model

Grameen model of microfinance emphasize on lending to villagers and keep loan lending on in smaller amount. The other core concept of model is formation of groups and these groups are eligible to take loan, no option of loan for individuals. Idea of progressive lending (Agion&Morduch, 2005, pp.119) introduced to lend loan to individuals with group lending. Amount of loan will increase after completion of every repayment schedule. But other characteristics of Grameen model (Group lending) are included in this method, like targeting to poor, women, group formation, and public payment. No doubt, progressive lending is an extension of group lending (Grameen Model) but now many MFIs are adopting this approach. In this model of "Progressive lending", microlenders are flexible about collateral and lend loan to group with individuals also.

This method is very helpful in areas with low population densities or highly diverse population where group forming is not so easy due to different ratio of safe and risky borrowers. This model is adopted by Banco Sol in Bolivia. In Bolivia, there was different situation when populist regime left government and there were high ratio of unemployment in urban areas. To come to fulfill the need of time, Banco Sol started operations in microfinance with progressive lending. Therefore we can say that microfinance approaches are evolved due to different political, ideological and social conditions. According to Weiss Montgomery (2004, pp.3) "Microfinance in Latin America developed under quite different conditions. In Bolivia, a collapsing populist regime led to widespread unemployment. Banco Sol, a pioneering microfinance institution in the region, developed to address the problem of urban unemployment and provide credit to the cash-strapped informal sector. The notion of commercial profitability was embraced relatively early in this approach."

Bangladesh–Grameen Bank

In Bangladesh, where about one third of the world's estimated 30-40 million micro borrowers reside, the growth has come from specialised microfinance NGO's and Grameen Bank. What began with a few small grants and loans from international donors, has now provided over 100 million dollars in loans. The most distinctive feature of the credit delivery system is the absence of middle men between the credit supplier and end user. The bank's cumulative recovery rate is an astounding 98 percent. Grameen Bank has its own special legal structure, and does not fall under regulatory oversight of the central bank. The bank also aims to raise health and environmental consciousness. Each of its members must plant at least one sapling a year as part of an afforestation programme. Grameen is perhaps the only bank in the world that encourages birth control, sanitation and a clean environment as part of its lending policy (Yunus, 2001).

India–SHG Bank Linkage

In India, despite the large size and depth of its financial system, the majority of the rural poor do not have access to formal finance and financial services. For this reason, innovative microfinance initiatives pioneered by nongovernmental organizations strove to create links between commercial banks, NGOs, and informal local groups to create the "SHG Bank Linkage".

The success of SHG Bank Linkage has been largely attributed to good policy and strong leadership, in conjunction with facilitating government policy and legal framework. India's approach to microfinance – making it profitable and so widely available – helped the country reduce the incidence of poverty from about 40 percent of the population in the mid-1970's to about 11 percent in 1996 (Robinson, 2002). Members of SHG recognise that "several challenges lie ahead," but still believe it has "the right ingredients to be scaled-up into offering mass access to finance for the rural poor while improving sustainability." (World Bank, 2003)

Foundation for International Community Assistance in Peru (FINCA)

FINCA is a small, non-profit, but financially sustainable, microfinance institution that has been operating in Peru since 1993, and was associated with FINCA International, a large USbased, non-profit organization responsible for creating and replicating the village banking methodology around the world. FINCA's mission is to improve the socio-economic situation of the poor and empower women through the promotion of the village-banking methodology. By providing them with working capital to increase inventory and invest in their businesses, FINCA expects to increase the earned income of its clients, primarily poor women with no collateral.

In addition to providing credit, FINCA teaches its clients to save by requiring weekly or monthly savings deposits that correspond to the size of the loan the client has taken out and by encouraging additional voluntary savings for which they receive market interest rates. FINCA further aims to empower clients by giving them the opportunity to run their banks through their rotating participation on the village-bank board.

Thailand-KIAsia

KIAsia offers capacity development services for community microfinance groups and community enterprises to strengthen their management capability. The KIAsia approach focuses on building sustainability in targeted communities by enabling community members to have access to needed financial and basic non-financial services for community enterprises. KIAsia utilizes a training curriculum it has developed in partnership with an internationally renowned American expert.

The curriculum focuses on concepts and tools for microfinance management following best practices localized to meet the needs of Thailand's social and cultural environment. The microfinance team works closely with community leaders and the management committees of community saving groups to provide technical assistance, microfinance training, and entrepreneurship training. Follow-on consulting is provided to community member entrepreneurs who borrow from the funds to invest in community enterprises. Small grants are sometimes provided to qualified community (groups) to reinforce their lending capacity and accelerate their growth with an ultimate goal to develop a sustainable community financing mechanism equipped with know-how in microfinance and entrepreneurship.

The program is generally implemented at two levels as follows:

(1) Capacity building training and consulting for community leaders and managers of targeted community funds.

(2) Training and consulting assistance is provided to equip micro-business owners with appropriate business skills and guide them from start-up to sustainability. Housewives are encouraged, trained to start and run cooperative-style businesses.

Empowerment of women through microfinance

In the theoretical chapter two Ostergaard (1992) suggests that since gender relations are not biologically fixed they can be changed by policies with the aim to re-shape opinions. Around the world, there are microfinance programs designed to empower women. This is often done, not only because when women control the income of the household children get more education and health care as Lundberg et al. (1996) suggest, but also because empowerment of women is important for the sake of the women themselves.

This part examines if microfinance could be a way of empowering women in Serbia. Marjanovic (2006-06-15) states that in Serbia "Microfinance would of course be a way of empowering women both in the family and in the community". Kralj (2006-06-14) agrees and states that women get empowered by being the one in the household who is responsible for the borrowing. Further, when female entrepreneurs in villages in Serbia have been offered loans for some time, Kralj (2006-06-14) notices, the mentality of the community usually changes somewhat to being more positive to female entrepreneurs. In accordance with Littelfield et al. (2003) in the theoretical chapter, Bukilica38 (2006-06-12) states that women get more of a say when they get to be the ones in the households taking the loans (Bukilica, 2006-06-12).

WEAKNESSES OF EXISTING MICROFINANCE MODELS

One of the most successful models discussed around the world is the Grameen type. The bank has successfully served the rural poor in Bangladesh with no physical collateral relying on group responsibility to replace the collateral requirements. This model, however, has some weaknesses. It involves too much of external subsidy which is not replicable Grameen bank has not oriented itself towards mobilizing peoples' resources. The repayment system of 50 weekly equal installments is not practical because poor do not have a stable job and have to migrate to other places for jobs. If the communities are agrarian during lean seasons it becomes impossible for them to repay the loan. Pressure for high repayment drives members to money lenders. Credit alone cannot alleviate poverty and the Grameen model is based only on credit. Micro-finance is time taking process. Haste can lead to wrong selection of activities and beneficiaries.

Another model is Kerala model (Shreyas). The rules make it difficult to give adequate credit (only 40-50 percent of amount available for lending). In Nari Nidhi/Pradan system perhaps not reaching the very poor.

Most of the existing microfinance institutions are facing problems regarding skilled labour which is not available for local level accounting. Drop out of trained staff is very high. One alternative is automation which is not looked at as yet. Most of the models do not lend for agriculture. Agriculture lending has not been experimented.

Risk Management: Yield Risk and Price Risk

Insurance & Commodity Future Exchange could be explored. All the models lack in appropriate legal and financial structure. There is a need to have a sub-group to brainstorm on statutory structure/ownership control/management/taxation aspects/ financial sector prudential norms. A forum/network of micro-financier (self regulating organization) is desired.

A NEW PARADIGM

A new paradigm that emerges is that it is very critical to link poor to formal financial system, whatever the mechanism may be, if the goal of poverty alleviation has to be achieved. NGOs and CBOs have been involved in community development for long and the experience shows that they have been able to improve the quality of life of poor, if this is an indicator of development. The strengths and weaknesses of existing NGOs/CBOs and microfinance institutions in India indicate that despite their best of efforts they have not been able to link themselves with formal systems. There are, however, certain unresolved dilemmas regarding the nature of the intermediary institutions. There are arguments both for and against each structure. These dilemmas are very contextual and only strengthen the argument that no unique model is applicable for all situations. They have to be context specific.

Dilemmas

Community Based	*Investor Owned*
Community Managed	Professionally managed
Community (self) financed	Accepting outside funds for on-lending
Integrated (social & finance)	Minimalist (finance only)
Non profit/mutual benefit	For profit
Only for poor	For all under served clients
'Self regulated'	Externally regulated

The four pillars of microfinance credit system (Figure. 1) are supply, demand for finance, intermediation and regulation. Whatever may the model of the intermediary institution, the end situation is accessibility of finance to poor. The following tables indicate the existing and desired situation for each component.

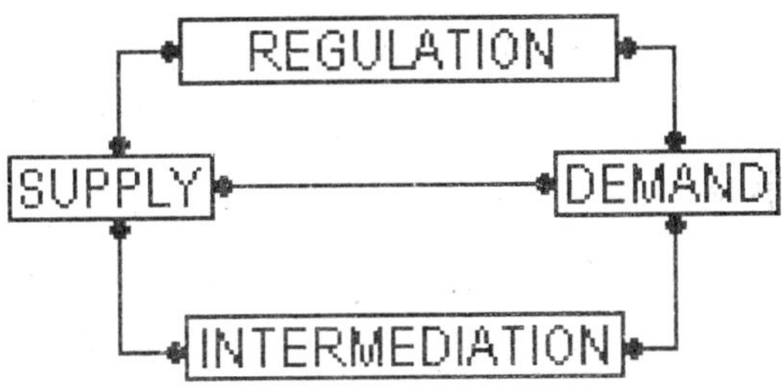

Figure 1

Demand

Existing Situation	*Desired Situation*
fragmented	Organized
Undifferentiated	Differentiated (for consumption, housing)
Addicted, corrupted by capital & subsidies	De addicted from capital & subsidies
Communities not aware of rights and responsibilities	Aware of rights and responsibilities

Supply

Existing Situation	Desired Situation
Grant based (Foreign/GOI)	Regular fund sources (borrowings/ deposits)
Directed Credit - unwilling and corrupt	Demand responsive
Not linked with mainstream	Part of mainstream (banks/FIs)
Mainly focused for credit	Add savings and insurance
Dominated	Reduce dominance of informal, unregulated suppliers

Intermediation

Existing Situation	Desired Situation
Non specialized	Specialized in financial services
Not oriented to financial analysis	Thorough in financial analysis
Non profit capital	For profit
Not linked to mainstream FIs	Link up to FIs
Not organized	Self regulating

Regulation

Existing Situation	Desired Situation
Focused on formal service providers (informal not regulated)	include/informal recognize e.g. SHGs
regulating the wrong things e.g. interest rates	Regulate rules of game
Multiple and conflicting (FCRA, RBI, IT, ROC, MOF/FIPB, ROS/Commerce)	Coherence and coordination across regulators
Negatively oriented	Enabling environment

CHALLENGES AHEAD

A World Bank study assessing access to financial institutions found that amongst rural households in Andhra Pradesh and Uttar Pradesh, 59% lack access to deposit account and 78% lack access to credit. Considering that the majority of the 360 million poor households (urban and rural) lack access to formal financial services, the numbers of customers to be reached, and the variety and quantum of services to be provided are really large. Vijay Mahajan, Managing Director of BASICS, estimated that 90 million farm holdings, 30 million non-agricultural enterprises and 50 million landless households in India collectively need approx US$30 billion credit annually.[4] This is about 5% of India's GDP and does not seem an unreasonable estimate.

A tiny segment of this US$30 billion potential market has been reached so far and this is unlikely to be addressed by MFIs and NGOs alone. Reaching this market requires serious capital, technology and human resources. However, 80% of the financial sector is still controlled by public sector institutions. Competition, consolidation and convergence are all being discussed to improve efficiency and outreach but significant opposition remains; for example, the All India Bank Employees Association has threatened to strike if the Government proceeds with its policy of reducing its capital in public sector banks, merging public sector banks or even enhancing Foreign Direct Investments in Indian private banks. There is a significant and growing gap between surging growth in South India, which contrasts with the stagnation in Eastern, Central and North Eastern India. Microfinance on its own is unlikely to be able to address formidable challenges of underdevelopment, poor infrastructure and governance.

The Self Help Group movement is beginning to focus on issues of quality and there were some interesting discussions on embedding social performance monitoring as a part of the regular management information systems.

The reality of the high transaction costs of serving small customers, their continuing dependence on the informal sector, the fact that most bankers shy away from retailing to this market as a business opportunity, and the poor quality of services currently provided does not figure prominently in this discourse. While the central bank has deregulated most interest rates, including lending to and by MFIs, interest rates restrictions on commercial bank for retail loans below US$5,000 (all microfinance and beyond) remain and caps on deposit rates also discourage sharing transaction costs with customers.

If the right indicators are monitored and operational freedom and incentives are clear, both public and private banks will have the capacity to rapidly address the remaining challenges.

CONCLUSION

Some valuable lessons can be drawn from the experience of successful Microfinance operation. First of all, the poor repay their loans and are willing to pay for higher interest rates than commercial banks provided that access to credit is provided. The solidarity group pressure and sequential lending provide strong repayment motivation and produce extremely low default rates. Secondly, the poor save and hence microfinance should provide both savings and loan facilities. These two findings imply that banking on the poor can be a profitable business. However, attaining financial viability and sustainability is the major institutional challenge. Deposit mobilization is the major means for microfinance institutions to expand outreach by leveraging equity (Sacay et al 1996). In order to be sustainable, microfinance lending should be grounded on market principles because large scale lending cannot be accomplished through subsidies.

A main conclusion of this paper is that microfinance can contribute to solving the problem of inadequate housing and urban services as an integral part of poverty alleviation programmes. The challenge lies in finding the level of flexibility in the credit instrument that could make it match the multiple credit requirements of the low income borrowers without imposing unbearably high cost of monitoring its end-use upon the lenders. A promising solution is to provide multi-purpose loans or composite credit for income generation, housing improvement and consumption support. Consumption loan is found to be especially important during the gestation period between commencing a new economic activity and deriving positive income.

Eventually it would be ideal to enhance the creditworthiness of the poor and to make them more "bankable" to financial institutions and enable them to qualify for long-term credit from the formal sector. Microfinance institutions have a lot to contribute to this by building financial discipline and educating borrowers about repayment requirements. Microfinance is not yet at the centre stage of the Indian financial sector. The knowledge, capital and technology to address these challenges however now exist in India, although they are not yet fully aligned. With a more enabling environment and surge in economic growth, the next few years promise to be exciting for the delivery of financial services to poor people in India.

REFERENCES

Barry, N.(1995), "The Missing Links: Financial System that Works for the Majority," Women's World Banking, New York.

Barry, Nancy, Armacost, Nicola and Kawas Celina (1996), "Putting Poor People's Economics at the Center of Urban Strategies," Women's World Banking, New York.

Chriseten, R.Peck Rhyne, Elisabeth and Vogel, Robert C. (1994), "Maximizing the Outreach of Microenterprise Finance: The Emerging Lessons of Successful Programs," September IMCC, Arlington, Virginia.

Churchill, C. F. (1996), "An Introduction to Key Issues in Microfinance: Supervision and Regulation, Financing Sources, Expansion of Microfinance Institutions," Microfinance Network, Washington, D.C. February.

Ghate, P. *et. al* (1992), Informal Finance: Some Findings from Asia, Oxford University Press, Hong Kong.

Grameen Trust (1995), Grameen Dialogue No.24, Dhaka, October.

Kim Kyung-Hwan (1995), "Access to Credit, Term of Housing Finance and Affordability of Housing," Housing Finance International 9(4), June 22-27.

Otero, M. and Rhyne, E. (1994), The New World of Micro-enterprise Finance-Building Healthy Financial Institutions for the Poor, Kumarian Press, West Harford, Connecticut.

Phelps, P. (1995), "Building Linkages Between the Microenterprise and Shelter Sectors: An Issues Paper," GEMINI, Betuesda, Maryland.

UNCHS and ILO (1995) Shelter Provision and Employment Generation, Geneva.

Women's World Banking (1994) "United Nations Expert Group on Women and Finance," New York.

23

ROLE OF SERVICE QUALITY IN MICROFINANCE IN THE INDIAN CONTEXT

Pinaki Ranjan Bhattacharyya & Sumita Bhattacharya

INTRODUCTION

The world of finance has undergone a sea change in the last two decades. This change has not taken place in the quality of the richer or well-to-do class. But this has more occurred in the lower strata of the society, where there has been a trend amongst the poor to save, to borrow and also to help others in the same social strata to sustain and make a proper living. This new trend has been considered as microfinance.

According to Robinson(1998), "Microfinance refers to small-scale financial services for both credits and deposits-that are provided to people who farm or fish or herd; operate small or microenterprises where goods are produced, recycled, repaired or traded; provide services; work for wages or commissions; gain income from renting out small amounts of land, vehicles, draft animals, or machinery and tools; and to other individuals and local groups in developing countries, in both rural and urban areas." The definition speaks volumes for the tremendous scope that this sector has thrown open to financial institutions, who at one point of time were more interested to extend credit to the bigger players and in the process, had huge amount of NPAs. The experimentation with the subsidised credit turned out to be failure as the concept of accessing the credit by the poor was totally overlooked. Studies revealed that the poor section could not access the credit, contrary to the belief that poor are concerned about the interest rate. It was also found that poor can and will save and can use wide variety of financial services such as remittances facilities and insurance products (Srinivasan and Sriram, 2003). It has been found that this concept can be addressed by those institutions that are able to provide financial services to poor people on a sustainable, profitable basis. As Littlefield, Morduch and Hashmi (2003) has mentioned, "Microfinance has demonstrated its potential to assist the poor to make significant strides towards reducing their vulnerability, improving their livelihoods, paying for basic health care and financing their children's education." The vast majority of Microfinance Institutions (MFIs) having the same functional credentials to offer short-term credit products, the clients have an option to stay or leave the current service provider at the end of every loan cycle or exercise their choice.

In India, microfinance has become an important developmental and economic tool that has caught the imagination of banks and other financial institutions on one hand and NGO's on the other. The structure of MFIs have made NGO's to convert themselves into self-help groups (SHGs) or banks. According to Deep Joshi (2003), NGOs are more concentrated in forming SHG's that function independent of promoters. These NGO's either access to revolving funds from donors or may link groups to banks for small sums where repayment history is yet to catch up and has no direct consequence. In the process, these NGOs have now adopted to the facilitator role rather than the lender role. Another important point that can be noted is that Banks and Insurance companies have realised that NGOs offer a gateway to the huge market generated by the households belonging to the lower-income households, and have established business alliance with them. Agri-input and processing companies such as EID

Parry, FMCG major Hindustan Lever and consumer durable companies Philips have realised the potential of this huge market and are actively using SHG's as entry points for business development. Grameen Banks in Bangladesh can also be considered to be using a model for reaching the masses which is known as Grameen Model. According to Harper (1999), "Grameen Bank and some of its "replicators" outside and within India have introduced more flexible products for farming, housing and other purposes. But this model is more time consuming for its execution, and the only decision to make as a group is whether or not to accept their fellow members' loan proposals, though a formality, since loans are disbursed on a strict quota basis".

Another model in this area is SHG model which starts off with savings as base. The model works on the lines of Grameen Model but is not so regimented. The essential design elements of the SHG model are as follows:

(1) Homogeneous affinity group of 15-20 members

(2) Regular meetings

(3) Regular savings

(4) Lending Decisions are of the group

(5) Group selects their leaders

(6) Group accessed external funds

PROBLEM DEFINITION

The different models which we have mentioned above are all effective but they are not free from limitations. Since there is no single external agency channeling credit, there is every danger that groups might wither away after a while, if not supported by the leading institutions. This may create a gap which will lead to degradation of service quality. The managers face tremendous pressure to demonstrate that their service is customer-focused and continuous performance improvement is being delivered. According to Brown and Bond (1995), "the gap model is one of the best received and most heuristically valuable contributions to the services literature". The model identifies seven key discrepancies or gaps relating to managerial perceptions of service quality, and tasks associated with service delivery to customers. The first six gaps (Gap1, Gap 2, Gap 3, Gap 4, Gap 6 and Gap 7) are identified as functions of the way in which service is delivered, whereas Gap 5 pertains to the customer and as such is considered to be the true measure of service quality. Measurement of service quality in the service sector should take into account customer expectations of service as well as perceptions of service. As Robinson (1999) mentioned, "it is apparent that there is little consensus of opinion and much disagreement about how to measure service quality". The most extensively used approach being used for measuring the service quality is the SERVQUAL method (Parasuraman et al 1985, 1986, 1988, 1991, 1993, 1994; Zeithaml et al 1990), to compare customer's expectations before a service encounter and their perceptions of the actual service delivered (Gronroos 1982; Lewis and Booms 1983). The 5(five) generic factors- Tangibles, Reliability, Responsiveness, Assurance, Empathy measures the customers expectations and perceptions.

This method if adopted for Microfinance may not be appropriate as it will not be able to reflect the true image if there is lack of information or the customers are unable to explicitly express their problem

METHODS ADOPTED

Service Quality had been assured by ensuring that the MFI's follow the following steps:

(1) Framing a proper marketing strategy

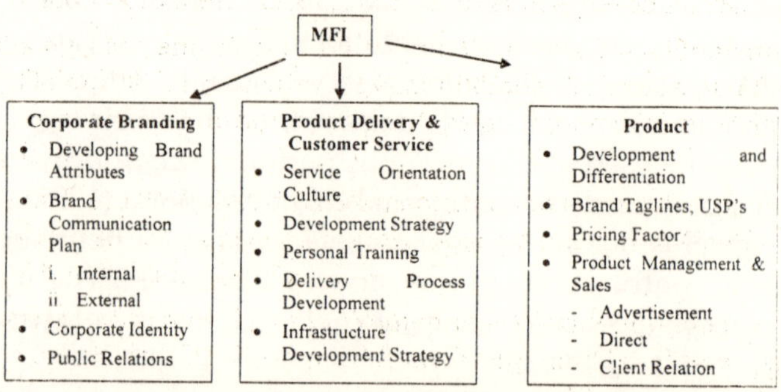

(2) Analysing the market-The following points should be considered while analysing the market.

   (a) Sizing the market and its growth characteristics in terms of (i) market size (ii) potential growth drivers (iii) potentially important sub-markets or segments (iv) segments reflecting more sustained demand and less sustained demand

   (b) Market Cost Structure and profitability in terms of (i) attractiveness of the market segment (ii) substitute products and competitor intensity profile (iii) bargaining strength of customers and suppliers

   (c) Distribution Channel–whether existing channels are optimal or whether alternate channels are changing and if so, their implication

(3) Analysing whether there exists a competitor or not– This is done by scanning the nature of the competitor environment with reference to the different P's in marketing for primary competition

(4) Analysing the customers–This refers to understanding the customer base with reference to (i) customer profile and demographic trends (ii) product usage patterns and their demand drivers (iii) profitability analysis for customers in terms of segment and profitability (iv) customer satisfaction with supplier service (v) product attribute satisfaction etc.

(5) Analysing the macro-environmental factors (PEST)– These relate to Political, Economic, Social and Technological factors

In order to measure these different factors for judging the quality of service effectively and to measure the impact of this differentiation, a number of methods have been developed to measure customer satisfaction. *Servqual*, one of the most popular methods was developed in 1988 to calculate the differences between customer expectations and perceptions on a number of pre-specified criteria. Due to perceived shortcomings in the *Servqual* approach, a performance based approach to measure service quality called *Servperf* was introduced in 1992, on the presumptions that service quality is an antecedent to consumer satisfaction. In fact, these different approaches have to measure quality of service to customers but no proper method have been recognized.

MFI's also suffer from the same problem. The MFI's are not so recognized to provide quality service to the SHG's or NGO's to cater the needs of the rural consumers. Hence, the service quality provided cannot be effectively measured by the standard methods in practice.

SUGGESTIONS

To measure the role of service quality in microfinance in India, the most coveted approach could be using Fayol's method of management. The fourteen principles of Fayol- (1) Division of work (2) Authority and Responsibility (3) Discipline (4) Unity of Command (5) Unity of Direction (6) Scalar Chain (7) Subordination of individual interest to group interest (8) Order (9) Remuneration (10) Centralisation (11) Initiative (12) Equity (13) Stability of tenure of personnel and 14) Esprit de corps–if effectively applied can reduce the gap between service expectation and perception. This will also enforce clarity in decision making, utilising the skills which can be used to improve the basic effectiveness in delivering quality service as expected by its consumers.

REFERENCES

Anyango E, Sebstad J. and Cohen M. (2002), "Assessment of the Use and Impact of Microsave's Market Research for Microfinance Toolkit", Microsave, Nairobi.

Brand M. and Gershick J. (2000), "Maximising Efficiency in Microfinance: The Path to Enhanced Outreach and Sustainability", ACCION International, Washington.

Brown S. W. and Bond E. U. III (1995), " The Internal/External Framework and Service Quality: Toward Theory in Services Marketing", *Journal of Marketing Management,* February, pp. 25-39.

Cronin J. J. Jr., Taylor S. A. (1992), " Measuring Service Quality: A Reexamination and Extension", *Journal of Marketing*, Vol. 56, pp. 13-55.

Cronin J. J. Jr., Taylor S. A. (1994), "SERVPERF versus SERVQUAL: Reconciling Performance-based and Perceptions-minus-Expectations Measurement of Service Quality", *Journal of Marketing*, Vol. 58, pp. 125-126

Brown T. J., Churchill G. A. and Peter J. P. (1993), "Improving the Measurement of Service Quality", *Journal of Retailing*, Vol. 69, No. 1, pp. 13-27

Gronroos C. (1982), Strategic Management and Marketing in the Service Sector, Swedish School of Economics and Business Administration, Helsingfors.

Kotler P., Andreasen A. R. (1996), "Strategic Marketing for Non Profit Organisations", Prentice Hall, New Jersey.

Littlefield E., Morduch J., Hashemi S. (2003), "Is Microfinance An Effective Strategy to Reach the Millennium Development Goals?", CGAP Focus Note.

Parasuraman A., Zeithaml V. A., Berry L. L. (1994), "Reassessment of Expectations as a Comparison Standard in Measuring Service Quality: Implications for Further Research", *Journal of Marketing*, Vol. 58, pp. 111-113.

Parasuraman A., Zeithaml V.A. and Berry L. L. (1993), More on Improving Service Quality Measurement", *Journal of Retailing*, Vol. 69, No. 1, pp. 140-147.

Robinson M. S. (1998), "Microfinance: The Paradigm Shift From Credit Delivery to Sustainable Financial Intermedation", in Mwangi S. Kimenyi, R. C. Wieland and J. D. Von Pischke (eds) Strategic Issues in Microfinance, Ashgate Publishing, Aldershot.

Robinson S. (1999), "Measuring Service Quality: Current Thinking and Future Requirements", *Marketing Intelligence and Planning*, Vol. 17, No. 1, pp. 21-32

Srinivasan R .and Sriram M. S. (2003), "Microfinance: An Introduction", *IIMB Management Review*, June, pp. 52-53.

Wanchho R. (2007), "Microfinance in India: The Changing Face of Micro-credit Schemes", *MPRA*, No. 3675

Websites

www.Microsave.org

www.ifmr.ac.in

www.microfinancegateway.org

24

MICROFINANCE AND SUSTAINABILITY OF SHGS-COPING WITH POVERTY ALLEVIATION AND GENDER EQUALITY

Twinkle Prusty & Silpi Sahoo

Microfinance as a sustainable resource is potentially a very significant contribution to gender equality and women's empowerment, as well as pro-poor development and civil society escalation. Through their contribution to the women's ability they have been able to initiate a consensus of economic empowerment, increased well-being for women and their families and wider social and political empowerment. Micro finance services and groups involving men also have potential to question and significantly change men's attitudes and behaviors as an essential component of achieving gender equality. Banks and micro finance institutions intend to finance the poor women because there is no fear of migration and the repayment percentage of the loans given to women are very high approximating 98%.Thus, an enduring system of participatory consultation, involving various stakeholders is obligatory for influencing their decision making.

SHG-Bank Linkage programmes are currently being promoted as a key strategy for simultaneously addressing both poverty alleviation and women's empowerment. Microfinance has been professed to be helpful to the women folk rendered helpless. By virtue of this, providing independent sources of income outside home tends to reduce economic dependency of the women on their spouses and thus help to enhance autonomy. At the same time, independent sources of income together with their exposure to new set of ideas, values and social support will make these women more assertive of their rights. If empowerment would be followed by a democratization process, it would likely to commence from below, because the poverty alleviating credit schemes are targeting individuals and not structures. The women of world's poorest families require credit for self-employment and other financial and business services. The issue of women's empowerment has thus started to constitute the cornerstone of any discussions on planned interventions for poverty alleviation. The unique aspect of such a strategy is through the viability of its financial intermediation in the form of credit for the poor which results in social upliftment.

SCHEMA OF MICROFINANCE

In the development strategy, for alleviating poverty and enhancing production and productivity, microfinance services have been perceived to be a powerful instrument for the expansion of the institutional structure, overcoming the disadvantages for the borrowers and provide subsidies for the interest rates. This would definitely ensure wider physical access of financial services to the poor and help to build a broad base for the delivery and deployment of credit. In order to increase the outreach of the rural credit institutions for the poor and stimulate additional flows to the financial sector, the reforms in this sector motivated the policy planners to search for strategies and products for delivering the financial services in a sustainable manner. Thus, the schema of microfinance is currently being promoted as a key strategy for simultaneously addressing both poverty alleviation and women's empowerment. The potential impacts of the financial services could be realized for:

(1) Enhancing economic independence of women's income levels and self control,

(2) Accessing information and possibilities through networks and markets in the development of social and political roles,

(3) Increased perceptions of women's contribution to household income and family welfare,

(4) Increasing women's participation in household decisions about family budget and other related financial issues, and,

(5) Upgrading attitudes in women's role in the welfare of the household as well as community.

Microfinance programmes while focusing on financial liberalization have also been used as a corrective device to the prior neglect of women's productive role. In some or the other contexts, women in microfinance programmes have indeed set in motion a process of empowerment where all the above elements have been mutually reinforcing.

ROLE OF SHGS IN MICROFINANCE

Micro finance has evolved over the past quarter century across India into various operating forms and to a varying degree of success. One such form of micro finance has been the development of the self-help movement. Based on the concept of "self-help," small groups of women have formed into groups of ten to twenty and operate a savings-first business model whereby the member's savings are used to fund loans. The results from these self-help groups (SHGs) are promising and have become a focus of intense examination as it is proving to be an effective method of poverty reduction.

Self help groups (SHGs) have been professed as the largest microcredit operation in the world with an estimated figure of more than 1.5 million groups that are formed consisting of an estimated 16 million clients. The microfinance providers have also considered the SHG approach to be beneficial from the profitability point of view and hence they can be visualized as the instruments through which the rural poor can be easily accessed. At the same time, the long-term viability of SHGs linking through banks and other financial intermediaries have emerged as the credit strategies for meeting the credit needs of the poor by combining the elasticity, sensitivity and receptiveness of the informal credit system with the strength of technical and administrative competencies and financial resources of the formal credit institutions. A most notable milestone in the SHG movement was when NABARD launched the pilot phase of the SHG Bank Linkage programme in February 1992. NABARD's corporate mission was to make available microfinance services to 20 million poor households, or to link 1 million SHGs to banks by 2008.This was the first instance of mature SHGs that were directly financed by a commercial bank. The informal thrift and credit groups of poor were recognized as bankable clients. Soon after, the RBI advised commercial banks to consider lending to SHGs as part of their rural credit operations thus creating SHG Bank Linkage programme. The SHG bank linkage model experienced a massive growth in recent years. The annual report of NABARD 2004/2005 states that the programme has now linked more than 1,6 million SHGs to banks, thus their 2008 target has already been achieved by far. The active participation of women (90%) and the timely repayment rates (95%) remain prominent features of the programme.

According to NABARD, a SHG consists of an average size of 15 people from a homogeneous social or economic class, all of who come together for addressing their common problems. The SHGs meet regularly and save small sums of money. They rotate these small-pooled savings as loans within the SHG. They maintain records of such financial transactions and slowly learn the basic aspects of financial management. They then approach a bank and leverage their accumulated savings for higher loans, which they then intermediate within the SHG. The groups are promoted either by banks or non – governmental organizations (NGOs) and are credit linked to various models developed by banks.

However, the SHG Linkage model faces several challenges, as various researches indicate that sustainability of the SHGs is a critical issue, as many remain dependent on promoter organizations such as NGOs for even routine tasks such as bookkeeping. SHGs having a membership of 10-20 are small and informal groups for which it would be difficult to negotiate with higher level structures, to get access to large amount of loans and to create a bargaining power .To address these challenges, SHG federations have emerged. .The structure can vary from informal to formal and from 15-20 SHGs under a federation to 150-200 SHGs under a federation with or without a secondary structure of SHGs at village level. Similarly, SHG federations can have various functions, ranging from strictly financial intermediation to only non-financial services at broader institutional level and the whole arena between these.

Thus, the alliances of SHGs should contribute to:

(1) Ensuring sustainability of SHGs whereby the maintenance cost of SHGs have to be permanently borne by the promoter, mostly a donor funded NGO, making the system inherently unsustainable. Federations could take over this role from the initial promoters.

(2) Capacity building of SHGs

(3) Ensuring quality while scaling up the number of SHGs.

(4) Economies of scale, reducing transaction costs and default rates, providing value added services like micro-insurance and input supply, while increasing the outreach and simultaneously reducing the promotional costs

(5) Increasing empowerment beyond that achieved by the SHGs by producing leaders and providing opportunities to deal with power and bureaucratic structures at a higher level, where mainstream organizations and governments offices exist.

The significance of SHGs can also be felt by the functions they perform in carrying out the microfinance activities like:

- Creating a common fund by the members through their regular savings.
- Flexible working system and pooling the resources in a democratic way.

- Periodically meeting for the decision making through group meeting.
- Repaying in easy installments particularly on time with affordable rate of interest.
- improving saving habits among women
- increasing the total family income
- fulfilling the economic needs through self-employment of women
- utilizing bank loan and government welfare schemes
- helping the members to escape from the clutches of moneylenders; and
- mobilizing financial resources.

According to the NABARD, at the end of March 2007, 2.92 million SHGs cumulatively received bank loans of Rs.180,410 million (US$4.5 million). In total, 40.95 million poor households have been provided with credit from formal financial institutions. And, given that the average size of the Indian family is five, this indicates that over 200 million people have been provided credit by the banking sector through SHGs, though not all of them would be active borrowers. The majority of them were, hitherto, out of the purview of mainstream financial institutions. The state of Andhra Pradesh is on the way to achieve near-universal financial inclusion because of SHGs. Other southern states are moving quickly in that direction as well and all other states have realized the potential of SHGs in financial inclusion and are adopting the model. Over 90% of the bank-linked groups are women groups and about four-fifth are situated in rural areas, a traditionally under-served area. It is clear that SHGs are doing their work efficiently and providing support to raise the living standards of the poor, low-income level people.

From the following table, it is evident that SHG-bank Linkage Programme is going positively to achieve its set objectives.

Table 1
SHG-Bank Linkage Programme–Cumulative Progress

Year	*March,03*	*March,04*	*March,05*	*March,06*
SHGs linked (financed)	107553	174666	343691	540481
No. of beneficiaries	1233660	2150752	4811674	7568842
Amt. Disbursed (RS. Crore)	324.84	614.87	1131.45	2262.95
Amt.outstanding (Rs. Crore)	269.43	462.77	872.08	1459.89
No. of SHGs maintaining Saving A/cs in the bank	279466	369568	508396	636067
Amount in saving A/cs (Rs. Crore)	261.36	348.31	411.82	434.07

Source: Nabard News Letter, March 2007.

According to the deliberations made by the SBI chairman Sri.O.P.Bhatt on 19 September, 2008, the bank has set itself a target of 33 per cent growth in agri-advances to Rs.13, 400crore in 2008-09. It also plans to issue 1crore SBI Tiny Cards by end-March 2010, of which 40lakh will be issued in the current financial year. One lakh un-banked villages will be covered by 2010, of which 40,000 will be taken up this fiscal. SBI also has plans for additional credit linkage of 2lakh Self Help Groups (SHGs) in 2008-09. The bank has already credit linked more than 10lakh SHGs till March 2008. Bhatt informed that the number of branches in rural and semi-urban centers will be raised from nearly 7,000 branches at present to 10,000, of which 1,000 will be opened this fiscal.

Poverty Alleviation and Gender Equality: The Focal Point of Microfinance

Microfinance being the effectual mechanism in poverty alleviation, is recognized as a key to the success of SHGs and other micro credit deliverance sculpt in selected regions of the country with an approved reflection for the microfinance sector. The annual demand for credit support from estimated 75 million poor households has been assessed at Rs. 450 billion, which is expected to be met by the formal banking sector and the Micro Finance Institutions (MFIs). This confrontation has been taken up by the conventional banking institutions and the microfinance sector to bridge the huge gap created due to the incessant dependency of the poor on informal sector accounting for 40% to 60% of the household demand. The assorted programmes or schemes for the underprivileged introduced by successive governments have failed to make apt impact on the poverty ladder. The government's intervention as being the regulator for microfinance along with the banking sectors' effort and with the intermediaries has necessitated the task of accumulating the capacity of the existing system of NGOs and MFIs to outreach larger number of poor households in the urban and rural areas. According to Friends of Women's World Banking (FWWB), in India (1982), the focus on women especially the economically active ones should be made, which accounts for 80% of the growing informal sector and have not been able to access the formal banking sector for their working capital needs. Therefore, it is imperative that the women in collectives (SHGs) should be encouraged as being bankable with capacity building for the reason that they contribute substantially to the income in poor households and the preferred impact on the household economy could be studied by the intervention through a woman's will. Hence the SHG methodology should be geared towards strengthening the capacity of these women in managerial and leadership skills. However, the quality of the SHGs in terms of time and resources in building the capacity of the members of the SHGs may be reduced with the increasing emphasis on organizing more poor women SHGs at a faster rate because of their ultimate focus on short term vision to access credit from banks, government and non-government agencies. The SHG models if implemented efficiently will have a multi-faceted impact on amelioration of the socio economic conditions of the rural poor. It would definitely provide an impetus to micro-entrepreneurship and generate a huge band of veterans for setting up micro-enterprises. NABARD has decided to intensify the micro finance programmes due to the buoyant response of banks in India to the linkage projects and favorable reports received as per their actions taken up. Besides improving the outreach of the formal banking system, it would also enhance the quality of credit in rural areas by promoting people's participation, self-help and grass roots institutions. However, substantial numbers of SHGs in many states have not been credit linked and they need to be assessed for bringing the required improvements to consolidate the gains so that incipient problems are analyzed and addressed.

THE AGENDA OF SHG-BANK LINKAGE

The achievement under the SHG-Bank Linkage Programme have been uneven in different regions of the country and NABARD has initiated actions to speed up progress which have large poor rural households and and according to its estimates, more than one lac SHGs should come up in the poverty-inflict areas of Orissa, Assam, Bihar, West Bengal, Madhya Pradesh, Rajasthan, Maharastra and Uttar Pradesh.

At the national level, a Government sponsored micro-finance model the Swarnjayanti Gram Swarozgar Yojana (SGSY), being implemented in rural India since the financial year 1999-2000 and dedicated to the rural poor, envisaged increasing outreach of micro-finance through small and informal SHGs formed with the support of 5 to 20 persons from relatively homogenous backgrounds. Micro-finance has been extended under the programme to only those SHGs who have passed a subjective grading test and are involved in regular thrift and credit activities for not less than six month. To improve the quality of life of the SHGs and their productivity, the programme has tried to firm up their financial and economic norms meant for selection of appropriate beneficiary and subsequent disbursement of credit to the needy. This micro-finance driven self-employment programme has been also expected to help in beneficiary identification through participatory methods. Subsidy given by Government to SHGs under this programme is back-ended.

However, the analysis of the State-wise poverty in India and credit flow under SGSY during 2004-05, suggests that poverty ratio for Orissa is 47.2% (1999-2000 estimates) which has been the highest in the country. Though credit flow under SGSY depends on the proportion of poor living in a State concerned, yet Orissa, being the most backward State has only got 5.88% of total SGSY credit for onward disbursement to its poor through SHGs during the year 2004-05. The largest gainer of the SGSY credit is Uttar Pradesh followed by Bihar, Madhya Pradesh and Maharashtra. The per capita SGSY credit disbursement to poor during the year was only Rs. 63.4 in the country. There were 8 states where the disbursement was lower than the national per capita credit disbursement under SGSY.

The UN-Solution Exchange has launched the micro finance community which has been the need of the hour since the mellowness of the women federations has to take form and need to be strengthened in the areas of microfinance which shall be a platform to introduce the learning and support of the expansion of SHGs. Recent surveys made by the development banks in Andhra Pradesh points out that there are about 2000 NGOs in India with substantial microfinance activities, and if Mutually Aided Cooperative Societies are included the numbers spurts to around 3800. Apart from outreach and amount outstanding, the Micro credit Summit Campaign Report published every year as a centralized mapping for microfinance activities around the world, measure the percentage of poor and poorest of the poor served by microfinance institutions and the corresponding figures for women borrowers.

It is well recognized that microfinance in India continues to be skewed in its geographical distribution due to the general malaise in the economy of central, eastern and north-eastern states, with very little resultant demand for credit, and the absence of quality NGOs that are willing to initiate microfinance programs in these states. Expanding the reach of microfinance services cannot be met overnight and overall economic growth has to pick up and public investments are essential in areas such as watershed development, small-scale irrigation, livestock up-gradation and forest regeneration. Long-term lumpy public investments in these areas can unlock the potential for enhancing the livelihoods of millions of poor people.

A proposal for increasing the number of quality NGOs like that of existing in the southern states, in the lesser served states was made by the Tenth Five Year Plan Working Group on

Poverty Alleviation Programs (Planning Commission 2002), which recommended that well established NGOs be asked to set up branches in selected poor districts and they be funded for this on an assured though declining basis for the first three to five years. The experience of Rashtriya Gramin Vikas Nidhi and Rashtriya Mahila Kosh in supporting hundreds of small NGOs all over the eastern region is a useful experience which needs to be taken into account. Another proposal has been to incubate microfinance institutions in poorer districts under the guidance of established microfinance institutions. Although the Linkage Bank Program still remains biased towards the southern region, the latest figures are an improvement over early years. NABARDS's emphasis on scaling up the SHG-bank linkage programme in 13 priority states accounting for 70 per cent of the country's rural poor has resulted in two and a half fold increases in the number of SHGs credit linked during the period 2003-05. Significant increases have been witnessed in the economically backward states like Assam, Bihar, and Orissa. As a result, the share of the 13 priority states excluding all the southern states, in the total number of SHGs credit linked, increased from 30.7 per cent by March 2002 and to 41.26 per cent by March 2005.

However, Orissa has been accorded as one of the poorest and the organic agrarian state in India having very high incidences of conjectural poverty due to the climatic crisis like flood, cyclone and drought etc causing destitution.As per the estimates made in 1999-2000 by the Modified Expert Group of Planning Commission, Orissa has the highest proportion of population living below the poverty line wherein the percentage of people living below the poverty line in the state was 47.15, whereas, it was 42.6 per cent in case of Bihar. On the other hand, the all India average was found to be 26.1 per cent. The lowest poverty ratio was seen in Jammu and Kashmir, (3.5%) followed by Punjab (6.2%), Himachal Pradesh (7.6%) and Haryana (8.7%). Moreover, the scheduled tribe (ST) and scheduled caste (SC) population and more particularly the ST population are very backward because of their tradition bound nature, ignorance, illiteracy, lack of awareness, dwelling in the inaccessible areas, etc with very poor living conditions. They are unable to afford the bundle of goods and services including food, education and health, which are necessary for minimum existence. The SC/ST households, being disadvantaged, have a considerably higher incidence of poverty than other groups and the percentage of SC and ST population to total population of the state was about 38 per cent in all the three censuses, i.e., 1971, 1981 and 1991. On the other hand, the corresponding figure for India was about 24 per cent. The percentage share of SC population was more or less same in all the three censuses both in Orissa and India. So, it is the scheduled tribe population, which is mainly responsible for the poor living condition of the people of the state. In Orissa the percentage of scheduled tribe population was about 23 per cent in the three censuses as against about 8 per cent in India. The poverty-hub regions need the outreach of the microfinance for promoting opportunity in stimulating overall growth, capacity building, and facilitating empowerment by removing the social barriers and enhancement of security from the outburst of economic shocks and policy induced dislocations.

CONCLUSION

There have definitely been significant advances in recent years and the concept and practice of SHG-based microfinance activities have now developed deep roots in many parts of the country. It is tough to gauge and enumerate the impact of the review of this Indian micro-credit experience on the poverty situation in India. Nevertheless, a lot needs to be accomplished in terms of outreach to make a serious dent on poverty. However, the logic and rationale of SHG-based microfinance have been established firmly enough that micro-credit has effectively graduated from man experiment to a widely-accepted paradigm of rural and developmental financing in India. The most realistic feature of this form of financing, that justifies its admittedly higher costs, is the near-perfect repayment rates. The biggest challenge in the rural development, however, is the simultaneous development of investment potential and improvement of skill levels of the borrowers. A superfluity of low-skilled services is an unwelcome substitute for scarcity of credit. As micro-credit alleviates the credit scarcity problem, the need for micro-consulting, business planning and services like marketing, are being felt with greater acuteness. There is a very real need of investments that yield higher returns than the sustainable micro-credit interest rates for the micro-credit initiative to be truly successful.

In particular, empowerment of women and the inculcation of financial training and discipline amongst the poor will undoubtedly have long-term socio-economic benefits. The principles of self-help and microcredit thus hold the key to economic and socio-cultural freedom for Indias' millions of poor, opening the gates of a hitherto untapped reservoir of human enterprise.

Eventually, the whole evolution of microfinance has instilled in keeping women's role to be the important one, in having control over the usage of the loans and ownership of the assets created through loans. Hence, it is crucial that such micro credit should be promoting livelihood opportunities and developing their skills to undertake micro-enterprises which will help in increasing the household income. It is of essence that the ways and means of improving and sustaining the quality of SHG with their consistency and balanced sustainability for credit access is to be identified. They are resolute keeping the vital requirements for every poor household in regard to meeting the survival and essential needs and sustainability of the revenue engendering capability.

Thus, there is urgent need to widen the scope, scale and reach of micro-finances through the qualitative performances of SHGs so as to pull off the vast inaccessible population in the low income group from financial exclusion. There is significant potential for micro-finance to enable women to challenge and change gender inequalities at all levels if there is a strategic gender focus. Nevertheless, benefits cannot be assumed and even financially sustainable micro-finance if it is gender blind may seriously dis-empower women and increase inequality. It is clear that most micro finance programmes have a long way to go before they make their full potential contribution to gender equality and empowerment. Many of the strategies promoted for financial sustainability may exacerbate the negative impacts of debt, because of over-rapid expansion, rigid product design inappropriate to women's economic activities, cutting of necessary support services and lack of attention to local economic contexts. There is also a need for innovation to ensure that access translates into a significant and sustainable contribution to women's empowerment. In view of providing impending paybacks to women, there is an urgent need for vigilance to the strategies espoused for women's empowerment.

REFERENCES

Bansal, Hema, (2003), "SHG-Bank Linkage Program in Indian: An Overview", *Journal of Microfinance*, Vol. 5, Number 1.

Basu, Priya and Verma, Niraj. (2004), Improving Access to Rural Finance in India:An Overview, Conference paper on Impoving Access to Rural Finance, New Delhi.

Bhatt, Nitin and Y.S.P. Thorat, (2001), "India's Regional Rural Banks: The Institutional Dimension of Reforms", *Journal of Microfinance*, Vol. 3, Number 1.

Damodaran, Harish, (2003), "Banks More Shy of Rural Lending", *Hindu*, July 12, 2003.

Dasgupta, Rajaram.(2005), "Microfinance in India: Empirical Evidence, Alternative Models and Policy Imperatives", *Economic & Political Weekly*, Vol. XL(12), March 19, pp. 1229.

Dreze, Jean and Sen, Amartya.(2002), "India: Development and Participation", Oxford University Press, New Delhi.

Fisher, Thomas and M. S. Sriram ed., (2002), *Beyond Micro-credit: Putting* Development Back into Microfinance, New Delhi: Vistaar Publications; Oxford: Oxfam.

Ghate,P.B.(1992), "Informal Finance. Some Findings from Asia".Oxford University Press.

Goetz, A.M. and R. Sen Gupta (1996), "Who Takes the Credit? Gender, Power and Control over Loan Use in Rural Credit Programmes in Bangladesh", World Development, Jan.

Hannover,Wolfgang May (2005), "The Impact of Microfinance Linkage Banking in India on the Millennium Development Goals(MDG)", Summary of Major Reports From Existing Studies, NABARD/GTZ

Harper, Malcolm, (2002), "Promotion of Self Help Groups under the SHG Bank Linkage Program in India", Paper presented at the Seminar on SHG-bank Linkage Programme at New Delhi, November 25-26, 2002.

Harper,Malcolm (2002), "Promotion of Self-Help Groups under the SHG-Bank Linkage Programme in India". Paper presented at the seminar on SHG-Bank Linkage Programme, New Delhi, November 25 and 26.

Hashemi, S. M., Schuler, S. R. and Riley, A. P. (1996), "Rural Credit Programs and Women's Empowerment in Bangladesh.", *World Development*, Vol. 24, No. 4.

Johnson, S. and B. Rogaly (1996), "Microfinance and Poverty Reduction" Oxford: Oxfam Kabeer, N and Murthy, R. K. (1996) "Compensating for Institutional Exclusion? Lessons from Indian Government and Non-Government Credit Interventions for the Poor" IDS Discussion Paper No. 356.

Johnson, S. and Rogaly, B. (1997), "Microfinance and Poverty Reduction", Oxford, OXFAM.

Jonathan and Rutherford, Stuart (2003), "Microfinance: Analytical Issues for India".Essay for the World Bank,South Asia Region,Finance and Private Sector Development Unit.

Kropp, Erhard, W. and B.S. Suran (2002), "Linking Banks and (Financial) Self Help Groups in India -An Assessment", Paper presented at the Seminar on SHG-bank Linkage Programme at New Delhi, November 25-26.

Mayoux, L. (1995b), "Beyond Naivety: Women, Gender Inequality and Participatory Development-Some Thorny Issues" Development and Change, 26 (2).

Mayoux, L (1997a), "Microfinance Programmes and Women's Empowerment: Towards a Framework for Participatory Planning", Background Discussion Paper, ActionAid UK

Montgomery, R. (1996), "Disciplining or Protecting the Poor? Avoiding the Social Costs of Peer Pressure in Micro-Credit Schemes", *Journal of International Development*, Vol. 8 No. 2, Wiley, U.K.

Nanda,Y.S. (1995), "Significance of Establishing Linkages with Self-Help Groups and Banks".

Otero, M. and E. Rhyne (eds) (1994), "The New World of Micro-enterprise Finance: Building Healthy Financial Institutions for the Poor" IT Publications, London.

Satish,P.(2001), "Institutional Alternatives for the Promotion of Microfinance:Selp-Help Groups in India", *Journal of Microfinance,* 3,no.2:p.49-74

Seibel, Hans D. and H.R. Dave, (2002), "Commercial Aspects of SHG Banking in India", Paper presented at the Seminar on SHG-bank Linkage Programme at New Delhi, November 25-26.

Sinha Sanjay (2003), "Financial Services for Low Income Families:An Appraisal", *IIM-B Management Review,* June.

Srinivasan, R. (2003), "Self-Help Groups as Financial Instituions: Policy Implications Using a Financial Model", *Journal of Microfinance,* Vol. 5, No. 1

Throat Y.S.P and Bhatt, Nitin. (2000), "India's Regional Rural Banks:The Institutional Dimension of Reforms", *Journal of Microfinance,*Vol. 3, No. 1.

Websites

http://www.altavista.com

http://www.cgap.com

http://www.economictimes.com

http://www.enterweb.com

http://www.financialexpress.com

http://www.fwwbindia.com

http://www.google.com

http://www.grdc.org

http://www.icrier.org

http://www.microfinancegatework.org

http://www.microinsurencecentre.org

http://www.nabard.org

http://www.nzu.edu

http://www.rbi.org

LIST OF CONTRIBUTORS

Prof. Akinchan Buddhodev Sinha, Faculty Member & Academic Coordinator, Icfai School of Financial Studies, Hyderabad, *Email:akinchanbsinha@gmail.com*

Mr. Arun Tiwari, Student of IBS-PUNE, *E-mail:aruntiwari93@gmail.com*

Prof. Anil Kumar Mishra, Sr. Lecturer, Academy of Management Studies, Bhubaneswar, *E-mail:anilmishra5555@gmail.com*

Dr. Abhijit Dutta, Associate Professor, Amity Global Varsity, Kolkata, *E-mail:abhijitdutta069@gmail.com*

Dr. Amiya K. Mohapatra, Faculty Member, Icfai Business School, Jaipur, *E-mail:amiyaeco@gmail.com*

Mr. Abhishek Tiwari, Institute of Business Management & Technology, Bangalore, *E-mail:abhishek_2725@yahoo.com*

Dr. Biraj Kumar Mohanty, Faculty Member, Icfai Business School, Bhubaneswar, *E-mail:biraj@winning.com*

Dr. Bibhudatta Nayak, Assistant General Manager (Economic Services), NABARD, Orissa.

Prof. Biswo Ranjan Mishra, Asst. Professor, Institute of Management and Information Science (IMIS), Bhubaneswar, *E-mail:biswomishra@gmail.com*

Mr. Dushmanta Mallick, Icfai Business School, Bhubaneswar, *E-mail:dushmantamallick@yahoo.com*

Prof. Gazia Sayed, Faculty Member,IES Management College and Research Centre-Mumbai, *E-mail:gaziasayed@rediffmail.com*

Prof. G.A. Narasimham, Faculty Member, INC, Visakhapatnam, *E-mail:narsimhaincvizag@gmail.com*

Dr. Hareram Mohanty, Associate Dean–Research, Icfai Business School, Bhubaneswar, *E-mail:harerammohanty@hotmail.com*

Dr. Jyotirmayee Kar, Faculty Member, Icfai Business School, Bhubaneswar, *E-mail:Jyotirmayee_k@yahoo.co.in*

Prof. Manidatta Ray, Asst. Professor, Institute of Management and Information Science (IMIS), Bhubaneswar, *E-mail:manidatta_ray@yahoo.co.in*

Prof. Manoranjan Dash, Sr. Lecturer, IBCS, Siksha 'O' Anusandhan University, Bhubaneswar, *E-mail:manoranjanibcs@gmail.com*

Dr. Munmun Mohanty, Asst. Professor, Institute of Business and Computer Studies, S 'O' A University, Bhubaneswar, *E-mail:munmunmohanty@rediffmail.com*

Mr. N. K. Mohanty, World Bank Consultant.

Dr. Pradeepta Kumar Samanta, Faculty Member in the Area of Finance, Icfai Business School, Bhubaneswar, *E-mail: pksamanta2005@yahoo.co.in*

Dr. Pinaki Ranjan Bhattacharyya, Faculty Member, Icfai Business School, Kolkata, *E-mail:pinakirb@rediffmail.com*

Prof. Pradip Banerjee, Faculty Member, Icfai Business School, Bhubaneswar, *E-mail:pradip-2002in@yahoo.com*

Prof. Sumeet Gupta, Faculty Member, Icfai Business School, Jaipur, *E-mail: sumeetbgh2007@gmail.com*

Ms. Sumita Bhattacharya, Research Associate, Icfai Business School, Kolkata, *E-mail:sumita_2006_202@yahoo.co.in*

Prof. Sunanda Asuti, Faculty of Economics, IES Management College and Research Centre, *E-mail:asuti_sunanda@yahoo.co.in*

Prof. Silpi Sahoo Faculty Member, Centre of Women Studies, Utkal University, Bhubaneswar.

Dr. S.C. Bihari, Sr. Manager, Allahabad Bank, Bhubaneswar, *E-mail:scbihari@gmail.com*

Dr. Sukanta Chandra Swain, Faculty Member, Icfai Business School, Bhubanesw ar,*E-mail:sukanta_swain@yahoo.com,sukanta@ibsindia.org*

Prof. Seshadev Sahoo, Faculty Member, Institute of Management and Information Science, Bhubaneswar, Orissa, *E-mail:seshadev@vgsom.iitkgp.ernet.in ,seshadev@rediffmail.com*

Prof. Shradhanjali Panda, Lecturer in Finance at Global Institute of Management , Bhubaneswar, *E-mail:shradha313@yahoo.co.in*

Dr. Twinkle Prusty, Faculty of Commerce, Banaras Hindu University, *E-mail:twinkle_prusty@rediffmail.com*

With Best Compliments from:

NATIONAL BANK FOR AGRICULTURE AND RURAL DEVELOPMENT

Mission

To Promote Sustainable and equitable agriculture and rural prosperity through effective credit support, related services, institution development and other innovations initiatives.

MAJOR ACTIVITIES

Credit Functions: Refinance for production credit (Short term) and investment credit (Medium and long term) to eligible Banks and financing institutions.

Development Functions: To reinforce the credit functions and make credit more productive development activities are being undertaken through.

- Research and Development Fund
- Soft Loan Assistance Fund
- Agricultural and Rural Enterprises Incubation Fund
- Rural Promotion Corpus Fund
- Credit and Financial Services Fund
- Watershed Development Fund
- Kisan Credit Cards and Linking SHGs to credit institutions
- Rural Infrastructure Development Fund

Supervisory Functions: NABARD shares with RBI certain regulatory and supervisory functions in respect of Cooperative Banks and RRBs.

We also provide comprehensive consultancy services relating to Agriculture & Rural Development. (nabcon@vsnl.net)

NABARD

Head Office: Plot No.- C-24, G-Block,
Bandra-Kurla Complex, Post Box No. - 8121
Bandra (E), Mumbai-400 051
visit us at : *www.nabard.org*

TWO DACADES OF COMMITTED SERVICE TO RURAL PROSPERITY

THIS VOLME IS PRINTED WITH FINANCIAL ASSISTANCE FROM
NABARD